Caribou and Conoco

Caribou and Conoco

Rethinking Environmental Politics in Alaska's ANWR and Beyond

ROBERT J. MCMONAGLE

LEXINGTON BOOKS

A division of
ROWMAN & LITTLEFIELD PUBLISHERS, INC.
Lanham • Boulder • New York • Toronto • Plymouth, UK

LEXINGTON BOOKS

A division of Rowman & Littlefield Publishers, Inc.
A wholly owned subsidiary of The Rowman & Littlefield Publishing Group, Inc.
4501 Forbes Boulevard, Suite 200
Lanham, MD 20706

Estover Road, Plymouth PL6 7PY, United Kingdom

British Library Cataloguing in Publication Information Available

Library of Congress Cataloging-in-Publication Data

McMonagle, Robert John.
  Caribou and Conoco : rethinking environmental politics in Alaska's ANWAR and beyond / Robert
J. McMonagle.
    p. cm.
  Focuses mainly on ANWAR, but includes discussion of drilling in the Eastern Gulf of Mexico
(EGOM) off the coast of Florida and the Cape Wind project in New England.
  Includes bibliographical references and index.
  ISBN-13: 978-0-7391-1961-7 (cloth : alk. paper)
  ISBN-10: 0-7391-1961-3 (pbk. : alk. paper)
  1. Energy industries—Political aspects—United States—Case studies. 2. Energy
industries—Environmental aspects—United States—Case studies. 3. Oil well
drilling—Political aspects—Alaska—Arctic National Wildlife Refuge. 4. Oil well
drilling—Environmental aspects—Alaska—Arctic National Wildlife Refuge. 5. Energy
policy—United States. I. Title. II. Title: Environmental politics in Alaska's ANWAR
and beyond.
  HD9502.U52M395 2008
  333.8'232140973—dc22   2008001486

Printed in the United States of America

⊖™ The paper used in this publication meets the minimum requirements of American
National Standard for Information Sciences—Permanence of Paper for Printed Library
Materials, ANSI/NISO Z39.48–1992.

To my wife, Tilottama, and the memories of our families.

Contents

Figures

Tables

Abbreviations

AFL-CIO	American Federation of Labor-Congress of Industrial Organizations
ANCSA	Alaska Native Claims Settlement Act of 1971
ANILCA	Alaska National Interest Lands Conservation Act of 1980
ANWR	Arctic National Wildlife Refuge
ARCO	Atlantic Richfield Company
ASRC	Arctic Slope Regional Corporation
BLM	US Bureau of Land Management
BP	British Petroleum
CAFÉ	Corporate Average Fuel Economy Standards
CMAL	Citizens for the Management of Alaska
CPG	Conditional Party Government
CRS	Congressional Research Service
DOE	US Department of Energy
DOI	US Department of the Interior
DOJ	US Department of Justice
EGOM	Eastern Gulf of Mexico
EIS	Environmental Impact Statement
EPA	US Environmental Protection Agency
FEMA	Federal Emergency Management Agency
FTC	Federal Trade Commission
LCM	Life Cycle Model
MMS	US Minerals Management Service
NEPDG	National Energy Policy Development Group
NPR-A	National Petroleum Reserve-Alaska
NRDC	Natural Resources Defense Council
NWF	National Wildlife Federation
OMB	Office of Management and Budget
OPEC	Organization of Petroleum Exporting Countries
PVM	Partisan Voting Model
TAPS	Trans-Alaska Pipeline System
USFWS	US Fish and Wildlife Service
USGS	US Geological Survey

Preface

The death of my former college roommate Captain John Beving, USMC, in or near Iraq after the Gulf War in 1992 piqued my interest in exploring an energy-related research topic when I was a graduate student in political science at Temple University in the early 2000s. That research forms the basis for this book.

I knew that the war was largely about oil and our economic way of life in the West. John saw action in the Battle of Kafji early in the war as a Cobra helicopter pilot and survived. Ironically, he was redeployed back to the Kuwait-Iraq border in 1992 where he died keeping the peace. John, you are a great American and will always have a place in our hearts.

Some will argue that the frequency of redeployment after that war pales in comparison to redeployments in the current and seemingly endless war in Iraq. Perhaps the bipartisan *brilliance* of downsizing the military during the 1990s accounts in part for this trend, but that would be the story of another book.

In this book, I emphasize the relationships between political and social forces that drive the policy-making process for contemporary environmental-energy policy debates and the implications of those decisions. Using the dual lenses of congressional partisanship and broader societal forces as conceptual underpinnings, and using empirical data rather than an advocacy approach per se, the four case studies in this book hopefully will shed much needed light on what is really transpiring beneath the surface of these often contentious public policy debates. In an era of rising energy prices, global warming, and political unrest, citizen activists, students, scholars, and lawmakers need a better understanding of the often confusing processes for crafting policy decisions. This book aims to help clarify this small, but important, piece of the world around us.

Policy for the Arctic National Wildlife Refuge in Alaska (ANWR) represents the core case. I also include recent debates over drilling in the Eastern Gulf of Mexico (EGOM) and on Western public lands, plus the unusual case of a proposed offshore wind farm in Massachusetts to help us better understand patterns of decision making in this critical area of public policy making.

Acknowledgments

I am especially thankful to Joseph Parry and the acquisitions team at Lexington Books for their confidence in my work. I am equally grateful to professors Chris Bosso (Northeastern University), Walter "Tony" Rosenbaum (University of Florida), Rob Mason (Temple University), and Paul Steinberg (Harvey Mudd College) for their chapter comments. And Kyle Kreider (Wilkes University) delivered timely and thorough feedback.

My wife Tilottama, Sylvia Macey, and Mike Silverstein deserve special thanks for their editorial support as does Jim Rogers (Temple University) for his suggestions on the selection of case studies. Librarian Larry Milliken (Neumann College) and the staff at Swarthmore College Library were reliable as always in helping me locate sources. Temple University professors Gary Mucciaroni, Robin Kolodny, and Conrad Weiler deserve recognition for aiding my scholarly growth during the oftentimes painful years as a doctoral student. Last but not least, Paris Coleman (Neumann College) did outstanding work designing the cover. I bear any and all responsibility for weaknesses in this book, and I welcome critiques from readers (email: <mcmonagr@neumann.edu>).

Chapter 1
Introduction: Rethinking Environmental-Energy Policy Studies

> Great minds discuss ideas; average minds discuss events; small minds discuss people.—Eleanor Roosevelt

Conservation has been an issue in American politics since Teddy Roosevelt's time. It merged with a broader range of environmental health and safety issues in the late 1960s and 1970s after the publication of Rachel Carson's ground-breaking *Silent Spring*, the first Earth Day in 1970, and the Love Canal fiasco.[1]

Energy became a major part of the national political debate at roughly the same period in the wake of the 1973 Arab Oil Embargo. Energy supply shortfalls and periodic price spikes have been a feature of American life ever since.

In recent decades environmental and energy issues have interacted in many ways and generated all manner of political disagreements and dueling policy nostrums. So frequently have these two policy imperatives interacted, in fact, that many experts now believe it is usually impossible to evaluate one of these issues without considering the other. This book seeks to help clarify these often highly contentious and confusing interactions for policy makers, for activists on both sides of the pro-environment and pro-energy divide, and for students seeking guidance on these matters.

In order to do this, a number of well-established (though too long underused) analytical methodologies are applied in these pages, first to the long-running disagreements about the Arctic National Wildlife Refuge (ANWR), and then to three other contested issues with both energy and environmental implications. The aim of this book's approach is to help cultivate real understanding of the choices in this realm—choices often obfuscated (deliberately or otherwise) by other approaches.

How obfuscated? One way has been to have these issues viewed strictly either in terms of direct costs to energy producers, or in terms of more diffuse and often more difficult to fiscally quantify environmental benefits such as preservation of a prized habitat. Political observers and political partisans often focus on just one of these perspectives, and not surprisingly, arrive at very different conclusions in consequence.

The scientific uncertainties surrounding many issues in this field are another major conflict generator. Data concerning environmental matters may be unavailable, may be incomplete, or depending on the source, may be just plain suspect. Experts on ANWR policy making, for example, have long been hindered in their efforts because scientific analyses vary so greatly concerning the amount of recoverable oil and gas in the refuge, and whether drilling would harm the Porcupine Caribou herd or other species and their habitats.

Economic and environmental analysis of data with conflicting energy and environmental implications has thus often been subject to manipulation by politicians and interest groups hoping to skew policies in their own favor. Government agencies that are ultimately charged with implementing these policies may be further hampered by their own fiscal budgetary pressures, and by laws and regulations that mandate measuring standards that don't always allow for the best policy formulation.[2]

For all such reasons, using strictly cost-benefit analysis to "solve" conflicts with conflicting energy and environmental implications is a problematic way to go. Actual costs and benefits in these equations tend to be too nebulous or demonstrably one-sided. The perceived distributional impacts of policies therefore represent a more plausible approach.

ANWR is a tract of federal land located in northeast Alaska (see fig. 1.1 below) that some people believe has large energy reserves. How to manage this tract and for what purposes has long been a subject of debate in the national political arena.

For decades, policies toward ANWR largely exhibited a pro-environment perspective (i.e. the view that keeping it in a pristine form offered greater benefits to the public than tapping its energy resources). The political upshot of such an analysis was that ANWR was not drilled for oil and natural gas because Congress did not allow it to be drilled. This approach, however, has been seriously challenged in recent years both by an Administration-controlled federal bureaucracy and in the US Congress.

ANWR is thus an obvious study for a book such as this one—an excellent core study of the underlying political forces driving policies with seemingly contradictory environmental and energy implications. Such a study clearly demonstrates, in part, that when a political and ideological shift occurs in Washington, arguments that had seemed of secondary importance can suddenly get a far more favorable hearing. It also clearly demonstrates that such a shift can occur without any fundamental change in the available information on which policy is supposedly based.

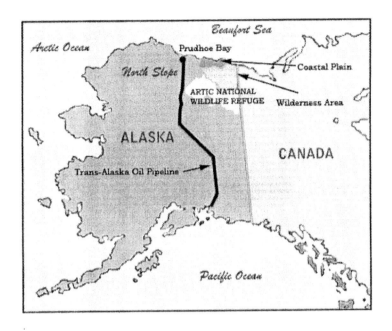

Figure 1.1, The Arctic National Wildlife Refuge (ANWR)
Source: no date <http://www.pbs.org/newshour /bb/environment/energy/#>

What did change since 1995 was not the nature of the information available about this issue but the importance assigned to elements of that information. Long-standing priorities on this issue had given more weight to environmental protection benefits and less to the benefits lost by aspiring drillers and oil consumers. The growing dependence of the United States on foreign oil suppliers, though long recognized, has in recent years also been given a higher priority in discussions about ANWR within policy circles in ways that favor the drilling side of the debate.

Generally, pro-environment policy priorities in Washington began to weaken in 1995 in large measure because a Republican majority took control of Congress. That year Congress passed a pro-drilling bill, though this was vetoed by President Clinton. After the election of George W. Bush in 2000, however, a GOP-led Congress passed various pro-drilling bills although none made it to the president's desk for his signature.

The book's core case study, it should be noted, began as an unusual "subsystem" in some respects, or a semi-autonomous decision-making structure within Congress. Decisions on ANWR policy were centered in a House subcommittee since 1977 but that dynamic later changed since oil companies and their allies certainly weren't without access of their own and the subsystem began to unravel. Pluralistic politics took root, with battling coalitions of organized and active interests trying to recruit allies from among the members of Congress and the mass public.

Although the core of this book is an examination of the underlying political forces and decision-making structure that have driven the evolution of policies toward ANWR, its last three chapters seek to apply the book's perspective to other important environment-energy debates. One of these involves drilling in the Eastern Gulf of Mexico (EGOM) off the coast of Florida. My goal again is to facilitate understanding of the patterns of political forces such as issue redefinition and partisan voting in Congress and their impact on policy shifts.

EGOM is another unstable subsystem where pro-environment arguments were not seriously challenged for many years. EGOM was largely off limits to drillers much as ANWR was off limits in accordance with pro-environment views about not drilling in ecologically sensitive territories. In 2006, however, Congress passed a law expanding the area within EGOM to allow drilling—the so-called "lease sale 181 area," with an estimated 1.26 billion barrels of crude oil and 5.8 trillion cubic feet of natural gas (see fig. 1.2).

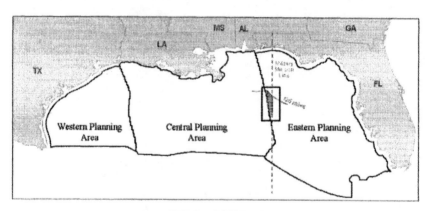

Figure 1.2, The Eastern Gulf of Mexico (EGOM),
Source: Minerals and Management Service, 2007.

This was seen as an important precedent at the time because nearly one-quarter of all domestically produced oil and natural gas comes from federal lands or coastal waters under federal protection. Companies typically pay a 12 to 16 percent royalty on their hydrocarbon sales to the federal government for rights to drill there (though these payments are somewhat offset by tax breaks for deepwater drilling).

A special factor that sets this case history apart and has made it a hot button issue in recent years involves these royalties. The federal government has been losing a large number of royalty payments because of a contractual blunder by mid-level US Department of the Interior (DOI) employees during the Clinton Administration.[3]

In addition to ANWR and EGOM case studies, where environmentalists historically prevailed until recent years, this book presents the case study of an arguably classic pro-development subsystem. It is referred to as *classic* here because it is a situation in which the battle between environmental and pro-development forces (over drilling for oil and gas on public lands in the Western United States) has historically seen a small group in the oil production industry or an entire industry itself benefit at the expense of the American public.

These pro-development forces have prevailed to an even greater extent in recent years. During the tenure of the George W. Bush Administration, the Bureau of Land Management (BLM), which is part of the DOI, issued a surge of leases to energy companies exploring in Western states, almost twice as many drilling permits, 7,018, in 2005 as President Clinton did in 2000, for instance.[4]

This book's last case study is the Cape Wind proposal to construct a large offshore wind farm in Massachusetts's Nantucket Sound, comprised of 130 wind turbines in a 24-square-mile area. It is a rather unusual case because here two different environmental coalitions are opposing each other, each claiming greater benefits for the American public if its views are adopted.

One of these coalitions supports wind power as an energy source. It asserts that wind turbines could reduce soaring electricity costs in New England in coming years, and could do so without seriously harming the environment. The second coalition focuses on alleged sweetheart deals with energy companies, and on the potential threat to birds. For now, let us focus on the core case study of this book, ANWR.

Background on the ANWR Case

One reason that ANWR has been the subject of so many heated disagreements over the years is that this ostensibly straightforward pro-environment versus pro-development dispute is anything but straightforward. There is a lot of history here, more special interests in play than most people realize, and a surprising lack of some critical data.

ANWR is located in Alaska, geographically the largest state in the nation with a very modest population of 626,000, 100,000 of whom are indigenous people.[5] Just by itself ANWR's present 19-million-acre size is larger than South Carolina.[6]

The ANWR story begins in 1959, the same year Alaska became a state. The Tanana Valley Sportsmen's Association proposed that Congress set aside lands in the northeastern part of Alaska to create an "Arctic National Wildlife Range." Then President Eisenhower responded by ordering his secretary of the Interior to designate a coastal plain in that part of Alaska extending over 8 million acres as a national wildlife range. This directive was approved and codified as Public Land Order 2214 on December 6, 1960.[7]

Initially this seemed like a decision that only involved environmental preservation. Preservation priorities were much in vogue during the early 1960s. A broadly supported Wilderness Act became law in 1964. It was only in 1968 that this Arctic Range emerged as an important energy-environmental controversy in the wake of the discovery of huge oil reserves at the state-owned Prudhoe Bay lands on Alaska's North Slope. This area is adjacent and to the west of the designated range.

Since then environmental interests have urged the federal government, which owns most of this land, to concentrate on protecting the migratory Porcupine Caribou Herd that breeds and flourishes along the coastal plain. They also have lobbied hard for protection of this habitat for many other species, some unique to the area, which live there for at least part of the year, species that include snow geese, polar and grizzly bears, wolves, and eagles.

On the development side, Chevron, the British Petroleum Corporation, the State of Alaska, and the Kaktovik Inupiat Corporation all share data derived from a single exploratory well jointly drilled years ago on privately owned land along the coast of ANWR.[8] Though the production potential of this lone exploratory well could be quite important in determining the value of drilling in this area, the findings remain largely secret for competitive market reasons.

How secret? When asked in 2003 if he was aware of the findings in that study, Andrew Lundquist, formerly of Vice President Cheney's 2001 energy task force, replied that he had been working on the issue 17 years and even he did not know.[9]

There are other, more readily accessible indications that the area might have considerable hydrocarbons. Oil seepage along the coastal plain and US Geological Survey (USGS) seismic data from the 1980s provide some support for a belief that the area has a large energy potential.[10] Opponents of drilling counter, however, that the USGS's non-invasive seismic activities do not necessarily indicate the presence of a vast, centralized reserve such as the one found at Prudhoe Bay.[11] Further, seismic activities produce estimates of economically recoverable oil based on oil prices that are always fluctuating.

The ANWR debate has been made even more complicated by two pieces of legislation passed during the 1970s. Indigenous Alaskans and the state government have made their own land claims that conflict in some ways with efforts to protect ANWR. A controversial 1971 statute (ANCSA) distributed roughly 44 million acres across the state to indigenous Eskimos and Indians.[12] Also in 1980 during the final months of the Carter Administration, President Carter signed into law the Alaska National Interest Lands Conservation Act (ANILCA), a measure that enlarged the Arctic Range from 8.9 to 19 million acres, and gave the range its present ANWR name.

The acreage that enlarged ANWR included an additional strip of the coastal plain, a narrow span 15 to 40 miles wide and 100 miles long, which because of the indications cited above made drillers anxious to tap reserves they believed (or at least hoped) were there in abundance. Most of the original 8.9 million acres within ANWR had been officially designated "wilderness," the most stringent level of environmental protection designated by the federal government.[13]

The House of Representatives voted twice to designate the new coastal plain area "wilderness" and thus protect it from petroleum-related development. The final version of the law passed by the Senate in 1980, however, permitted seismic (i.e., sound wave) exploration in the area, though not exploratory drilling or full-scale development near the coast.[14] ANILCA in its final form also called for further study by the Department of Interior (DOI) to determine the coastal plain's environmental and hydrocarbon resources. Politically, the ANILCA law passed this hot potato to a future Congress to decide whether to drill or not.

Historians and political observers have both asserted that these two statutes permanently altered the ANWR policy debate. ANSCA forced Alaskans to contend with the concerns of Eskimos and Indians; ANILCA seemed to legitimize economic values as applied to ANWR as long as these are deemed consistent with wilderness values.[15]

Since the end of the first Gulf War in 1991, ANWR has risen to the top of the congressional agenda many times.[16] And in recent years, there's been a noticeable shift in Washington on priorities on the issue. A largely pro-environment decision structure governing ANWR faced a major challenge in 1995 when a newly Republican-dominated Congress voted for a budget measure that included a provision to drill on the expanded reserve's coastal plain.

This policy revision was short-lived. President Clinton vetoed that bill. Two years later, he even signed a measure that legally clarified that the mission for refuges in general was to promote conservation and plant and animal restoration (P.L. 105-57). This measure managed to get bipartisan support, in part, because lawmakers believed the refuge system lacked adequate funding and managerial oversight, something this law would help provide.

By 1997, ANWR was one of 509 wildlife refuges in the US covering 92 million acres. The DOI permits hunting in 283 of these refuges and fishing in 276. Most refuge acreage is located in Alaska, though some other refuge lands are adjacent to West Coast subdivisions and south of Washington, DC at the Chincoteague National Wildlife Refuge.[17]

The legislative and administrative debate over drilling in ANWR has only intensified in the present decade. On August 1, 2001, the House again voted (240-189) to allow drilling on a segment of the ANWR coastal plain as part of an energy package (HR 4). The bill would have also provided $33.5 billion in tax incentives over 10 years to energy producers and users to develop new energy sources and to conserve existing supplies.

Similar legislation that included an ANWR-drilling provision passed the House in 2003, 2005, and again in 2006. The Senate, however, on occasion with the help of a filibuster (e.g., in April 2002), has consistently rejected plans to open part of ANWR to drilling.

The push to drill in ANWR now focuses on just eight percent of the refuge's 19 million acres. This is the so-called "1002 Area," named for the section of the 1980 ANILCA law dealing with the 1.5-million-acre coastal plain.

Energy and labor interests cite as their rationale for development here an estimated 11.6 billion barrels of oil in untapped reserves, which with new extraction technology could provide more than 30 years worth of reliable oil production. This figure is a 1998 estimate from the USGS and is based on intricate geological and fluid economic assumptions. Supporters of drilling likewise claim 750,000 new jobs would be created across America by this drilling.

Environmentalists argue the need for continued protection of various species and their habitat. They also cite geologists who estimate the volume of oil reserves in this area to be a mere 5.6 billion barrels or less, which translates into as little as a 6-month supply of oil.[18]

Questions Addressed by This Book

At a macro level, this book seeks to understand the determinants and structures of environmental-energy policy change or lack of it. It seeks to empower scholars, the policy-making community, and students to think anew about the forces underlying today's contentious debates in environmental-energy policy, including ANWR.

The new conventional wisdom suggests that it is difficult, if not impossible, to discuss most environmental topics without considering the energy implications, or vice versa. I will do so not only by exploring the policy evolution of ANWR, but also by considering three additional cases: proposals to construct wind farms in Massachusetts; expanded drilling for oil and natural gas in the Gulf of Mexico; and drilling on public lands in the West during the *Bush 43* years.

The results will yield answers to important questions such as Why hasn't ANWR been drilled but the Eastern Gulf of Mexico has or will be soon? What accounts for *big oil* gaining access to drill in more public lands in the Western United States in recent years? What forces are driving the debate between environmental groups over proposed wind farms in New England? How do these cases differ in terms of their decision-making structures? Do those structures impact policy outcomes?

At a micro level, I define policy *arena change* as the strengthening or weakening of a pro-environment decision-making structure or subsystem that is arguably favorable for those promoting environmental agendas, and resulting policy shifts.[19] Use of this concept enables the researcher to identify the underlying political forces driving ANWR and similar debates in Congress. Policy change can be explained

   This book is perhaps the first longitudinal case study of ANWR decision making based on hard data. In this case its central questions are What explains the existence and then unraveling of the ANWR subsystem (e.g., pro-drilling votes)? What explains the limited extent to which challenges to the subsystem have been effective? Are these phenomena best understood as arising out of legislative party politics and the Partisan Voting Model (PVM), as manifestations of changes in the broader political environment in which public policy is made and the Life Cycle Model (LCM), or some combination of the two? Or, does neither model separately or in combination capture fully the reasons for policy continuity and arena change? Finally, can we apply the findings in the ANWR case to other disputed issues in environment-energy policy making?

A Dual Framework for Explaining Policy Change

My research uses two analytical tools to construct a wide stage to clarify environmental-energy policy shifts in the United States. The Life Cycle Model (LCM) and the Partisan Voting Model (PVM) may help to explain the changing policy arena for ANWR and other conflictive policy issues. Each model has a foundation in the public policy literature in political science. The PVM employs a popular method of roll call analysis to determine whether partisan voting in Congress led to establishment of the subsystem and policy shifts favoring drilling. The LCM offers a more sophisticated analysis since it uses three separate explanations rather than one. These include Executive Branch activity, issue redefinition favoring drilling, and public opinion shifts in the same direction.

   The purpose of these case studies is to explain why certain policy arenas change or fail to change.[20] The primary case, ANWR, argues that the pro-environment subsystem weakened and temporarily lost the political battle; this is reflected in the clear tilt toward pro-drilling ANWR votes in one or both chambers of Congress since 1995. This section is directed primarily to students and introduces the PVM and the LCM models. Chapters 4 and 5 apply them to ANWR and other cases. For now, consider the basic framework of the PVM and the guiding scholarship that I applied in the four cases beginning with ANWR.

The Partisan Voting Model (PVM)

The Partisan Voting Model (PVM) represents a narrow explanation for ANWR arena change between 1977 and 2006. It uses roll call analysis to answer whether partisan congressional voting explains the existence of the ANWR subsystem, its weakening, and resultant policy shifts. Conventional wisdom suggests that

Democratic Party control of both chambers of Congress in 1980 and Republican Party control of one or both chambers of Congress in 1995, 2001, 2003, 2005, and 2006 led to very different vote outcomes on ANWR. Chapter 4 tests this position using empirical data. This rubric, like the Life Cycle Model, should prove to be a useful tool in clarifying these often confusing and heated debates in environmental-energy policy.

The PVM uses roll call analysis to detect the presence or absence of partisanship, or the extent of party line voting on ANWR votes in the House and Senate over time. As detailed in chapter 4, the explanatory power of the PVM depends on finding a pattern of partisanship on critical votes on an issue. This book hypothesizes that political party behavior influences policy outcomes for ANWR and topics in the environmental-energy subfield.

Several key research findings support the PVM as an explanation for ANWR arena change. The basis for this model is two major bodies of literature on legislative behavior theory. Both sets of literature employ roll call analysis. The first group of works summarized below addresses group (i.e., party) voting behavior. The second group concerns the behavior of individual legislators. These works are included here because chapter 4 investigates why certain legislators' votes on ANWR undermined the partisan explanation or made it indeterminate. Below I summarize the scholarship on institutional differences between the House and Senate and their impact on partisan voting in the two chambers.

We can divide research on the role of national political parties in voting behavior into studies that define and explain inter-party cohesion and inter-party conflict on the one hand, and those that examine voting cleavages involving broad policy coalitions and their impact on legislative voting on the other. Both scholarly strands share an emphasis on party serving as the dominant cleavage in Congress, or shifting partisan cleavages in the House and Senate over time.

Lawrence A. Lowell (1901) paved the way for modern scholarship on American political party behavior through his classic work, "The Influence of Party upon Legislation in England and America." He found that party voting in Congress is difficult to predict, and that it is contingent upon having a sharply divisive question on the agenda.[21]

Lowell established a foundation for Rice's (1928) seminal work, which is integral to this book. Lowell and Rice "…assessed the strength or importance of partisan cleavages via two measures of party behavior, the level of intra-party cohesion and the incidence of inter-party conflict."[22] Rice's work is longstanding in the field and critical for construction of the Partisan Voting Model used to explain policy outcomes for ANWR and other cases (see chapter 4).

This book uses sociologist Rice's Index of Cohesion for several reasons. First, it has been a commonly used measure of group cohesion in political science for decades. Second, it will aid in determining whether intra-party voting cohesion was present on ANWR votes since 1977. Third, and most importantly, measurement of intra-party cohesion allows us to measure partisan voting across parties and test one of my key claims in the core case of ANWR, that partisan voting in Congress explains subsystem and policy shifts since passage of President Carter's ANILCA law 1980.

The term "partisanship" is used in this book in a straightforward way. It refers to majorities of both major political parties opposing one another's position on any given vote. Identification of levels of party cohesion on that vote simply determines the extent of partisanship. Rice's method, or cohesion index, is a means to evaluate both intra- and inter-party voting cohesion (see Methodological Appendix for illustrations and applications to the ANWR case). These inter-party comparisons aid in identifying degrees of partisanship.

Importantly, more recent scholarship on party voting as an explanation for policy change elucidates a debate between those who argue that party shapes voting behavior and rational choice scholars who assert that individual legislators' goals and incentives drive decision making (e.g., Krehbiel 1998). Rational choice thinkers argue the individual legislator is the key driving force.

The party-related scholarship is relevant to chapter 4, which tests the claim that party-line voting was a necessary condition for shifts in ANWR policy outcomes since 1977, especially in the US House of Representatives. Numerous scholars have found that "party does matter in American national government."[23] Specifically, some claim that parties have independent effects on legislative decision making and policy outcomes since parties dictate the "rules of the game."[24]

However, scholars tend to conceptualize party effects differently.[25] Cox and McCubbins (1993) maintain that party serves as a cartel to solve collective action problems within the majority party.[26] Aldrich and Rohde (2000) place conditions on their own version of party-governmental theory. They specifically claim that the hand of the majority party leadership in determining policy outcomes is strengthened when there is policy conflict and high partisan unity.[27] This is the theory of conditional party government (CPG).

Clearly, the polarization that started in Congress in the 1980s had an impact on policy through the 1990s.[28] Thus, it is reasonable to speculate that partisan forces in both chambers influenced ANWR policy outcomes after passage of the pro-environment, bipartisan ANILCA law in 1980 and that majority party leadership on these votes contributed to their party's legislative success.[29] The challenge for scholars is how to construct systematic means to measure the relationship between partisan voting and policy outcomes.[30]

The "parties matter" literature is critical in constructing the PVM. However, defections from partisan voting patterns weaken the explanatory power of the model. As we shall see, Republicans who affected policy outcomes are the critical defectors in the ANWR case.

To understand reasons for defections (and thus alternative explanations for arena change), we need to look at the variety of factors that may influence voting behavior in Congress. These include Members' constituencies; colleagues; interest groups; the party leadership; the administration; congressional staff; region; and conception of what constitutes "good public policy."

Scholars have not agreed on which of these or other factors has the most influence on voting behavior. Collie, who summarized the disparate body of literature related to individual voting behavior, found no consensus on what determines individual decision making in the American setting.[31] Kingdon's findings were similar, although he discovered that constituency and fellow congressmen likely were important influences on congressmen's votes.[32]

This book therefore also explores three explanations for why lawmakers did or did not vote in a partisan way: voting in a way that is consistent with a legislator's conception of *good public policy*, a legislator's concern about satisfying *pro-environment constituents*, and the *region* in which the legislator's state or district lies. It is tricky trying to gauge politicians' motives on votes, but these variables are commonly seen in the literature, although other explanations may exist, according to Kingdon (1989).

Part of this book therefore attempts to *get inside the minds* of lawmakers to see why they vote as they do on environment-energy issues such as ANWR. Determining reasons for defections on ANWR votes helps clarify why arena change may or may not be present. This book borrows three possible explanations from the literature in order to draw inferences about those changes in my core case study.

Deviations from partisanship may be related to chamber influences as well. The House or Senate may be more or less conducive to party-based voting patterns. If chamber differences exist and give rise to different voting outcomes, I will want to explore the reasons for them. As we will see, the House and Senate have voted differently on ANWR in recent years. This book seeks to find if institutional distinctions partly account for House passage of pro-drilling energy legislation in 2001, 2003, 2005, and 2006 and the failure of companion legislation in the Senate, for example. Essentially, did Senate procedures temper the effects of GOP majorities seeking to change ANWR to a pro-drilling policy? Research findings from other studies suggest that chamber differences exist and can be important.[33]

Focusing first on ANWR, the claim that I will test for the partisan framework is that if the PVM explains arena change (i.e., subsystem and policy shifts), then shifts in ANWR policy should coincide with shifts in party control or party voting in Congress. This study posits that Democratic control with partisan voting yielded a status-quo, pro-environment policy up until 1995. And Republican control of Congress accompanied by partisan voting produced arena change. So, in chapter 4 I will test the validity of the following proposition using roll call data:

> Pro-drilling decisions in Congress should be associated with Republican control of Congress.

We can reasonably expect testing of the partisan voting hypothesis to yield the most supportive data since party is thought to serve as the dominant cleavage in Congress, both by scholars and political observers. However, we cannot be certain which claim will be confirmed until they are tested.

The Life Cycle Model (LCM)

The Life Cycle Model is the more complex framework of the two that seeks to identify and explain the underlying political forces driving arena change in environmental-energy cases. Chapter 5 tests hypotheses based on the LCM by employing mixed methods: content analysis of media accounts and congressional hearings that define ANWR and the other cases; examination of public opinion data; and, document analysis of actors involved in the subsystem or decision structure. Here I introduce its basic idea for this model and its conventional yet eclectic data collection methods.

Life cycle scholars basically argue that a combination of underlying political forces can explain subsystem and policy change. In this book, support for the life cycle explanation requires uncovering specific evidence about three underlying political forces: issue redefinition, public opinion shifts, and new actors becoming involved in the policy-making process.

The model posits in my core case that ANWR was redefined as a pro-drilling issue either through the media, in Congress, by the President of the United States, or some combination of these actors. Issue redefinition began presumably prior to the GOP takeover of Congress in 1995 and continued thereafter to shape the pro-drilling policy that periodically emerged through 2006.

It also assumes that presidents rarely monopolize the process of issue definition for domestic issues such as ANWR. The model assumes that high-ranking political appointees rather than career civil servants in Executive Branch agencies tend to represent the president's position at congressional hearings and in news accounts.

The second explanation in the LCM concerns the role of public opinion, whether it favored environmental interests, and whether it shifted to a pro-drilling or neutral opinion. The explanation supports the LCM if public support for protecting ANWR fades after establishment of the subsystem even though the subsystem remains in place. A temporary period of "optimism and positive mobilization [leaves] a tremendous institutional legacy."[34]

The involvement of new interests or other actors in the policy-making arena is the third type of change that supports the LCM as a viable explanation for policy arena change. New or previously excluded actors should become involved in congressional decisions about ANWR, for instance, prior to policy decisions that are pro-drilling.

In short, the life cycle concept as often used is comprised of issue redefinition, shifting public opinion, and involvement of new actors in the policy-making process; it offers a more complex explanation for arena change than partisan voting in Congress alone. Chapter 5 and the appendix provide a more detailed discussion of this approach.

This book helps make sense of the forces driving environmental-energy policy changes ranging from the role of Congress in redefining policy issues and voting plus the influence of broader societal factors, all based in public policy scholarship in the field of political science. But there is another, related factor in understanding these policies—namely—the perceived distributional impacts of policy decisions.

Most political scientists have at least some familiarity with the body of literature on capture theory, iron triangles, and subsystems. In the core case of ANWR, they provide a plausible point of reference for studying how most congressional decisions have been made since 1960. These studies can also be used necessarily for probing subsystems for a plethora of contemporary environmental-energy policies. According to this approach, policy is made by a limited number of like-minded actors within a somewhat rigid decision-making structure, really, a policy configuration of mid-level actors who share a set of values or goals.

The life cycle literature, by contrast, addresses how and why these closed structures often change over time, and specifically the weakening or dismantling of iron triangles, decision-making monopolies, and the like. In this book, these works serve as a possible explanation for shifts in ANWR and other subgovernments.

The scholarship that mentions directly or implies that policies have life cycles has a lengthy history and offers rich content.[35] The literature begins with a static concept, a "subsystem." Various formal definitions exist for this term, but Fritschler and Hoefler (1996) provide a clear-cut designation as useful as any other. They define it as "a structure dependent upon a larger political entity but one that functions with a high degree of autonomy. ... It cuts across institutional lines and includes within it all groups and individuals who are making and influencing government decisions concerning" a given issue.[36]

Subsystems are often described as *subgovernments*, *whirlpools*, and *iron triangles*. They have been studied since Maass's work in 1951. An important strand of literature on subsystems discusses the perceived distributional impacts of their policy outputs. The importance of the distribution of policies' costs and benefits is illustrated through typologies that classify observations in terms of distributional variables. Lowi (1964) and Wilson (1980) base their typologies on common properties and perceptions regarding cost-benefit distributions of subsystem policy outputs. Typical of subgovernments is the distribution of monetary benefits to client groups. For Wilson (1980), some regulatory politics appears to be *client politics*, in which the costs of regulation are widely disbursed throughout society and its benefits are afforded to a select few, typically regulated industries.[37]

Examples of clientelistic policy monopolies of the kind Wilson describes are found in the life cycle literature. They range from the civilian nuclear power case (Baumgartner and Jones 1993), to tobacco (Fritschler and Hoefler 1996), to pesticides (Bosso 1987). These structures also tend to be characterized by a low public visibility, mutual accommodation among the interested political actors, minimal information dissemination, privatized conflict, and controlled issue definition. Their respective policies yield a distribution of monetary benefits to private interest clients and incremental policy change.[38]

Hugh Heclo (1978) provided a foundation for political science literature on life cycles of policies by identifying dynamic rather than static decision-making structures. He critiqued the earlier scholarship on iron triangles by arguing that "issue networks" offered a characterization of the policy-making process that is more fluid in its dissemination of information. He identified webs of influence comprised of additional actors (e.g., academic institutions, think tanks, policy specialists, etc.) who exchange information in a less predictable manner than iron triangles.[39]

Several scholars who have studied life cycles of issues frequently emphasize one or more explanations for shifts in decision-making structures and therefore policy outcomes. These include issue redefinition, changes in public opinion, and the role of actors who compete with those already established in the subsystem.[40] But it should be noted that other explanations for policy change may exist and that some works such as Steinberg's (2001) explain environmental policy changes in an international comparative context across countries.

For our purposes, Baumgartner and Jones (1993) studied the civilian nuclear power subsystem and borrowed Anthony Downs's (1972) contention that public opinion is cyclical and therefore usually declines after its peak. They likewise asserted that stable policy monopolies are "created and destroyed at critical junctures throughout the process of issue development."[41]

These changes are contingent upon changing "policy images" or issue definitions and shifting "institutional venues" or actors.[42] A combination of empirical information and emotional appeals determine issue definitions.[43] Institutional venues are "the institutional locations where authoritative decisions are made concerning a given issue."[44] The images (i.e., issue definitions) and institutions associated with a given policy are subject to rapid change if the right set of conditions exists.

Their study provides insight into the birth and death of policies and their respective subsystems. This study of ANWR arena change and other pro-environment subsystems utilizes the life cycle literature, but it also deviates from that scholarship to some extent.

Following Bosso and other LCM theorists, this book recognizes that many policy areas have grown much more pluralistic, and therefore much different than the vision of Lowi (1979) and others who emphasized isolated pockets of power (e.g., subsystems) that are immune from control by the populace, private armies of sorts.[45] What Lowi and others overlooked is the possibility that interest groups such as those in the environmental community can advance issues that are subject to and consistent with national public opinion (e.g., protecting ANWR from development).

Finally, studies of subsystems tend to overlook important institutional differences between the House and Senate. Interests seeking to challenge or bolster subsystems face different constraints in the House than in the Senate (e.g., the Senate filibuster and the House Committee on Rules).

Several research hypotheses based on the LCM follow with the goal of explaining the existence and unraveling of the ANWR subsystem since 1995. If the LCM explains arena change then policy decisions on ANWR should reflect a redefined issue favoring drilling, a shift in public opinion against environmental protection, and involvement of new or latent subsystem actors that supported drilling and expanded political conflict prior to 1995. The year 1995 is important since I hope to determine the impact of these political forces in policy shifts independent of change in party control in Congress.

Furthermore, each of these factors potentially can affect the salience of ANWR as a public policy issue. Chapter 5 tests the hypotheses that are introduced here for my core case, ANWR.

Issue redefinition represents the heart of the life cycle analysis. The first hypothesis concerns redefinition of ANWR by the media and in Congress:

> The tone and definition of the ANWR issue in the media and Congress should reflect a pro-drilling position prior to 1995, pre-dating the Republican takeover.

The next claim tested for the LCM concerns the role of the White House in issue redefinition. Specifically, President George W. Bush was a key political actor in redefining ANWR, in part, through congressional testimony by his agency representatives. The assertion is that:

> President George W. Bush's leadership on ANWR helped to redefine ANWR as a pro-development policy.

Even if Congress and the media redefined ANWR prior to President Bush's first term, he may have built on that momentum by persuading party moderates in Congress to support his definition of ANWR and thus weaken the subsystem by passing pro-drilling legislation, as his father sought to do.

The third proposition from the LCM concerns the role of public opinion:

> Public opinion favored the environmental position prior to creation of the ANWR subsystem, but it shifted against the environmentalists' view later.

If the LCM has explanatory power, we should expect the tone of public opinion surveys to favor ANWR protection and then shift to favor drilling over time as drilling bills passed.

The fourth contention from the LCM concerns involvement of new or latent actors in subsystem unraveling:

> The weakening of the ANWR subsystem and policy decisions in favor of drilling are associated with pro-drilling Executive Branch agencies and interest groups formerly not involved in the issue.

If the LCM is supported by the data, we should find that a federal agency or interest group served as a catalyst for arena change by expanding the scope of the debate. The US Department of Energy and the US Fish and Wildlife Service at the Department of Interior are two prospective actors in the ANWR case. This finding would be consistent with other life cycle studies that found, for example, that the Federal Trade Commission weakened the tobacco subgovernment during the early 1960s,[46] the Atomic Energy Commission and Nuclear Regulatory Commission weakened the civilian nuclear power subgovernment,[47] and the Food and Drug Administration diminished the pesticides monopoly.[48]

It is possible that the findings in chapters 4 and 5 applying the two models to ANWR and other cases will support either the Partisan Voting Model or the Life Cycle Model. Alternatively, the data may bolster both models as explanations for the existence and unraveling of the ANWR decision-making structure or changes in other public policies: drilling on public lands in America's West (see Rosenbaum 2002, chapter 9), in the Eastern Gulf of Mexico, and for the Cape Wind project in New England. Or, the data may support neither model. A final possibility is that one or both models could be supported by subsystem activity in one chamber of Congress but not the other.

Rethinking ANWR, Drilling in the Gulf of Mexico and in the West, and Wind Power

Chapter 2 identifies the policy evolution of ANWR and its pro-environment subsystem created in the US House of Representatives in 1977, including its actors, characteristics, and how it deviates from a classic subsystem (i.e., decision-making structure). Specifically, it recounts the role of the subsystem in the debate on the Alaska National Interest Lands Conservation Act (ANILCA), which President Jimmy Carter signed in 1980.

Chapter 3 discusses subsystem maintenance in the ANWR case and challenges to its dominance during three periods when drilling emerged on the congressional agenda (1991-1992, 1995, 2001-2006). It examines how the subsystem's key decision makers shifted from Congress to the Clinton White House after the 1994 congressional elections. Finally, this chapter discusses the structure of the subsystem and its opponents during George W. Bush's administration.

Chapter 4 uses roll call analysis of energy and budgetary votes to determine whether congressional voting in the ANWR case reflects legislative partisanship on ANWR under Republican and Democratic majorities. This chapter also explores the role of moderate *swing* voters in Congress as defectors from the partisan voting pattern, which either undermines or makes the partisan explanation indeterminate. It subsequently applies the partisan voting perspective to three contemporary environmental-energy debates.

Chapter 5 applies the life cycle approach to the ANWR case study to determine if ANWR was redefined, new actors became involved in the arena, and public opinion changed in ways consistent with congressional voting patterns. Finally, it examines the three additional cases in light of this framework.

Chapter 6 makes sense of the lessons from all of this book's case studies on the environmental-energy policy-making process: the ANWR case and proposals to construct wind farms in Massachusetts, the debates over expanded drilling for oil and natural gas in the Gulf of Mexico, and drilling on public lands in the West, by identifying patterns of the underlying forces at work in the policy-decision process.

This book varies the types of cases according to their perceived distributional calculus in order to critique classic subsystem politics discussed by Bosso (1987) and Baumgartner and Jones (1993), and to offer new insight into unique decision-making structures that scholars may have overlooked. They argue that subsystems benefit narrow interests and that their unraveling occurs through changes in broad-based forces, thereby leading to policy shifts. I analyze those assertions by identifying subsystems with different distributional impacts leading to policy shifts or lack of them. My goal with all of this is to prompt everyone who cares about energy and the environment to think anew about the political forces driving these public policy decisions, hopefully to better serve the American public.

Notes

1. See: David Vogel, "Representing Diffuse Interests in Environmental Policymaking," in *Do Institutions Matter? Government Capabilities in the United States and Abroad*, ed. R. Kent Weaver and Bert A. Rockman (Washington, DC: The Brookings Institution, 1993), 259-60.

2. See: Gary Bryner, *Blue Skies, Green Politics: The Clean Air Act of 1990* (Washington, DC: CQ Press, 1993), 24,34.

3. "Congress Approves Offshore Drilling Bill," Reuters, <http://www.msnbc.msn.com/id/16140704/print/1 /displaymode/1098/> (10 December 2006); "Another Energy Inquiry on Royalties Collection," the *New York Times*, 16 February 2007; "Oil Company Revives Suit on Avoidance of Royalties," the *New York Times*, 3 March 2007.

4.   Jennifer Weeks, "Domestic Energy Development," *CQ Researcher* 15, no. 34 (30 September 2005): 815; "Growing Coalition Opposes Drilling; In NM Battle, Hunters Team with Environmentalists," the *Washington Post*, 25 July 2006.

5.   Stephen Haycox, *Frigid Embrace: Politics, Economics and Environment in Alaska* (Corvallis, OR: Oregon State University Press, 2002), 8.

6.   Susan   McGrath,   "The   Last   Great   Wilderness." *Audubon.org*, <http://magazine.audubon.org/ features0109/arctic.html> (2001).

7.   Lynne M. Corn and Bernard Gelb, "Arctic National Wildlife Refuge: Legislative Issues," Congressional Research Service, 14 May 2002 (4).

8.   Telephone interview with Andrew Lundquist, The Lundquist Group (formerly with the George W. Bush Administration), 6 January 2003.

9.   Lundquist interview.

10.   Telephone interview with Alaska State Representative & Majority Leader Jeannette James (R), 12 December 2002 and general knowledge.

11.   Telephone interview with DOI Secretary Cecil Andrus, Ret., 16 December 2002 and 24 July 2003.

12.   This measure was controversial primarily due to section 17 (d) (2), which empowered the Secretary of Interior to protect up to 80 million acres of lands in Alaska (see the 1980 *US Code Congressional and Administrative News*, 5073-75, for an overview of this section of the 1971 ANCSA statute).

13.   McGrath, "The Last Great Wilderness."

14.   Hank Lentfer and Carolyn Servid, eds. *Arctic Refuge: A Circle of Testimony* (Minneapolis: Milkweed Editions, 2001), 7.

15.   Haycox, *Frigid Embrace*, 172.

16.   Major ANWR-development debates transpired in 1991, 1995, 2001, 2002, 2003, 2005, and 2006.

17.   "House Passes New Standards for Use of Wildlife Refuges," *CQ Weekly Report*, 7 June 1997: 1313.

18   See: Lynne M. Corn and Bernard Gelb, "The Arctic National Wildlife Refuge: The Next Chapter," Congressional Research Service, Updated 2 April 2001 (2,4); "GAO Report Sparks New Arguments over ANWR drilling," Associated Press State and Local Wire, 15 November.2001; John Cochran and Rebecca Adams, "Fresh From a Set of Hill Victories, Can Labor Keep the Momentum?" *CQ Weekly Report* (1 September 2001); "2001 Legislative Summary," *CQ Weekly Report* (22 December 2001): 3037; <www.anwr.org> (27 May 2007); <www.audubon.org> (27 May 2007).

19.   As detailed in chapter 3, it is apparent that a subsystem of sorts existed and that it has weakened considerably over time.

20.   Harry Eckstein, "Case Study and Theory in Political Science," in *Handbook of Political Science*, Vol. 7, ed. Fred I. Greenstein and Nelson W. Polsby (Reading, MA: Addison-Wesley, 1975), 99-104.

21.   Lawrence A. Lowell, "The Influence of Party Upon Legislation in England and America" (paper presented as part of the *Annual Report of the American Historical Association for 1901*) I: 336-37.

22.   Melissa P. Collie, "Voting Behavior in Legislatures," *Legislative Studies Quarterly* 9 (February 1984): 7.

23.   Jon R. Bond and Richard Fleisher, eds. *Polarized Politics: Congress and the President in a Partisan Era* (Washington, DC: CQ Press, 2000), 188.

24. See; Gary W. Cox and Matthew D. McCubbins, *Legislative Leviathan: Party Government in the House* (Los Angeles: University of California Press, 1993); John H. Aldrich and David W. Rohde, "The Consequences of Party Organization in the House: The Role of the Majority and Minority Parties in Conditional Party Government," in *Polarized Politics: Congress and the President in a Partisan Era*, ed. Jon R. Bond and Richard Fleisher (Washington, DC: CQ Press, 2000), 31-72.

25. David W. Brady, John F. Cogin, and Morris P. Fiorino, eds. *Continuity and Change in House Elections.* Stanford, Calif.: Stanford University Press/Hoover Institution Press, 2000. 4.

26. Also see Cox, Gary W. Efficient Secret: The cabinet and the development of political parties in Victorian England. Cambridge; New York: Cambridge University Press, 1987; D. Roderick Kiewiet and Matthew D. McCubbins, eds. Logic of delegation: Congressional parties and the appropriations process. Chicago: University of Chicago Press, 1991.

27. Also see David W. Rohde, *Parties and Leaders in the Postreform House* (Chicago: The University of Chicago Press, 1991).

28. See: Rohde, *Parties and Leaders*; John H. Aldrich, *Why Parties? The Origin and Transformation of Political Parties in America* (Chicago: The University of Chicago Press, 1995); Bond and Fleisher, *Polarized Politics*; Keith T. Poole and Howard Rosenthal, *Congress: A Political-Economic Theory of Roll Cal Voting* (Oxford University Press, 1997); Barbara Sinclair, *Legislators, Leaders, and Lawmaking: The US House of Representatives in the Postreform Era* (Baltimore: The Johns Hopkins University Press, 1995).

29. According to Paul Quirk (see Roger H. Davidson, ed. *Postreform Congress.* New York: St. Martin's Press, c1992, pp. 310-11) most scholarship on congressional reform recognizes that Congress willingly decentralized its power during the *reform era* of the 1970s, and proceeded to maintain that diffusion of power in committees, subcommittees, etc. while strengthening the hand of the majority party leadership during the so-called "post-reform era" that started in the 1980s.

30. Bond and Fleisher, *Polarized Politics*, 64.

31. Collie, *Voting Behavior*, 26-27.

32. John W. Kingdon, *Congressmen's Voting Decisions* 3d ed. (Ann Arbor, MI: The University of Michigan Press, 1989) 67,105.

33. See: Rohde, *Parties and Leaders*; Lawrence C. Evans and Walter J. Oleszek, *Congress Under Fire: Reform Politics and the Republican Majority* (New York: Houghton Mifflin Company, 1997).

34. Frank R. Baumgartner and Bryan D. Jones, *Agendas and Instability in American Politics* (Chicago: The University of Chicago Press, 1993), 88. Also see E.E. Schattschneider, *The Semisovereign People: A Realist's View of Democracy in America* (New York: Harcourt Brace Jovanovich College Publishers, 1975).

35. Scholars including Griffith (1939), Maass (1951), Cater (1964), Freeman (1965), McConnell (1966), Redford (1969), Lowi (1968), Fritschler (1974), Heclo (1978), Kingdon (1984), Sabatier (1993), Bosso (1987), Baumgartner and Jones (1993), and Fritschler and Hoefler (1996) not only constructed the iron triangle concept and its variants, but also identified their shortcomings, including oversimplification. This scholarship set the foundation for the study of life cycles of issues.

36. A. Lee Fritschler and James M. Hoefler, *Smoking & Politics: Policymaking and the Federal Bureaucracy* 5ed. (Upper Saddle River, NJ: Prentice Hall, 1996) 5.

37. James Q. Wilson, *The Politics of Regulation* (New York: Basic Books, Inc., 1980), 367-371. He distinguishes between majoritarian politics (widely distributed costs and benefits); interest group politics (narrowly distributed costs and benefits); client politics (concentrated benefits yet widely distributed costs); and, entrepreneurial politics (widely distributed benefits and narrowly imposed costs).

38. For a comparison of these subsystem characteristics with those of a more pluralistic policy-making type, see Table 13 in Christopher J. Bosso, *Pesticides and Politics: The Life Cycle of a Public Issue* (Pittsburgh: University of Pittsburgh Press, 1987), 257.

39. Hugh Heclo, "Issue Networks and the Executive Establishment," in *The New American Political System*, ed. Anthony King (Washington, DC: American Enterprise Institute, 1978), 88, 94-97, 105-106.

40. See Schattschneider, *The Semisovereign*; Baumgartner and Jones, *Agendas*; Bosso, *Pesticides and Politics*; Gary Mucciaroni, "Problem Definition and Special Interest Politics in Tax Policy and Agriculture," in *The Politics of Problem Definition*, ed. David A. Rochefort and Roger W. Cobb (Lawrence, KS: University of Kansas Press, 1994), 117-137; John W. Kingdon, John W. *Agendas, Alternatives, and Public Policies*, 2d ed. (New York: Harper Collins College Publishers, 1995); Sandra Suarez, *Does Business Learn? Tax Breaks, Uncertainty, and Political Strategies* (Ann Arbor, MI: The University of Michigan Press, 2000).

41. Baumgartner and Jones, *Agendas*, 22.

42. Baumgartner and Jones, *Agendas*, 25-35.

43. Baumgartner and Jones, *Agendas*, 26.

44. Baumgartner and Jones, *Agendas*, 32.

45. Baumgartner and Jones, *Agendas*, 5. Also see Theodore Lowi, *The End of Liberalism: The Second Republic of the United States*, 2d ed. (New York: WW Norton & Company, 1979), 33,35.

46. Fritschler and Hoefler, *Smoking & Politics*, 13.

47. Baumgartner and Jones, *Agendas*.

48. Bosso, *Pesticides and Politics*.

Chapter 2
The Case of the Arctic National Wildlife Refuge (ANWR): A History

By 1977, an environmentally friendly subsystem for ANWR policy making had been created and centered in the US House of Representatives. Before that story is told, however, it is important to review several earlier events that affected the Alaska lands issue and contributed to the debate that led to the Alaska National Interest Lands Conservation Act (ANILCA) of 1980. The energy–environmental debate over Alaska's northeast coastal plain, after all, had been at least a century in the making.

The United States purchased Alaska from Russia in 1867. At that time, "...nothing was done to settle the aboriginal claims of the indigenous residents, the Indians, Eskimos, and Aleuts, and for [the next] century Congress and the Executive Branch [would pass] the buck."[1] Land rights issues were to become inextricably linked with the complex energy-environmental debates that would ensue in the region. But it was not until the Nixon Administration that federal lawmakers would address this issue directly.

At the beginning of a new century, President Theodore Roosevelt established the first component in the National Wildlife Refuge System: Pelican Island, Florida, in 1903.[2] Since its inception, this System has aimed to protect wildlife and its habitat. Roosevelt's successor, William Howard Taft, established six additional national wildlife refuges along the Alaska coast between 1909 and 1913. This conservation approach toward Alaska lands continued when the Mt. McKinley Park (known today as Denali National Park and Preserve) became the first national park established in Alaska in 1917.[3]

Through the 1920s and 1930s, both governmental and non-governmental developments helped shape the fledgling debate between environmentalists and petroleum and national security interests. President Warren Harding signed an executive order establishing the Naval Petroleum Reserve (renamed the National Petroleum Reserve-Alaska, NPR-A, in 1976) west of the area that would become the Arctic National Wildlife Refuge.[4] At the same time, biologists Olaus and Margaret Murie were beginning to build a case for protecting lands in northeast Alaska as they explored, by boat and sled, various drainages in the Brooks Mountain Range.

Robert Marshall, who led the effort to form the Wilderness Society, struck up a friendship with Olaus Murie that provided the impetus for a long-term effort to establish an Arctic wildlife reserve. By 1938, Marshall recommended as part of a congressional study that most of Alaska north of the Yukon River be set aside permanently as wilderness.[5]

In 1943, the US Department of Interior (DOI) issued Public Land Order 82, which preserved a huge tract of land the size of North Dakota for national defense purposes, thus favoring the development side of the Alaska lands debate.[6] But six years later, the National Park Service at DOI began a series of pro-environment activities that would last into the late 1950s. The northeast corner of Alaska was recommended for preservation due to that area's wildlife, wilderness, recreation, scientific, and cultural value. In 1957, DOI also prepared a request for Congress to establish an 8,000-square-mile wildlife reserve in northeastern Alaska.

In the midst of all this Executive Branch activity, a high-ranking actor in the non-political branch of the federal government, US Supreme Court Justice William O. Douglas, visited biologists Olaus and Margaret Murie at their camp in Alaska in 1957. These three individuals led a campaign favoring conservation in the region. This campaign was instrumental in the creation by President Eisenhower of the Arctic Range three years later. Environmentalists have cited Justice Douglas as a champion of ANWR protection ever since.[7]

In many ways, the year 1958 was a watershed one in Alaska politics. President Eisenhower signed the Alaska Statehood Act into law on July 7th that year. In admitting Alaska as the 49th State, this measure also granted the state the right to select 102.5 million vacant, unreserved acres with accompanying mineral rights.[8] Energy development interests were pleased by these developments.

However, in the early years of Alaska's statehood, local institutions played a key role in protecting lands in the northeastern part of the state. The Tanana Valley Sportsmen's Association, Fairbanks Chamber of Commerce, parallelism *Fairbanks News Miner* proposed that Congress set aside lands in northeastern Alaska to create an "Arctic National Wildlife Range." The Alaska Department of Mines and the Anchorage Chamber of Commerce opposed the idea, believing it would hinder development.

On May 1, 1959, US Secretary of the Interior Fred Seaton submitted draft legislation to create a nearly 9-million-acre Range in northeast Alaska. Seaton hired and worked closely with a young former prosecutor from Fairbanks, Ted Stevens, after the two men had struck up a friendship. Stevens was to become a major player in ANWR policy making for decades to come. The efforts of these two men paid dividends in the US House of Representatives in 1960 when the lower chamber passed legislation that would create the Arctic Range. The Senate held hearings, but failed to pass a companion measure, largely because Alaska Senator Bartlett, who strongly opposed the measure, chaired the committee that handled the bill.[9]

This matter did not end there, however. On December 2, 1960, President Eisenhower ordered DOI Secretary Seaton to designate Public Land Order 2214. This action selected 8.9 million acres in northeast Alaska to be included in a national wildlife range.

Environmentalists were ecstatic. This Arctic National Wildlife "Range" would become an important building block for pro-environment forces that, two decades later, would enact legislation doubling its size and renaming it the "Refuge." The energy lobby was pleased too since the Eisenhower Administration also revoked Public Land Order 82 (1943), and opened 20 million acres on the North Slope to prospective energy-related development, including the area near Prudhoe Bay.[10]

The Kennedy and Johnson Administrations, for the most part, favored environmental protection. Although President Kennedy signed a measure (P.L. 87-714) authorizing DOI to set aside parts of national wildlife refuges and other conservation areas for public recreation activities, the Johnson Administration enacted a variety of statutes that advanced environmental causes nationally.[11]

For instance, in 1964 the Congress passed the Wilderness Act (P.L. 88-577). This law was "designed to preserve substantial land areas of the nation in a wild, unspoiled condition."[12] Presidents Kennedy and Johnson strongly supported the bill.

The following year, Congress passed the Land and Water Conservation Fund Act; and, in 1966, it enacted another environmentally friendly law, the National Historic Preservation Act.[13] The environmentalist cause was strengthened again two years later when President Johnson signed the Wild and Scenic Rivers Act, a measure that provided three designations, each with a different degree of protection for rivers—wild, scenic, and recreational.[14] Environmentalists subsequently utilized this law as a rationale for protecting certain areas in Alaska.

Yet, it took a non-statutory development in 1967 and 1968 to make the environmental-energy controversy in Alaska even more salient. The Atlantic Richfield Company (ARCO) discovered a deposit of 15 billion barrels of oil at Prudhoe Bay, Alaska, which is located west of the area that became known as ANWR's coastal plain, or 1002 Area (i.e., the key area of contention today between environmentalists and producer interests). The discovery of the Prudhoe field was the largest to date in North America. Shortly afterward, in 1969, the federal government hired its first manager for the Arctic Range.[15]

The early 1970s produced several new laws that aimed at raising national environmental standards, settling Alaska indigenous land claims, as well as increasing access to hydrocarbons on Alaska's North Slope. First, Congress established the Council on Environmental Quality and the Environmental Protection Agency by enacting the National Environmental Policy Act in 1970.[16]

A year later, a major piece of legislation in the ANWR saga became public law. President Nixon signed the Alaska Native Claims Settlement Act (ANCSA), which permitted "...Native villages and regional corporations. . . . to select 44 million acres of land, in addition to awarding them $962 million."[17]

This Act empowered the Secretary of Interior to protect up to 80 million acres of land in Alaska while Congress studied the land set-aside issue. In addition, the law established December 18, 1978, as the deadline for Congress to submit its study recommending lands to be designated for varying degrees of environmental protection. This deadline would become critical in the formation of the House subsystem in 1977 and passage of the Alaska National Interest Lands Conservation Act (ANILCA) in 1980 (i.e., the Alaska lands debate).

Historian Stephen Haycox asserts that the ANCSA (1971) and ANILCA (1980) laws changed Alaska "dramatically and permanently." ANCSA forced Alaskans to take the claims of indigenous groups seriously. Close to a decade later, ANILCA may have created a new type of American wilderness where human presence is permissible as long as it does not undermine wilderness values.[18]

After Congress approved ANCSA, the Nixon Administration handed environmentalists a setback in their efforts to protect Alaska lands when Vice President Spiro Agnew cast the tie-breaking vote (50-49) in favor of constructing the Trans-Alaska Pipeline (TAPS) in 1973. This development, by its close vote, is an early example of congressional partisanship or conflict on environmental-energy issues given the closeness of the tally.

Senator Mike Gravel (D), who later would run for President in 2008, and Ted Stevens (R) of Alaska supported the administration's position. Specifically, the vice president voted against the motion to recommit the Gravel-Stevens Amendment barring further court review of environmental questions raised by pipeline construction.[19]

The proposed pipeline route originated at Prudhoe Bay, moved south to Fairbanks, then to the southern port of Valdez, and ultimately to markets in the "lower 48." Prudhoe Bay had been selected by Juneau as state land several years prior to the discovery of major oil and gas reserves in 1968. State officials were eager to construct the oil pipeline since its existence would mean revenue for state and local coffers. The Arctic Range to the east was unavailable for extensive exploration or drilling since it remained in federal hands.[20]

The Alaska Public Interest Coalition was an umbrella group composed of environmentalists who opposed the pipeline.[21] They faced the disconcerting prospect that building a pipeline could provide a rationale for drilling along the coastal plain of the Arctic Range since the pipeline would increase market access. But the good news for environmental activists was that drilling on the North Slope would likely be limited for a time: pipeline construction would take several years to complete. Besides, the development of areas besides the Range, especially on state-controlled lands, would minimize the chances of near-term opening of the controversial Arctic Range to development.

During this period, Congress amended the National Wildlife Refuge Administration Act and granted the US Fish and Wildlife service (USFWS) primary administrative power over refuges.[22] Other agencies with some jurisdiction over the Arctic Range/ANWR since the 1970s included the Bureau of Land Management (BLM) and the US Geological Survey (USGS).[23] While these three agencies are each accountable to the Secretary of the Interior, there are some key distinctions between them. Importantly, the USFWS tends to manage federal lands by emphasizing protection of wildlife and their habitat. The BLM, on the other hand, advocates multiple uses for public lands.[24]

Internationally, the US experienced its first oil-price shock when the Organization of Petroleum Exporting Countries (OPEC) imposed an oil embargo as retribution for American support for Israel during the 1973 Yom Kippur War. Oil prices soon quadrupled. America's dependence on foreign oil became a means to define the ANWR issue for supporters of drilling for oil and natural gas. This definition was employed periodically from this period through the congressional debates of the early twenty-first century.

Overall, the Nixon Administration did not push for a statute aimed at designating Alaska lands into the four national conservation systems, and the succeeding Ford Administration showed no interest in pursuing this matter.[25] Congress likely obliged because the need for more energy resources during the early- to mid-1970s made environmental protection issues and Alaska lands protection per se less salient than they had been earlier.

In the wake of the first oil shock, an environmentally friendly Democratic congressman from Ohio, John Seiberling, led a congressional delegation to the wildlife range in northeast Alaska in 1975. The purpose of the trip was to see personally the lands that were set aside temporarily for environmental protection by Secretary of Interior Rogers Morton. The secretary used the (d)(2) provision in the 1971 ANCSA statute to set aside at least 80 million acres of Alaska lands for five years. At the same time, Congress was debating the issue.[26]

The congressman's trip would change the face of the ANWR debate beginning in 1977, the year that Seiberling became one of the principal congressional leaders advocating selection of Alaska lands as required under the 1971 statute. In late 1976, he joined fellow Democrat Mo Udall of Arizona and an official from the Sierra Club, Chuck Clusen, in a four-year campaign that led to passage of the ANILCA law in 1980.

The ANILCA Debate:
Forming a Pro-Environment Monopoly (1977-1980)

The creation of the ANWR subsystem is linked inextricably with the passage of the Alaska lands bill (HR 39) or ANILCA law in 1980. The 1971 ANCSA statute had mandated that Congress replace, by December 18, 1978, the interim protection of the lands set aside by the DOI. Permanent protection would be required for new national parks, wildlife refuges, and wild and scenic rivers to be established by Congress. Meeting this requirement had to *precede* distribution of additional lands to indigenous groups and to the state of Alaska.[27] These environmental land designations represented the core of the ANILCA, or Alaska lands debate that began in earnest in Congress in 1977.[28]

In the analysis that follows, I will identify the pro-environment ANWR subsystem that emerged during the ANILCA debate. The ANWR decision-making structure was comprised of both public sector and non-governmental actors. Moreover, the monopolistic, or quasi-monopolistic nature of the subsystem will become manifest. The term "monopoly" means that a core group of decision makers dominated the political process and tended to gain its preferred policy outcomes on the ANWR issue.[29] Pro-drilling forces are considered competitors of the subsystem. This book uses the term "subsystem" broadly to include actors that opposed and displaced the pro-environment/anti-drilling forces. Finally, I will review the characteristics of the ANWR decision-making structure during the pre- and subsystem periods and will explore the ANWR subsystem's deviations from a classic subsystem.

Public Sector Actors: Congress

The ANWR-environmental subsystem was established in the US House of Representatives in 1977 when the new House Interior Committee Chairman, Congressman Mo Udall (D-AZ), created the Subcommittee on General Oversight and Alaska Lands and appointed Congressman Seiberling (D-OH) to chair the panel. In 1975, Seiberling visited Alaska with a congressional delegation after having read a magazine article on the area. These two men are the chief public-sector political entrepreneurs in this case study. They would spur enactment of the ANILCA law for Alaska in 1980 by making conservation there a national issue.[30]

Long since retired in 2002, former Congressman Seiberling, who served in Congress from 1970 to 1987, reflected on that 1975 trip. He argued that "there were no politics" involved because the delegation was bipartisan. Seiberling also praised the National Park Service for providing airplanes to enable House Members to fly all over the region.[31] As will be discussed shortly, the driving forces behind Udall and Seiberling's creation of the House Subcommittee on General Oversight and Alaska Lands a few years later were the 1978 deadline and the work of Chuck Clusen from the Sierra Club, who chaired the pro-environment Alaska Coalition during the ANILCA debate.

Although Congressmen Mo Udall and John Seiberling are the two chief political entrepreneurs in this study, environmental activist Chuck Clusen is a non-governmental actor who helped them gain the chairmanships of the House Interior Committee and Alaska Lands Subcommittee respectively. A quarter century later, Clusen is still a political operative in environmental circles. In 2002, Clusen recounted how he and Congressman Udall "cooked up a scheme" to make Udall chairman of the full committee in late 1976 and early 1977.

At that time, Arizona Democrat Udall was the second-ranking member of the committee. In order to bypass the ranking member and become chairman, Clusen suggested that Udall threaten to run a campaign for the chairmanship outside of the Democratic Caucus. This threat, Clusen recalled, was enough to get the ranking member, Congressman Johnson (D-CA), to cede the post to Udall. The two strategists also included the oftentimes "dull" oversight functions in the subcommittee's jurisdiction, thus successfully dissuading senior committee members from serving on the committee.

At the same time, Clusen and Udall crafted a subcommittee that would have nearly full jurisdiction over Alaska lands issues. The non-profit umbrella group, the Alaska Coalition, lobbied senior members for this arrangement.[32] Besides the House Committee on Interior and Insular Affairs, other congressional committees shared jurisdiction over ANWR issues through Congressman Seiberling's final year in Congress (1986). These included the House Committee on Merchant Marine and Fisheries and the Senate Committee on Energy and Natural Resources.[33]

Once the subgovernment was formed and the ANILCA debate began to unfold, Congressmen Seiberling (D-OH) and Don Young (R-AK) emerged as two of the primary subsystem and opposition leaders respectively. Throughout the debate on the Alaska lands bill, the two men were on opposite sides of the fight. A former riverboat pilot from northeast Alaska who also used to check for fur traps, Young's style was direct, sometimes brash. Seiberling was subtler, but just as determined and likewise capable of expressing witticisms when he was unhappy. He grew adept at legislative "horse trading," and was known as a fair chairman.

Seiberling often faced intense lobbying in his subcommittee hearing room during markup of the bill with conservationists, oil and gas interests, Interior Department representatives, and other actors interested in legislation relating to the Arctic Range. Seiberling set the tone at hearings with his color photographs of Alaska displayed in the hearing room. In all, the corporate lawyer from Akron, Ohio and the former riverboat pilot from Fort Yukon, Alaska were leaders throughout House battles over HR 39.[34]

While a structure closely resembling a monopoly existed within the House Interior Committee, the Alaska lands bill also needed the approval of the Merchant Marine Committee, which had jurisdiction over refuges.[35] This was done in March 1978. The two committee chairmen reached a consensus on protecting 120 million acres, but it took a crafty Udall to kill a competing pro-development substitute measure during House floor debate in 1979; that bill earlier had been approved by the Merchant Marine Committee. Udall's actions maintained the power of his subgovernment.

Was the ANWR environmental subsystem highly monopolistic? On the one hand, the House subcommittee chaired by Seiberling, with the blessing of Interior Committee Chairman Udall, introduced the legislation that ultimately became ANILCA; this provides some evidence of a monopoly. On the other hand, at least one long-time political insider has suggested that the organizational structure for ANWR policy making was elastic or porous.

Don Barry is an Executive Branch official who worked on both sides of the ANWR issue for over twenty-five years. Barry claims that "floating coalitions" existed on any given issue during the ANILCA debate of 1977-1980. There was a tacit "three of four rule," or agreement between power blocs (e.g., Carter Administration officials and their congressional allies, indigenous peoples, Alaska state officials, and the environmental community) requiremed to act on each component of the ANILCA bill (HR 39).

However, Barry's analysis[36] seems to downplay the role of Congressmen Udall and Seiberling, who were determined to gain passage of a bill to protect Alaska lands. In fact, Barry does concede that these two congressmen were the "ringmasters" in the House, but that skillful staff was critical in negotiating each provision of the bill. While the subsystem did not exist exclusively within the House Interior Committee, that entity nevertheless dominated policy formation.

The Senate apparently did not have a companion monopolistic structure in place favoring the pro-environment position during this period.[37] There was an absence of a subgovernment in the Senate resembling the one centered in the House Subcommittee on General Oversight and Alaska Lands. Based on the above definition of "monopoly," the Senate lacked a dominant pro-environment group in the ANWR debate. Freshman Senator Paul Tsongas, for instance, although a leader on this issue, was unable to pass a measure in the Senate that matched the more environmentally friendly provisions of the House bill.

Things might have been very different in the Senate, according to environmental lobbyist Chuck Clusen, if Senator Lee Metcalf (D-MT) had not died in January 1978 (before either body had passed the ANILCA measure). Metcalf had served on the Senate Interior Committee, and had been the "champion" for Alaska lands issues in the upper chamber. His successor, John Durkin (D-NH) was "not the best champion" on the new Committee on Energy and Natural Resources (i.e., the reconstituted Interior Committee) during 1977-1978.[38]

Senator Henry "Scoop" Jackson of (D-WA) was also favorable toward the coalition's cause, but he attempted to remain neutral about the Arctic Range and Alaska lands in order to strike a compromise with the Carter Administration. By the 1979-1980 period, freshman Senator Paul Tsongas of Massachusetts became the "champion" for ANWR protection in the upper chamber.[39]

It is important to remember that while the subgovernment initially was not centered in the Senate, this does not mean that the Senate was impotent in its capacity to affect the House subsystem. Senate rules (e.g., the amendment process and the filibuster) as well as senatorial input at the conference committee level potentially could undermine the House's environmental subsystem. Chapter 3 illustrates why the Senate played a larger role in the subsystem beginning in 2001.

Former Congressman Seiberling recalled in 2002 a key distinction between House and Senate handling of Arctic Range/ANWR policy in 1977, the year that he became chairman of the Alaska Lands Subcommittee:

> I realized . . . the real problem was the way the Senate operates. . . . I tried to break the cozy relationships between Senators and [energy-related] interest groups [by making ANWR] a national issue. [We held] hearings in the lower 48 states [including] Washington DC, Chicago, Denver, and Seattle [with] 2,000 witnesses [testifying. We also] publicized it [in newspapers such as] the *Chicago Daily News, Denver Post,* and *Atlanta Constitution.*[40]

Seiberling and his House colleagues also held multiple hearings in Alaska. During the summer of 1977, the House Interior Committee held five public hearings and twenty town meetings in Alaska cities and villages. Approximately half of the one thousand Alaskans who testified supported the Udall-Seiberling bill, HR 39.[41] In short, Chairman Seiberling successfully expanded the scope of the conflict in order to increase the likelihood of success.[42]

Towards the end of this chapter, I will discuss the flurry of legislative activity that transpired in various forms during the three years after those initial hearings in 1977. But first, it is important to identify how other governmental and non-governmental actors on both sides influenced subsystem decisions. We already discussed the role of congressional actors. Next, consider the role of the White House and the Executive Branch.

Public Sector Actors: The Executive Branch

The White House, although not directly responsible for creating the pro-environment ANWR subsystem in the House in 1977, was critical in setting the tone for House creation of the Alaska Lands Subcommittee. President-elect Jimmy Carter invited CEOs from key environmental groups to his home in Plains, Georgia, and told them that the new administration would make protection of Alaska lands its top environmental priority. Carter reiterated his position to his future Interior Secretary, Cecil Andrus, when he interviewed for the position.[43]

President Carter was to remain consistent on this issue throughout his term in office. At one point during the 1980 Senate debate on ANILCA, Carter convened a kickoff event with "200 grass-rooters, VIPs, and citizen leaders,"[44] telling them that he had been on the phone with senators all morning, working to improve the legislation.

What role did Executive Branch agencies play during the early years of the ANWR-environmental subsystem? The Alaska Native Claims Settlement Act (ANCSA) of 1971 called for setting aside and studying for possible environmental protection up to 80 million acres of public lands in Alaska. The statute distinguished between four systems of environmental protection, each shielded from development to different degrees, and managed by a separate Executive Branch agency.

The National Park Service would manage national parks. The Bureau of Sport Fisheries and Wildlife (i.e., later renamed the Fish and Wildlife Service) would manage wildlife refuges. The Bureau of Land Management (BLM) would manage national forests (i.e., it would regulate grazing, mining, and other development). The Bureau of Outdoor Recreation, an agency that later was abolished, would regulate wild and scenic rivers.[45]

Interior Secretary Andrus evaluated the role of these agencies in Arctic Range policy making during his tenure (1977-1981). He said that the National Park Service was proactive in pushing for protection. Some civil servants at BLM, he continued, also worked with the pro-protection forces. Also, pro-environment forces utilized the United States Geological Service (USGS) for its scientific data in the 1980 debate. Andrus revealed that USGS scientists were careful not to appear to favor or oppose the Administration's position. Importantly, he also said that the US Fish and Wildlife Service helped in managing the Range. It is worth noting that many of these agencies remain part of DOI today, which has played a key role in subsystem decision making.

According to Secretary Andrus, DOI is a "strange mosaic" of smaller departments that are competitive with one another but answer to one secretary. Likewise, he called the Alaska lands bill (HR 39) "my baby" because it was handed to him by President Carter, which suggests a high degree of influence for DOI over the Alaska lands issue generally and ANWR policy specifically during the early years of the subsystem.[46]

Secretary Andrus used his authority to withdraw 40 million acres in Alaska from development in late 1978. President Carter withdrew another 56 million acres of land at that time. Andrus and Carter each invoked a different statute in order to pre-empt the December 1978 deadline for Congress to set aside Alaska lands (recall that this was a prerequisite for state and indigenous land claims).[47]

When asked whether he and President Carter had set aside these lands in order to pre-empt that deadline under the 1971 ANCSA statute, Andrus said, "That's why we did it." The impact of these land withdrawals, Andrus noted, was to bring "back to the table" those who opposed lands protection since the Senate had failed to act just prior to the deadline.[48]

President Carter could have used executive orders at this time to make monuments of all 110 million acres set aside for Congress to consider as wildlife refuges, parks, and other conservation entities. However, he opted to follow the advice of Secretary Andrus and make monuments of only 56 million acres, as Andrus believed that this acreage was most defensible under the Antiquities Act.[49]

The permanence of these orders was uncertain. Uncertain enough, at least, that Carter and his allies could not simply accept the 110 million acres of set asides in Alaska, claim victory, and move on. In theory at least, any President can overturn the executive orders of earlier Presidents; thus, Carter's pro-environment actions might have been reversible.

Yet, this case evidently was different: only an act of Congress could undo the permanent protected status of the monuments designated by President Carter.[50] Besides, the Administration desired more acreage for protection than the amount already set aside. Secretary Andrus later said that the administration's final acreage selections in ANILCA "were much larger."[51]

The various iterations of the ANILCA bill that were debated from 1977 to 1980 each set aside a certain amount of land in Alaska with particular degrees of environmental protection (see table 2.1 for a summary of the final versions of ANILCA in the House and Senate). Key issues of contention were the amount of land to be set aside as "wilderness" (i.e., the most protected designation), and whether ANWR per se would be designated "wilderness," thus precluding oil and gas development at the coastal plain.

The Carter Administration found a largely cooperative, environmentally friendly House in 1979 when that chamber rejected two pro-development bills in favor of the Udall-sponsored bill, but the President faced a less cooperative Senate in 1980. During this period and throughout his tenure at DOI, Secretary Andrus provided the president with weekly updates on the Alaska lands bill. The secretary called the president every Monday and passed along names of Members of Congress whom the president should telephone in order to pass the bill.

Andrus later described the president a "believer" in the cause who later became a "mover and shaker" on protection of Alaska lands, including those involving the Arctic Range. Carter and his team did not separate the Arctic Range proposals from the Alaska lands bill because they felt that many areas in the state were equally important. In short, Secretary Andrus said that passage of HR 39 would have been "impossible without [President Carter's] help."[52]

Public Sector Actors: The Alaska State Government

Federal officials were not the only ones who influenced ANWR policy decisions during the 1977-1980 period. The State of Alaska has been a strong advocate for drilling at ANWR since at least the 1970s when the state legislature appropriated five million dollars for a lobbying and advertising campaign against the pro-environment bill (HR 39) being considered by the national legislature.[53] Elected and appointed representatives from both political parties in the State of Alaska overwhelmingly opposed the pro-environment coalition.

This trend would continue for the next quarter century. Environmentalists have accused Alaska politicians at the state level of wanting more oil royalty money (i.e., from drilling at ANWR) in order to continue the flow of money into state and local coffers. The next chapter will discuss how, during periods when ANWR was on the national political agenda, the Alaska State Legislature and their oil company allies had their "water carried" in Washington DC, as one representative from the pro-development interest group Arctic Power phrased it. This group was created after the Gulf War to push for drilling at ANWR.

Public Sector Actors: The Canadian Government

The Canadian government is a secondary actor in ANWR subsystem politics. However, Ottawa's behavior and statements about ANWR clearly have been used by both sides in this debate to help define the issue. Canada has granted permanent wilderness status in its national parks in the Yukon to protect the calving grounds of the Porcupine Caribou Herd. American environmentalists contend that the US should follow suit and designate the coastal plain at ANWR "wilderness."

Yet, an official at Arctic Power called the Canadian record "hypocritical" for several reasons. First, Canada continues to explore offshore for oil and natural gas in the Beaufort Sea. Second, Canada leased all of its land in the area to oil companies during the 1960s and 1970s. Those firms drilled more than 90 wells that failed to yield economically viable hydrocarbons. Third, the government built the Dempster Highway, which runs through calving and migratory areas. Arctic Power officials also suggest that Canadian Gwich'in Indians never protested these development efforts.[54]

In short, American environmentalists have claimed for decades that the Canadian government opposes development of the ANWR 1002 Area. The opposing coalition supporting development has alleged Canadian duplicity in this matter.

Non-Governmental Actors: The Pro-environment Coalition

So far, the discussion has emphasized public sector actors and their involvement in the ANWR-environmental subsystem during its early years. But private and non-profit sector actors also played important roles. Here, I will consider both subsystem decision makers per se and their opposition, since each set of actors has influenced ANWR-related decisions.

By the end of 1977, with the House subcommittee in place, the core interest group component of this pro-environment subsystem was formalized. The Alaska Coalition was converted from an informal group to a formal entity that enabled HR 39 to get a "fast start" by "propelling the issue" forward, according to Chuck Clusen. By 1980, the Alaska Coalition expanded to include more than fifty environmental groups.[55]

The Alaska Coalition is an umbrella group that was set up during the early 1970s, and has existed in "various forms and structures" ever since, according to the group's National Outreach Director Dan Ritzman. The coalition transcends the ANWR issue, and breadth of this *group of groups* expanded steadily between 1980 and the early 2000s.[56] Sixteen environmental groups were original members of the coalition, and six of those were from Alaska. The number grew to 33 by 1978, and by 1980, the coalition had over 50 member groups. By 2002, the list had blossomed to roughly 670.

In part, the coalition's growth was due to the wily strategy of the subsystem leadership, aimed at gaining nationwide public support, and then congressional support, for their ANWR policy. This strategy was set in motion through the creation of a list of prospective grassroots supporters from the House Interior Committee field hearings held in 1977.[57] These membership figures do not necessarily include the myriad "housewives, schoolteachers, business people, clerks, construction workers, scientists, factory workers, doctors, lawyers, and students[58] who helped to gain passage of the ANILCA law and those who participated in ANWR-related debates in Congress during the 1991-1992, 1995, and 2000-2006 periods.

By the early 2000s, a symbiosis of grassroots activism and state-level strategizing was attained through creation of 23 non-national coalitions representing a plethora of groups in 25 states. These partnerships include the Alaska Coalition of California (i.e., representing 52 groups), the Alaska Coalition of the Dakotas (i.e., representing 15 organizations), the Alaska Coalition of Pennsylvania (i.e., boasting 53 associations), and so on (2002 Alaska Coalition membership list).

Not everyone sees the Alaska Coalition as stronger today than in the past. Some argue that counting various sub-national groups as members creates the impression that the coalition has more support now than it did in past. This counting can be misleading as these groups weren't even taken into account in the 1970s.

Despite this criticism, some recognize that new coalition members are unique people who should be afforded an opportunity to conduct business differently than it had been in the 1970s. Coalition leaders today might employ different tactics than their predecessors did to draw attention to Alaska lands issues.[59]

Yet, the question arises whether the Alaska Coalition still possessed the depth of political expertise today that it did a few decades earlier. The next chapter will address this and other questions regarding the relative strength of the subsystem over time.

It is clear to subsystem actors and to political observers that the Alaska Coalition had a core group of supporters. By late 1976, the fledgling Alaska Coalition (i.e., which only used this name when representatives from the various organizations decided to meet) was being sustained through the work and financial support of the affluent Larry Rockefeller, the Wilderness Society, the National Audubon Society, the Sierra Club, and Friends of the Earth. The latter two groups provided office space. These four organizations represented the heart of the coalition through the debate on the ANILCA bill in 1980.[60]

Conventional wisdom suggests that the Alaska Coalition was a vital actor in the passage of the Alaska lands bill, or ANILCA. However, some who shaped this legislation have differed on this point. DOI Secretary Andrus contends, for instance, that no single private interest group could be said to have been critical to the success of ANILCA. While the Alaska Coalition was a means to unite individual efforts, such as those provided by singer John Denver and many others, Andrus says that no one group played a key role.[61]

Interior Committee Chairman Udall, on the other hand, gives them great credit. Carson (2001) states:

> Udall heaped praise on the Alaska Coalition, saying its network of activists applied pressure quickly when needed...[by, for instance, having] five people from [a senator's] home state who had credentials as supporters [for amendments]...show up or...get on the telephone, Udall recounted. ...He also lauded [Congressman John] Seiberling...[as] the unsung hero.[62]

Most political observers contend that the Alaska Coalition did indeed play an important role in advancing this segment of the environmental agenda. Its influence over Congress was strong. For example, White House staff and their Alaska Coalition allies utilized a private room near the House floor to serve as a command post during the debate on HR 39 in 1979.[63] When asked about this arrangement in 2002, Chuck Clusen said

> [W]e had a room belonging to the House Democratic leadership that Mo Udall got for us to use. This was unusual to the best of my knowledge. However, the

Republicans since 1994 have brought [oil] industry lobbyists inside in all kinds of ways.[64]

The influence of the Alaska Coalition on Congress and ANWR probably peaked with passage of the ANILCA law in 1980 since the 1002 Area never has been designated "wilderness," which is the most stringent level of protection afforded to land.

Non-Governmental Actors: The Pro-Drilling Coalition

Several large oil firms, called the "big oil boys" by DOI Secretary Andrus, led the non-governmental opposition to the ANILCA bill.[65] They influenced subsystem decisions in various ways, beginning with the creation of that structure in 1977.

For example, subsystem actors have often been forced to consider the other side's definition of the ANWR issue and incorporate this knowledge into their political strategies. Again, pro-drilling interests influenced subsystem foes and defeated a variant of the Udall-Seiberling bill by a single vote in the House Interior Committee in 1979. The committee subsequently reported on a pro-industry bill sponsored by a sophomore House Member, Jerry Huckaby of Louisiana. That measure, which later was defeated on the floor, included a provision allowing oil exploration at the Arctic National Wildlife Range.[66]

Adversaries of the ANILCA bill (HR 39) included oil, timber, and mining firms, the National Rifle Association, the State of Alaska, and the umbrella group Citizens for the Management of Alaska Lands (CMAL). Industry interests organized CMAL in 1976 to promote a unified approach on Alaska lands issues. It hired a full-time staff of five by 1979, and accepted contributions from Alaskan businesses, industries, and trade associations; national contributing firms included Chevron, Exxon, Phillips Petroleum, Shell Oil, Standard Oil of Ohio, and Atlantic Richfield. Oil and mining interests developed a strategy to sway the seventy-five House seats that had changed hands in the 1978 congressional elections and appeal to their concern about the national energy crunch. Timber and gun interests offered their own arguments.[67]

In the next chapter I will discuss in more detail and over time the non-governmental actors supporting drilling. By 2001, the subsystem faced a strong competing coalition led by the permanent opposition group, Arctic Power. Industry created this umbrella group, representing oil companies and arguably the majority of Alaskans, after the Gulf War to focus on developing oil and natural gas resources at ANWR. It allied with the Teamsters Union, the Alaska State Legislature, and the Arctic Slope Regional Corporation, among others.[68] We shall examine the role of these actors in legislative and political developments from 1980 to 2006 in the next chapter.

Pre-Subsystem Characteristics

It is plausible to say that decision making for ANWR had three major characteristics prior to construction of the subgovernment. Prima facie evidence suggests that after President Eisenhower established the Arctic National Wildlife Range in 1960, but prior to debate over its expansion beginning in 1977, a relatively competitive but pro-environment decision-making structure existed between the Congress and the White House.

One piece of evidence is that during the Johnson Administration, Congressman Wayne Aspinall, "the powerful House Interior Committee chairman, was adamantly opposed to any use of the Antiquities Act [of 1906] by a President [to protect public lands] because it preempted the right of Congress to establish national parks."[69] Congress evidently coveted its power and downplayed prospective policy benefits of uniting with pro-environment forces in the Executive Branch.

The second characteristic or evidence for the ANWR decision-making structure prior to 1977 concerns the relationship between mid-level Executive Branch officials and environmental interests. The relationship evidently was becoming clientelistic. One scholar describes the cozy relationship between environmental interest groups and DOI as a classic *revolving door* between the National Park Service and the environmental interest groups during the late 1960s and early 1970s, with experts leaving one vocation to work in the other.[70]

Another scholar notes that during the first months of the Nixon Administration several dozen representatives of Alaska environmental groups and state and local officials met in Juneau for a "wilderness workshop." That meeting led to formation of the Alaska Wilderness Society.[71]

A third trait of the pre-subsystem decision structure is that its dominant actors linked Alaska lands issues inextricably with indigenous claims. The fact was that indigenous land claims were not paid serious attention until 1969 when a Senate bill based on a committee-commissioned study produced hearings in Alaska and in Washington, DC. This ultimately became the *d-2* provision of the indigenous claims law of 1971 (ANCSA). That controversial provision granted the DOI Secretary power to set aside lands.[72]

This discussion of the period prior to 1977 makes at least two points clear. First, clientelistic politics were present between mid-level Executive Branch officials and environmental groups prior to creation of the monopolistic House subcommittee. This trait may have facilitated the work initiated by Congressmen Udall and Seiberling since a network of potential supporters already existed. The second observation is that decision makers consistently linked Alaska lands issues with indigenous claims.

Subsystem Characteristics

Decision making continued to be characterized by private-public clientelism and decision makers' linkage of Alaska lands issues with the claims of indigenous groups after 1977. Inter-branch environmentalist competition, the third trait of decision making before the subsystem, evidently shifted toward a more cooperative relationship beginning with the Carter Administration.

President Carter organized a White House rally for environmental interests during the final days of the ANILCA debate. This is one example of clientelism after the Nixon years.

A more overt example of clientelism occurred when President Clinton tapped three leaders from the Wilderness Society for key posts in his administration in 1993. Alice Rivlin, who had been Chair of the Wilderness Society's Governing Council from 1988 to 1992, was appointed Deputy Director of the Office of Management and Budget. George Frampton, who had been President of the Wilderness Society from 1986 to 1992, became Assistant Secretary for Fish, Wildlife and Parks at DOI. Jim Baca, a member of the Wilderness Society's Governing Council, became Director of the BLM.[73] Also, after leaving the Clinton Administration in 2001, USFWS Director Jamie Rappaport Clark became Senior Vice President at the National Wildlife Federation.

In his memoirs, former President Carter concedes that part of the ANILCA debate concerned granting "special privileges for Native Indians and Eskimos." This is an illustration of the continued linkage between indigenous claims and Alaska lands matters since 1977.[74]

A second illustration is from the congressional debates on ANWR development during the George W. Bush Administration. During those debates (2001-2006), the pro-drilling forces frequently cited support of the Inupiat Eskimos; the pro-environment coalition likewise referenced their Gwich'in Indian supporters.

The inter-branch environmentalist competition that was present before 1977 was transformed during the Carter Administration through the creation of the House Subcommittee on Alaska Lands, which increased cooperation between environmentalists in the two political branches of government.

On November 15, 1978, DOI Secretary Andrus received a letter from House Interior Committee Chairman Udall urging Secretary Andrus to take "extraordinary measures" to protect Alaska lands since an "emergency situation" allegedly existed. The next day, Secretary Andrus used his authority under the BLM Organic Act (P.L. 94-579) to set aside over 50 million acres of federal land, thus precluding development.[75] Anti-environment opposition intensified because of this and other actions. Inter-branch environmental cooperation diminished during the next two administrations, but it returned to prevalence during the tenure of Democrat Bill Clinton.

In 1997, President Clinton had the support of many pro-environment Members of Congress when he invoked the Antiquities Act and announced the creation of the Grand Staircase-Escalante National Monument in Utah. Yet, this action "provoked the ire of the Utah congressional delegation, many Western Republicans and some Democrats."[76]

Although this illustration does not deal directly with ANWR per se, it nonetheless is relevant. Many political observers felt that President Clinton should have invoked the Antiquities Act with the support of like-minded congressmen, just as President Carter had done with Alaska lands prior to ANILCA, to protect the coastal plain at ANWR from energy producers. However, former DOI Secretary Andrus said in 2003 that President Clinton could not make ANWR a national monument because Congress would have to rewrite ANILCA.[77]

This analysis implies two things. First, environmentally friendly presidents after 1977 (i.e., typically Democratic administrations) have gained cooperation from environmentalists in Congress while facing greater opposition from pro-development congressmen. Second, and most importantly, the ANWR-environmental subsystem had become so powerful that it apparently supplanted, through enactment of ANILCA, the short-term application of a longstanding environmental statute (i.e., the Antiquities Act of 1906, which permits the use of executive orders) to the coastal plain at ANWR.

Deviations from a Classic Subsystem

Once the core of the ANWR subsystem was established in the US House in 1977, one can argue that several additional traits became manifest, characteristics that differ from those traditionally associated with subgovernments (e.g., the tobacco or pesticides subsystems).

First, the perceived benefits provided have non-monetary rather than monetary value.[78] That is, environmental benefits are afforded to the public. Second, the decision-making structure for ANWR policy clearly has had a wide scope of political conflict;[79] ANWR debates since the ANILCA period (1977-1980) have received wide media and public attention. A third and final deviant characteristic of the ANWR-environmental subsystem has been its dominance, at least initially, in a single chamber, the House. It is likely that Senate institutional norms and procedures frustrated subsystem expansion to that body until 2001, when President George W. Bush took office.

The following examples illustrate the capacity of senatorial procedures to hinder subsystem formation. The cloture rule, which requires a 60-vote super-majority to end debate and thus permit a vote on legislation, was a point of contention both during the ANILCA debate and 20 years later. The mere threat of a filibuster oftentimes is enough to dissuade senators, including those involved with subgovernments, from advancing legislation toward their preferred outcomes.

Besides, non-germane amendments are permissible in the upper chamber only. This rule can transform a passable piece of legislation into one that senators might run from like "scalded dogs."

At least part of the reason for this single-chamber subgovernment during the 1977-1980 period concerns the lack of advocacy for this issue among senators relative to House members. No clear champion for ANWR protection emerged in the Senate, unlike in the House where Congressmen Udall and Seiberling advocated ANWR protection. Policy entrepreneurs oftentimes are key to subsystem creation and maintenance (see chapter 3 for a more detailed analysis of this concept and its application to the ANWR case).

The ANILCA Debate Continued (1978-1980)[80]

Earlier in this chapter I demonstrated how the ANWR-environmental subsystem and its opposition were established in 1977 during the first year of the ANILCA debate. Table 2.1 provides an overview of the complex path of ANILCA in 1978, 1979, and 1980 respectively, including the provisions of the final versions of the bill in the House and Senate in 1979 and 1980. The table shows that the stronger subsystem in the House produced a stronger environmental law in that chamber than in the Senate.

On May 19, 1978, the House passed an Alaska lands bill (HR 39; 277-31) that was largely favorable toward environmental interests. It rejected two pro-development motions offered by Congressman Don Young (R-AK). In December 1978, the House passed a bill to extend the December 18th deadline for designating which Alaska lands to protect under Section 17 (d)(2) of the 1971 ANCSA statute. The upper chamber failed to act upon a bill reported by the Energy and Natural Resources Committee that year; and Alaska Senator Mike Gravel (D) threatened to filibuster the measure for the first of two consecutive years for reasons that will be discussed momentarily. As noted earlier, the Carter Administration responded by invoking two statutes, one by the president, and one by DOI Secretary Andrus that temporarily set aside roughly 110 million acres of Alaska lands as leverage for gaining an environmentally friendly bill.

The following year, the House again passed an Alaska lands bill. With the passage of a rule by the Rules Committee that was favorable to Congressman Udall (D-AZ) at the expense of Congressmen Huckaby (D-LA) and Breaux (D-LA), who each introduced an industry-backed bill, the full House approved an environmentally friendly version of the Alaska lands bill (HR 39; 360-65) on May 16, 1979. The two pro-drilling bills were absent from the debate the prior year, likely because industry had been focused on the Carter energy plan.

In the Senate, the absence of floor action in 1979 was largely due to what Senator Stevens (R-AK) viewed as the unacceptable Tsongas-Roth substitute. Stevens favored the more pro-development Energy Committee bill.

To be sure, contention over ANILCA in the Senate between Alaska's two senators contributed to legislative defeat in 1978 and 1979, although Senator Gravel agreed to cooperate in early 1979 with those who wanted to enact a bill before changing his mind. He was concerned that any conference version of the bill would enable the federal government to set aside additional lands in his state later, and that the Senate would cede to the environmentalist-House position.

Senator Gravel also hoped that election of a Republican administration in 1980 would yield a policy favoring the state's pro-drilling position. Ironically, he was precluded from working with the incoming Reagan Administration because Republican Frank Murkowski defeated him for election that year. As for Senator Stevens, he shared Senator Gravel's goals but differed on the route to legislative victory, believing that passing a bill before 1980 would yield a more pro-development bill because an election year could prompt senators to favor environmental constituencies.[81]

By the fall of 1980, in a lame duck session of Congress, environmental activists including Chuck Clusen and Doug Scott of the Alaska Coalition, favored waiting until 1981 for a bill that would be friendlier toward the environmentalist position. Congressman Udall, Secretary Andrus, and President Carter were among those who were unwilling to wait. They recognized that the House had already passed a bill and that the Reagan Administration likely would not support a pro-environment position.[82] Failing to approve the Senate version of the bill might result in no bill at all in 1981.

When all was said and done, a variant of the Alaska lands measure that was introduced by subsystem actors in 1977 was accepted by vast majorities of both chambers of Congress, by the Carter Administration, and by many in the environmental community.

It is worth noting that besides the election of Ronald Reagan and a Republican Senate in 1980, international events ostensibly could have precluded enactment of ANILCA. One might suppose that the second oil shock, which was triggered by the Islamic revolution in Iran in 1979, would have thwarted environmentalists' efforts to protect various regions in Alaska from energy development in 1980 as oil prices doubled when Iran temporarily halted oil production and OPEC raised prices. Nonetheless, the Congress acted to protect Alaska lands. Why?

Congressman Seiberling recounted part of the likely answer two decades after ANILCA became law. Seiberling argued that, during the second oil shock of 1979, he and his colleagues portrayed environmental protection as compatible with energy production.[83] This page in their playbook was borrowed and reverse engineered by the Bush-Cheney team years later.

The Carter Administration and likeminded lawmakers promoted an energy policy that focused on conservation rather than on increasing supplies of oil and natural gas. The United States, they argued, could meet its energy needs while simultaneously expanding the acreage of federal lands to be set aside for environmental protection. They also believed that it would be easier to push for Alaska lands protection in 1980, since Congress had approved major energy legislation already before final consideration of the Alaska lands bill. The two bills therefore would not compete with one another for a spot on the agenda.

In all, the ANILCA debate finally was resolved on December 2, 1980, during the final months of the Carter Administration, when Congress enacted the Alaska National Interest Lands Conservation Act (ANILCA, P.L. 96-487). This statute, among other things, enlarged the Refuge from 8.9 million to 18 million acres. The law also renamed the "Arctic Range" the "Arctic National Wildlife Refuge" (ANWR).

Although the coastal plain was not designated as a wilderness area, eight million acres at ANWR received that distinction and three rivers were designated "wild," the most protected status. Section 1002 of the statute mandated a Department of Interior study of the energy and biological resources located along the 1.5-million-acre coastal plain. Section 1003, which was crafted by Congressman Udall (D-AZ), required Congress to first authorize future oil and natural gas exploration at the refuge.[84] Table 2.1 below compares provisions in the House- and Senate-passed versions of ANILCA.

There are several key observations from Table 2.1 that suggest the existence of a strong subsystem centered in the House. First, the full House seemed to favor environmental protection more than the full Senate (i.e., as evidenced by overall acreage protection). Subsystem leader Mo Udall (D-AZ) incorporated the 127.5 million acres into the 1979 House bill. He skillfully utilized the House Rules Committee to his advantage and successfully ended the bidding of pro-development interests when he defeated two competing bills (i.e., sponsored by Louisiana Democrats Huckaby and Breaux respectively) on the House floor in 1979.

The Huckaby bill would have permitted DOI to conduct some oil and gas exploration at the Arctic Range as part of a six-year, energy-wildlife study. The Breaux bill would have permitted private industry to explore for oil and gas as part of a seven-year study.[85]

A second observation based partly on the table is that the Alaska lands bill (HR 39) that originated in the House Interior Committee in 1977 ultimately added 9.5 million acres to ANWR to total nearly 19 million acres, and 8 million of those were afforded the most stringent level of protection—wilderness. This also suggests the presence of a strong pro-environment subsystem since that structure drove the policy outcome.

Table 2.1: Comparing Key Provisions on Final Versions of ANILCA

Legislative (or administrative) provisions	New acreage protected across AK (in millions)	Acreage protected at ANWR (in millions)	New acreage at ANWR designated "wilderness" (in millions)	"Wilderness" designation for Arctic Range/Refuge (i.e., exploration for hydrocarbons prohibited)	Development/drilling for hydrocarbons precluded unless authorized by Congress
Second bill passed by House (1979)	127.5	18.8	13.43	Yes	n/a
Final ANILCA bill passed by Senate and accepted by House (1980)	104.3	18.4	8	Not completely, seismic exploration permitted at coastal plain	Yes (Section 1003)

In addition, Congressman Udall persuaded his colleagues in the Senate to include Section 1003 in their bill (i.e., requiring congressional authorization to drill) in order to balance the Senate's provision permitting seismic oil and gas exploration at ANWR, but not full-scale drilling, five years after enactment. Udall's proactive policy making guaranteed that no development at ANWR could transpire unless a future Congress explicitly granted permission to drill.

Finally, the ANWR subsystem clearly was monopolistic as indicated by the broader policy outcome favoring environmental interests. That is, the ANILCA law of 1980 more than doubled the size of national parks, wildlife refuge systems, and wilderness areas in the US.[86] This victory for environmentalists both in and outside of government would need continued sustenance into the 1980s and beyond.

Summary

The ANWR-environmental subsystem was not created in a political and historical vacuum. The subsystem is a decision-making structure that was decades if not a century in the making. Political entrepreneurs such as President Teddy Roosevelt, President Eisenhower, President Carter, and environmentalists Robert Marshall and Chuck Clusen positioned the building blocks for what would become a subgovernment for ANWR policy making.

Congressmen Seiberling and Udall established the subsystem per se in 1977. It was centered, but not exclusively located in the House Interior Committee. The Senate's pro-environment influence within this subsystem would not increase significantly for another two decades.

In addition, international and domestic developments served as "focusing events" that made ANWR a more salient issue over time.[87] On the one hand, the national environmental movement began to take root during the 1960s and 1970s. Advocates of protecting the Refuge piggybacked this broader cause. On the other hand, the discovery of a huge oil reserve to the west of ANWR at Prudhoe Bay in the late 1960s and two oil embargoes served as a means for pro-development forces to intensify their arguments.

Finally, this subsystem can be characterized as monopolistic because it controlled the ANWR agenda over time and exhibited private-public clientelistic relationships. Yet, this subgovernment seems to be unlike any other in the political science literature since it expanded rather than minimized political conflict. The subsystem's structure is unique because the perceived beneficiaries of its policy outcomes have been public rather than special interests, and because it originally was based in a single chamber of Congress. The power of the ANWR-environmental subsystem clearly was in evidence in 1980 when it championed enactment of the

ANILCA law, a statute that doubled the size of the Refuge and protected many
additional areas in Alaska.

Notes

1.   Robert Cahn, *The Fight to Save Wild Alaska* (Washington, DC: National Audubon
Society, 1982) 11.
2.   "Arctic National Wildlife Refuge: TimeLine," Department of the Interior, USFWS,
1997.
3.   Cahn, *The Fight to Save*, 8; "Congress Clears Alaska Lands Legislation," *CQ
Almanac*, 1980: 575-584; *CQ Weekly Report*, 19 May 1979: 976.]
4.   The NPR-A has been explored numerous times since 1944 in order to search for
hydrocarbons and to test modern exploration methods, but no drilling has been permitted.
Some today advocate drilling there in order to decrease pressure for drilling at the ANWR
coastal plain (USGS website, 1 Jul. 2003, *The National Petroleum Reserve Alaska—Legacy
Data Archive*).
5.   "A History of the Arctic National Wildlife Refuge" and "National Petroleum
Reserve-Alaska," Alaska Wilderness League website (29 Aug. 2002); American Geological
Institute website (1 Jul. 2003).
6.   "A History."
7.   One Earth Adventures website (1 Jul. 2003); Union of Concerned Scientists
website (1 Jul. 2003); Department of the Interior, "ANWR: TimeLine."
8.   "Congress Admits Alaska as 49th State," *CQ Almanac*, 1958: 281.
9.   "A History"; Stephen Haycox, *Frigid Embrace: Politics, Economics and
Environment in Alaska* (Corvallis, OR: Oregon State University Press, 2002): 87; "Capitol
Briefs: Arctic Wildlife," *CQ Weekly Report*, 8 May 1959: 624; "CQ's Presidential Boxscore
Through Sept. 1 Adjournment," *CQ* Almanac, 1960: 97; "A History," Wilderness League,
9.
10.   "History of the Arctic National Wildlife Refuge," Alaska Coalition internal
document, no date; "A History," Wilderness League, 12-13.
11.   "Recreation in Wildlife Reserves," *CQ Almanac*, 1962: 465.
12.   "Congress Passes Wilderness Act," *CQ* Almanac, 1964: 485.
13.   Alston Chase, *Playing God in Yellowstone: The Destruction of America's First
National Park* (Boston: The Atlantic Monthly Press, 1986), 43.
14.   Department of the Interior, "ANWR: TimeLine."
15.   Stephen Haycox, *Frigid Embrace: Politics, Economics and Environment in Alaska*
(Corvallis, OR: Oregon State University Press, 2002), 83; Department of the Interior,
"ANWR: TimeLine."
16.   Chase, *Playing God*, 43.
17.   Cahn, *The Fight to Save*, 6.
18.   Haycox, *Frigid Embrace*, 172.
19.   "Congress Completes Action on Alaskan Pipeline Bill." *CQ Almanac*, 1973: 599-
600; "A History."

20. "Congress Completes," 597; "A History," Wilderness League, 13.

21. "Congress Completes," 605.

22. Cahn, *The Fight to Save*, 31.

23. United States Department of the Interior. *Arctic National Wildlife Refuge, Alaska, Coastal Plain Resource Assessment: Report and Recommendation to the Congress of the United States and Final Legislative Environmental Impact Statement*, 21 April 1987.

24. Important examples of management jurisdictions in Alaska are the BLM manages the NPR-A; the USFWS manages ANWR; and, the State of Alaska manages the land at Prudhoe Bay (Inforain website, 1 July 2003).

25. Cahn, *The Fight to Save*, 14.

26. Telephone interview with The Honorable John Seiberling, Member of Congress (D-OH), Ret., 18 September 2002 and 24 September 2002.

27. Cahn, *The Fight to Save*, 15; Donald W. Carson and James W. Johnson, *Mo: The Life and Times of Morris K. Udall* (Tuscon, AZ: The University of Arizona Press, 2001), 195,198-99; *US Code and Administrative News*, 96th Congress, Second Session, 1980, 5: 5070-79.

28. The 1958 law designated over 102 million acres to the state. The 1971 statute provided 44 million acres to Alaska's indigenous peoples. Failing to meet the December 1978 deadline would have precluded state and indigenous claims to another 80 million acres of land.

29. Examples of the primacy of this subsystem are numerous. Congressman Udall, for instance, worked with the House Rules Committee in 1979 to bring his Alaska lands measure to the floor, despite its defeat earlier in the Interior Committee that he chaired. Also, the Alaska Lands Subcommittee coordinated policy making with environmental groups and Interior Secretary Cecil Andrus; they pressured House Members to support their policy position on Alaskan natural resources issues, including ANWR. This monopolistic decision-making structure was created in 1977 and, by 1979, ostensibly ceased to exist in the same form. An important caveat is that the chairman of this subcommittee, John Seiberling (D-OH), became chairman of another Interior-related subcommittee in 1979. An examination of respective years of the *Congressional Staff Directory* indicates that Seiberling took the bulk of the committee staff with him, which suggests that a jurisdictional shift for Alaska lands issues likely transpired. In short, a variant of the subsystem continued to exist.

30. Carson and Johnson, *The Life and Times*, 195.

31. Seiberling interview.

32. Telephone interview with Chuck Clusen, NRDC (former Chairman of the AK Coalition), 1 November 2002.

33. Seiberling interview.

34. *CQ Almanac*, 1978: 727.

35. *CQ Almanac*, 1979: 663.

36. Telephone interview with Don Barry, 6 January 2003.

37. An examination of the *Congressional Staff Directory* from 1977 through 1980 reveals that no companion subcommittee was established. The Senate version of HR 39 was passed by a 17-1 vote on Oct. 30, 1979, by the Senate Committee on Energy and Natural Resources (see *US Code 1980*: 5079). Neither Alaska senator officially served on the

committee until Senator Stevens became a member in 1979. This committee was created in 1977, along with the Committee on the Environment and Public Works. The Committee on Interior and Insular Affairs was disbanded that same year.

38. Clusen interview.
39. Clusen interview.
40. Seiberling interview.
41. Cahn, *The Fight to Save*, 18-19.
42. See E.E. Schattschneider, *The Semisovereign People: A Realist's View of Democracy in America* (New York: Harcourt Brace Jovanovich College Publishers, 1975).
43. Clusen interview.
44. Cahn, *The Fight to Save*, 5.
45. Cahn, *The Fight to Save*, 3; Clusen interview; *CQ Almanac*, 1978: 727.
46. Telephone interview with DOI Secretary Cecil Andrus, Ret., 16 December 2002 and 24 July 2003.
47. Mr. Andrus invoked his authority under the BLM Organic Act of 1976 (P.L. 94-579) to set aside 56 million acres of federal lands. President Carter set aside other lands through the Antiquities Act, a 1906 law that permits the president to use executive orders to create national monuments (i.e., these have the same land-use status as national parks); monument creation may only be reversed by an act of Congress (see Carson and Johnson, *The Life and Times*, 201; *CQ Almanac*, 1978: 725,741).
48. Andrus interview.
49. *CQ Almanac*, 1978: 742.
50. *CQ* Almanac, 1978: 741.
51. Andrus interview.
52. Andrus interview.
53. Cahn, *The Fight to Save*, 19.
54. "Features: The Canadian Government, Arctic Power website (3 Oct. 2002).
55. Clusen interview.
56. Telephone interview with Dan Ritzman, National Outreach Director, Alaska Coalition, 16 September 2002.
57. See Cahn, *The Fight to Save*, 1,16,20. Members of the Alaska Coalition in 1980 included Alaska Center for the Environment; Alaska Conservation Society; American Institute of Architects; American League of Anglers; American Littoral Society; American Rivers Conservation Council; American Wilderness Alliance; Americans for Democratic Action; Appalachian Mountain Club; Arctic International Wildlife Range Society; Brooks Range Trust; Center for Action on Endangered Species; Cousteau Society; Defenders of Wildlife; Denali Citizens Council; Environmental Action; Environmental Defense Fund; Environmental Policy Center; Fairbanks Environmental Center; Federation of Flyfishermen; Federation of Western Outdoor Clubs; Friends of the Earth; The Garden Clubs of America; International Backpackers Association; International Ecology Society; International Association of Machinists and Aerospace Workers; National Audubon Society; National Intramural Recreational Sports Association; National Land for People; National Parks and Conservation Association; National Recreation and Parks Association; National Speleological Society; National Wildlife Refuge Association; Natural Resources Defense

Council; North American Wildlife Park Foundation; Oil, Chemical and Atomic Workers International; The Ozark Society; Public Lands Institute; Rivers Unlimited; Sierra Club; Southeast Alaska Conservation Council; Trout Unlimited; Trumpeter Swan Society; Trustees for Alaska; United Automobile Workers of America; United Electrical, Radio and Machine Workers; United Mine Workers of America; United Steelworkers of America; Wilderness Society; Wilderness Watch; Wolf Sanctuary; and, the World Wildlife Fund. Other supportive organizations included Americans for Alaska, Izaak Walton League of America, and the National Wildlife Federation.

 58. Cahn, *The Fight to Save*, 4.

 59. Clusen interview.

 60. Andrus interview; Cahn, *The Fight to Save*, 16; Clusen interview.

 61. Andrus interview.

 62. Carson and Johnson, *The Life and Times*, 201.

 63. Cahn, *The Fight to Save*, 25.

 64. Clusen interview.

 65. Andrus interview.

 66. Cahn, *The Fight to Save*, 24.

 67. Cahn, *The Fight to Save*, 19,24; *CQ Weekly Report*, 28 April 1979.

 68. Telephone interview with Adam Kolton, National Wildlife Federation (formerly with Alaska Wilderness League), 12 September 2002.

 69. Cahn, *The Fight to Save*, 9.

 70. Chase, *Playing* God, 43.

 71. Cahn, *The Fight to Save*, 10.

 72. Cahn, *The Fight to Save*, 11.

 73. *Wilderness Watch*, Spring 1993, 4.

 74. Jimmy Carter, *Keeping Faith: Memoirs of a President* (New York: Bantam Books, 1982) 582.

 75. *CQ Almanac,* 1978: 725,741.

 76. *CQ Weekly Report*, 3 May 1997: 1016.

 77. Secretary Andrus evidently has a different view regarding this matter than his one-time boss, President Carter. In August 2000, the two men visited Alaska in honor of the twentieth anniversary of passage of the ANILCA law. The former President called on President Clinton to declare ANWR a national monument (Andrus interview); Haycox, *Frigid Embrace*, 158.

 78. Hank Jenkins-Smith and Gilbert K. St. Clair, "The Politics of Offshore Energy: Empirically Testing the Advocacy Coalition Framework," In *Policy Change and Learning: An Advocacy Coalition Approach*, ed. Paul A. Sabatier and Hank Jenkins-Smith (San Francisco: Westview Press, 1993): 151,171.

 79. See Schattschneider, *The Semisovereign People*, 1975.

 80. Much of the discussion here comes from a variety of sources including the Andrus interview; Seiberling interview; Clusen interview; Cahn, *The Fight to Save*, 16; Carson and Johnson, *The Life and Times*, 197-200; *CQ Almanac*, 1979: 663-70; CQ *Almanac,* 1980: 575-84; *CQ Weekly Report*, 3 March 1979; 392; *CQ Weekly Report*, 24 March 1979: 507; *CQ Weekly Report*, 19 May 1979: 978; P.L. 96-487. In order to simplify the text, some

sources are cited here instead since combinations of sources frequently are utilized in a single passage.

81. *CQ Weekly Report*, 10 February 1979: 248; *CQ Weekly Report*, 8 September 1979: 1960.

82. Andrus interview.

83. Douglas R. Arnold, *The Logic of Congressional Action* (New Haven: Yale University Press, 1990): 224,236; Seiberling interview.

84. "A History;" Department of the Interior, "ANWR: TimeLine;" internal Senate Energy and Natural Resources Committee documents (2002).

85. *CQ Weekly Report*, 5 May 1979: 821.

86. *CQ Almanac*, 1979: 663-64; *CQ Almanac*, 1980: 575.

87. John W. Kingdon, *Agendas, Alternatives, and Public Policies*, 2d ed. (New York: Harper Collins College Publishers, 1995), 94-100.

Chapter 3
Advance to Go: The ANWR Policy Monopoly Unravels Then Regroups

In political science literature, the term subsystem *maintenance* refers to sustained influence on policy making. It depends upon the persistence and ingenuity of policy entrepreneurs: public or private sector actors who advance issues onto the congressional agenda and deflect political opposition.

No better illustration of maintenance exists in the ANWR case than Congressman Mo Udall turning defeat on the Alaska lands bill in the Interior Committee into victory on the floor, thus maintaining the power of his fledgling policy monopoly, or subsystem, in 1979. Udall lost a vote on his own version of the Alaska lands bill in the House Interior Committee that he chaired, and subsequently executed a parliamentary maneuver, substituting his bill for the bill that was pending on the floor.

This chapter addresses subsystem maintenance after the passage of the ANILCA statute in 1980 through 2006, focusing on the 1991-1992, 1995, and 2001-2006 legislative voting periods. During those critical junctures, ANWR again rose to the top of the congressional agenda. The power of the pro-environment ANWR subsystem arguably peaked with the enactment of ANILCA in 1980. After that, no laws were enacted that would have designated the coastal plain at ANWR "wilderness," therefore precluding drilling. At the same time, pro-environment actors managed to prevent drilling every time this issue arose on the agenda through the present. Their decision-making structure remained a force on Capitol Hill and in the public square for a long period.

Political entrepreneurs or triggering events were critical factors in subsystem maintenance. Entrepreneurs in the ANWR subsystem have tended to be leaders of a political party or members of committees with jurisdiction. However, high-ranking officials in the Executive Branch, including Democratic Presidents Carter, Clinton, and their political appointees at DOI and one of its key divisions, the US

Fish and Wildlife Service (USFWS), have also taken the initiative periodically in protecting ANWR's coastal plain from development.

Historically, ANWR jurisdiction in the House has been split between the Interior Committee and the now defunct Merchant Marine and Fisheries Committee, with the former having greater influence in the subsystem since it addressed on-land matters. In the Senate, a single committee consistently had jurisdiction: the Senate Interior and Insular Affairs Committee, renamed the Energy and Natural Resources Committee in 1978. During the ANILCA debate, the influential Washington Senator Henry "Scoop" Jackson was chairman of this committee. [1]

The political science literature confirms this nexus between political activists and subsystem maintenance. Both Suarez (2000) and Baumgartner and Jones (1993) assert that subsystems tend to be maintained largely through influential and activist Members of Congress. They might, for instance, lobby colleagues on behalf of subsystem interests, or shield subsystem benefits from criticism, thereby sustaining the subgovernment.

Those scholars also note that other types of actors are less involved in subsystem maintenance. For instance, while political parties, the White House, and the media tend to be involved with subsystem creation or destruction, typically they are less involved with subsystem maintenance. And while interest groups are important in the life of a given subsystem, private interests may also provide an impetus for the destruction of subgovernments. [2]

Scholars also discuss the importance of the use of symbols by political entrepreneurs who either maintain or oppose subsystems and their preferred policies. [3] It is commonly understood that public policies by definition are supposed to serve the interests of the citizenry. We therefore can ask whether the evolution of ANWR as a policy issue has served the masses in a tangible way since 1977, or whether it has been more of a symbolic issue.

This book found evidence that actors on both sides of the issue have defined ANWR symbolically and have tried to maintain or broaden their respective decision-making structures to gain policy victories. The debate largely centered on environmental protection versus environmentally sound drilling (see chapter 5).

Pro-environment witnesses in both chambers of Congress consistently advanced the policy images of the Porcupine Caribou Herd (i.e., which are not listed as endangered species) and the coastal plain as a pristine wilderness or the "crown jewel" of wildlife sanctuaries to maintain the anti-drilling position. Similarly, pro-drilling witnesses defined ANWR symbolically in House and Senate hearings by saying that drilling would leave a small "footprint" on the habitat used by caribou and other species, or that only a small portion of the refuge would be drilled. So, we can conclude that both chambers of Congress, despite their different procedures, treated ANWR symbolically and as a pro-drilling issue at the committee level. Overall, actors in the ANWR-environmental subsystem and their opponents each have utilized real, concrete and objective phenomena symbolically by making emotive appeals to gain support for their respective policy stances.

The evidence therefore suggests that ANWR has been a largely symbolic issue since 1980. Neither coalition has delivered substantive benefits to the public. Both the environmental movement and the energy industry have maintained a presence in Washington, DC and have used that presence to engage in symbolic politics in the ANWR debate. Failure to offer symbols might weaken their respective positions of influence though. Now let us examine the political context for the maintenance of ANWR's pro-environment decision structure and the entrepreneurs who led that effort.

Subsystem Maintenance: 1981-1992

The influence of the ANWR-environmental subsystem that was centered in the US House of Representatives peaked with enactment of ANILCA in 1980, since ANILCA clearly was its greatest success by doubling the size of the refuge. Certainly, a greater achievement would have been to persuade a future administration and the Congress that the controversial "1002 Area" of ANWR deserved the highest possible degree of environmental protection, that is, "wilderness" status. While they did not succeed in this, subsystem actors were nevertheless influential enough to maintain a status-quo policy between 1981 and 1992. At least some of this maintenance was due to unforeseen events rather than the activity of political entrepreneurs.

The 1980s

At least until the mid-1980s, the subsystem appeared strong, or at least unchallenged, as measured by continued protection of the Refuge and the 1002 Area. In 1983, for instance, the federal government added roughly one million acres to the refuge when the State of Alaska opted not to retain control of certain lands chosen under the Statehood Act of 1958. Again, the US and Canada signed a document in 1987 aimed at managing and protecting the Porcupine Caribou Herd. The following year, Congress added 325,000 acres to ANWR, and the total acreage rose to 19.8 million acres.[4]

The pro-environment subsystem retained strength in the House in part because Congressman Bruce Vento (D-MN) continued John Seiberling's strong pro-environment position when Vento replaced him as chairman of the House Interior Subcommittee on National Parks and Public Lands in 1986.[5]

The evidence that the ANWR subsystem was relatively strong during the Reagan years bolsters Vogel's (1993) broader claim that, "throughout the decade [of the 1980s], Congress continued to pass new environmental statutes, in many cases strengthening the standards it had passed during the 1970s."[6] Vogel also asserts that both states' rights and fund-raising played a role in enabling environmental groups to mitigate opposing policy-making efforts in the Executive Branch during the 1980s. These groups were able to gain enactment of more stringent environmental laws or regulations at the local level rather than the national level. Again, membership and solicitations increased partly due to identification of strong opposition in the White House as well as the deployment of new direct mail techniques. [7]

Despite all the evidence for subsystem maintenance during the 1980s, the political waters clearly would become stormy for environmentalists during the first half of President Reagan's second term. Political entrepreneurs who possessed a pro-drilling agenda for ANWR began to challenge the clout of the subsystem during the late 1980s and early 1990s. Key events also put the issue back on the agenda.

Consider the period preceding the Exxon Valdez oil spill in 1989. On April 21, 1987, the DOI submitted its environmental impact statement (EIS) on the 1002 Area to the Congress, as it was required to do under the 1980 ANILCA law. Section 1002 of that law mandated that the DOI Secretary prepare this EIS "on exploration activities." The report "recommend[ed] to the Congress of the United States that it enact legislation directing the Secretary [of the Interior] to conduct an orderly oil and gas leasing program for the 1002 Area at such pace and in such circumstances as he determines will avoid unnecessary adverse effect on the environment." [8] And in 1988, the relatively pro-environment House Merchant Marine and Fisheries Committee approved a bill that would develop the 1002 Area, thus improving the chances for House passage.

The entire dynamic changed when the Exxon Valdez ran aground in Alaska's Prince William Sound in 1989. [9] Over 10 million gallons of oil spilled from the vessel on March 24, 1989, extensively damaging 1,500 miles of beaches and killing thousands of birds, seals, otters, and other wildlife for years to come. [10] The grave damage caused by the spill seemed to point clearly to the possible environmental consequences of development, and so helped to preserve the political status quo against developing ANWR.

Proponents of the conservation at ANWR were now afforded an opportunity to define the 1002 Area as needing continued federal protection against oil and natural gas interests. In a broader sense, the Exxon Valdez incident may have been a significant factor in the second wave of environmentalism that emerged in much of the industrialized world, including the United States, during the late 1980s. [11] At any rate, the influence of environmentalism remained strong until the next threat emerged, namely the danger posed by Saddam Hussein's Iraq to American and Western oil supplies.

The Early 1990s

By early 1991, policy-making momentum shifted back in favor of pro-drilling interests. In the wake of the Persian Gulf War, President Bush called for a national energy plan that included leasing at the 1002 Area, or ANWR coastal plain, to oil and natural gas interests. Senators Bennett Johnston (D-LA) and Malcolm Wallop (R-WY), both from oil-producing states, introduced the legislation with the support of a variety of energy and business groups.

However, the momentum shifted again when the bill was defeated in the US Senate by Democratic Senator and political entrepreneur Tim Wirth of Colorado, who filibustered the measure. This action was a forerunner to full-fledged senatorial influence within the subsystem that took root beginning in 2001 and the morphing of the subgovernment into a more fluid *issue network*. Unexpectedly, disgruntled utility firms and several organizations that opposed an increase in Corporate Average Fuel Economy (CAFÉ) standards joined Senator Wirth and his likeminded colleagues.[12]

According to Becky Gay, who worked in the Alaska governor's office on political mobilization for ANWR development during the early 1990s,[13] a second reason why the energy bill was toppled from the agenda in 1991 was the allegation by Anita Hill against US Supreme Court nominee Clarence Thomas.[14] That issue dominated the agenda late that year.

In short, the subsystem was able to fend off a pro-drilling threat to its existence in 1991 by having activist Members of Congress utilize the rules of the Senate (e.g., the filibuster) to their advantage. Although the controversy about Clarence Thomas had subsided by 1992, the mere threat of a filibuster to the entire energy bill was enough to trigger removal of the ANWR-drilling provision from the legislation. Congress soon passed the bipartisan Energy Policy Act of 1992.

Although pro-drilling forces suffered legislative defeat after the Gulf War, they would live to fight another day. The inability of the oil industry, or at least certain firms, to schedule a vote on drilling at ANWR in 1991 prompted them to create Arctic Power in April 1992, a single-issue organization with bipartisan membership.

This interloper in the ANWR subsystem now boasts over 10,000 members. Established to target Members of Congress and the White House to permit development of the refuge, the group also maintained a close working relationship with Alaska Senators Ted Stevens and Frank Murkowski,[15] Congressman Don Young, Governor Tony Knowles, and the Alaska Legislature (who all favored drilling). This organization, however, never aimed to dictate the terms of future drilling leases, which is the job of the owners of ANWR, the federal government.[16]

A variety of actors have supported and funded Arctic Power since then. Chief among these have been oil firms with longstanding interests in Alaska, such as British Petroleum (BP), as well as the State of Alaska. Arctic Power has worked to maintain a presence in Congress even during periods when ANWR drilling was not on the congressional agenda. This strategy would enable the pro-drilling *issue network* to retain a capacity for political mobilization when the ANWR issue reemerged on the agenda. By definition, issue networks are decision-making structures that have both fluid membership and the capacity to mobilize when issues resurface on the government agenda.[17] According to its website, Arctic Power is

> [a] grassroots, non-profit citizen's organization that advocates jobs and energy for Americans through development of ... ANWR resources. The organization is committed to securing congressional and presidential approval of legislation opening the coastal plain of the ANWR to responsible oil development. [It is comprised of] citizens from Alaska and across the nation who hail from a full economic spectrum including miners, fishermen, tourism operators, transportation companies, labor unions, Alaska Native corporations, elected officials and more. The organization is governed by a board of directors representing all regions of Alaska."[18]

Soon this threat to subsystem maintenance would face a formidable political force in the Clinton-Gore Administration as pro-environment forces shifted their weight to the White House.

Bill Clinton and Al Gore were important political entrepreneurs who helped to maintain the ANWR subsystem during the 1990s. In their 1992 book, *Putting People First*, the two candidates vowed to "[p]rohibit drilling in Arctic National Wildlife Refuge (ANWR) in Alaska [and] work instead to expand the ANWR to include the 1.5-million-acre Arctic Coastal Plain"[19] This statement implies that the two men aimed to designate that area wilderness. They never achieved this goal though. Yet, subsequent events during the first Clinton-Gore Administration would demonstrate clearly that the subsystem had a new leader, the man in the White House.

Subsystem Maintenance: 1993-1995

The ANWR-environmental subsystem remained strong during the first three years of the Clinton Administration, culminating in a legislative victory over pro-drilling forces in 1995. The early months of that year brought the appointment of pro-environment operatives to various posts, including Bruce Babbitt as Secretary of the Interior, and the Wilderness Society's Alice Rivlin as Assistant Budget Director at the Office of Management and Budget. Two other leaders from the Wilderness Society, Jim Baca and George Frampton, were named Bureau of Land Management (BLM) Director and Assistant Secretary for Fish, Wildlife and Parks (DOI) respectively.

Each of these positions would critically influence future ANWR policy decisions. Specifically, these and other decision makers later would support wholeheartedly President Clinton's decision in 1995 to veto a budget reconciliation package, a measure that included a provision for the BLM to issue leases for oil and natural gas exploration at ANWR's coastal plain, as will be explained momentarily.

Network Control Shifts to the White House

By 1993, it was evident that the hub of the evolving ANWR decision-making structure was shifting from Congress to the Executive Branch. There were at least two reasons for this.[20] First, pro-environment Members of Congress did not object to the "bully pulpit" of a new environmentalist president providing them with a means to justify votes with constituents on controversial environmental issues. President Clinton, DOI Secretary Babbitt, and others in the new administration generally promoted protection of public lands (e.g., near environmentally sensitive areas), including protection of the coastal plain at ANWR. Second, environmental interest groups supported this change since they clearly had an ally in the White House and now could devote their resources to lobbying Congress.

This shift in subsystem control created an opportunity for pro-drilling interests led by the State of Alaska and several major oil companies to regroup. They were able to strengthen their network of decision makers by raising the profile of the fledgling Arctic Power, which would become an ally of pro-drilling members in the soon-to-be Republican Congress in 1995.

When Clinton became President, Arctic Power and other advocates of drilling began to adopt some tactics of their opponents. For instance, they brought more Democrats into the information network (just as environmentalists had recruited moderate Republicans) and distributed information more widely.[21] Subsystem forces and pro-drilling advocates each would have a high-profile political target by the mid-1990s: Arctic Power (i.e., "the face of big oil") and President Clinton respectively. This elevation of a limited number of visible opponents may have added to the increasingly acrimonious characteristic of the ANWR debate.

One result of the 1994 congressional electoral landslide for the GOP was that two Alaskans were appointed to the key committees in the House and Senate that had jurisdiction over ANWR issues. Congressman Don Young (R-AK) became chairman of the House Resources Committee (formerly the Interior and Insular Affairs Committee). Senator Frank Murkowski chaired the Energy and Natural Resources Committee.

Importantly, each chairman required his respective committee members to debate Alaska lands issues at the full committee rather than subcommittee level, thus minimizing prospective subcommittee opposition and affording each committee chair greater authority over ANWR policy.[22] This replacement of pro-environment committee chairs with pro-development chairs (i.e., political potential entrepreneurs) in Congress in 1995 represents one of two structural changes that challenged the pro-environment network for ANWR during this period.

A second effect of the 1994 elections was the dismantling of the pro-environment House Committee on Merchant Marine and Fisheries by the incoming Speaker of the House, Newt Gingrich, as part of a broader effort to centralize authority in the lower chamber. Since this committee had been comprised primarily of Republicans who were liberal-to-moderate on environmental issues, the reorganization effectively tilted the dynamic of the ANWR debate against environmentalists. By 1995, its partial jurisdiction over ANWR was folded into the increasingly pro-development House Resources Committee, which was comprised increasingly of conservative Members from Rocky Mountain and Western states.[23]

Certainly, the full House had become more conservative by 1995, but the Speaker now had the power to appoint and remove committee chairs. Assumedly, Speaker Gingrich appointed conservative chairs that favored his policy positions and removed or threatened to remove chairs with liberal policy tendencies.

In short, the structure of the ANWR-environmental network, which was seated in the Executive Branch beginning in 1993, was threatened by an opposing structure within the congressional committee system beginning in 1995. The notion of shifting policy stances and decision structures is an important one since a central question of this book is whether partisan voting in Congress of the more complex *life cycle* concept (or some combination) best explains these shifts in the ANWR case. The next chapter will explain the impact of alleged Republican partisanship in detail, especially beginning in 1995, and its potential impact on these structural and policy shifts.

Veto of FY 1996 Budget Bill with ANWR Rider

Amid a partisan political environment in 1995, President Clinton vetoed the FY 1996 omnibus budget reconciliation package (HR 2491) partly because the Senate included a provision that would have permitted drilling at ANWR.[24] The Senate arguably has less influence over budget reconciliation legislation than it does on typical bills because although senators may attach non-germane amendments on both budgetary and non-budgetary measures, they are precluded under Senate rules from using the filibuster on a budget resolution.[25] The vote on the resolution is taken early in the reconciliation process, typically in late winter or early spring. Pro-development forces in the Senate traveled this path in 1995 but failed as President Clinton's veto proved the final line of defense for the pro-environment team.

Alice Rivlin, who was elevated from OMB Deputy Director to Director in 1994, recounted that ANWR "was important" in President Clinton's decision to veto the measure and that a strong consensus existed within the Clinton Administration against drilling at ANWR since the 1992 presidential campaign. This issue, she said, was "not contentious within the Administration at all."

In fact, ANWR was an "environmental bottom line" in 1995 when the issue arose in "various forms." Rivlin added that a "solid phalanx of environmental groups" supported ANWR protection during the 1995 budget debate. The list included the usual network of actors, the Wilderness Society, the Sierra Club, the National Resources Defense Council, and the League of Conservation Voters to name a few. Yet, she did not recall any high-profile activity on the other side by the Teamsters Union.[26]

All political observers do not share this view of a "solid phalanx" of environmental interests. Andrew Lundquist,[27] who served as a Senate committee staffer on ANWR issues during the 1995 debate on the budget reconciliation bill, and later headed Vice President Dick Cheney's energy task force in 2001, described a somewhat divided environmental community during the budget debate.[28]

Lundquist hinted that environmentalists were unable to identify and rally against a specific enemy, such as oil companies, in 1995. Environmentalists' opponents included larger oil companies, but one group that later would serve to weaken the network, the Teamsters Union, was not particularly active during the 1995 ANWR debate.[29] The importance of this union in the 2001 House debate, among other factors, will be discussed shortly.

Subsystem Maintenance: 1996-2006

Overview

During the 1996-2006 period, the ANWR subsystem, by now a more fluid network of decision makers, continued to face intensified political opposition. The pro-environment position on ANWR clearly was weakened by several factors: congressional reorganization of 1995 and change in party control of the Congress; the election of a pro-drilling Republican to the White House in 2000; and, House passage of an energy bill in August 2001 permitting drilling at ANWR.

Subsystem allies in the Senate, however, managed to counter this largely pro-drilling momentum in April 2002. Taken as a whole, this power shift favoring energy development transpired despite the nearly unanimous enactment of a law (P.L. 105-57) during the Clinton Administration in 1997 that overhauled the nation's wildlife refuge system by affording refuges a clearly defined legal purpose for the first time.

The remainder of this chapter will analyze policy and subsystem developments during President Clinton's second term and outline key events that transpired from the election of George W. Bush until consideration of the budget and defense spending bills in 2005. In this analysis, I will identify network actors and their opponents during the Bush years and compare them with public and private interests that were prevalent during earlier periods. Finally, I will explore how political entrepreneurs managed to preserve the subsystem in the face of competitors who threatened its survival.

ANWR and the Second Clinton Term

In April 1996, the final year of President Clinton's first term in office, the House passed legislation (HR 1675; 287-138) that would have overhauled America's wildlife refuge system by, among other things, codifying the mission of the refuge system. The Clinton Administration and some Democrats in both chambers expressed concerns about the bill. Advocates of reform would have to wait until the next Congress to gain passage of a refuge reform law.[30]

A broad consensus had developed among members of the House Resources Committee by April 1997 that the National Wildlife Refuge System needed improvement. The system lacked funds and managerial oversight, and most refuge policy makers and close observers concurred that a singular legal mission was needed to replace a nebulous term, "compatible," which appeared in current law. This term permitted uses of lands that were consistent with the major (but still vague) purposes of the refuge system.[31] On June 3rd, Congress passed a bill (HR 1420; 407-1) aimed at establishing new standards for the use of the nation's wildlife refuges, including ANWR; the Senate later would amend the bill and pass it on a voice vote.[32]

Despite overwhelming support for this measure in both chambers of Congress, some opposition existed among interest groups. On the one hand, the legislation included provisions that pleased congressional conservatives and liberals. On the other hand, although pro-development interests such as the Wildlife Legislative Fund of America (i.e., a group that was lobbying for access to public lands for hunters) supported the legislation, environmental groups provided mixed reviews.

This partial opposition to the 1997 refuge law among the environmental community did not preclude the building of a temporary bridge between some environmentalists and pro-development forces. In 1996, President Clinton had threatened to veto a refuge reform bill at the behest of DOI Secretary Babbitt. This time, though, the president was satisfied with the bill and its legal establishment of the mission for the refuges: namely, promoting conservation, plant, and animal restoration.

Jamie Rappaport Clark, the former Director of the USFWS (1997-2001) and a career DOI employee, characterized the measure as the "clarification of who makes the science [of refuges] into law," and contrasted the bill's conservation provisions with BLM-administered areas where land can be used for multiple purposes. She asserted that environmentalists believed that the bill could help to protect the ANWR coastal plain because any drilling provision would be incompatible with the new statutory mission of the refuge system.

Conservatives, including Alaska's sole House Member and Chairman of the House Resources Committee, Don Young, applauded the bill as well, especially for the provisions that offered recreation to hunters and fishermen. In the past, hunters and fishermen had failed to gain support for a provision to increase their access to national wildlife refuges and other public lands.[33]

Although the 1997 refuge law bolstered the ANWR-environmental subsystem only indirectly, another action in that year directly strengthened the issue network's position on ANWR. The US Supreme Court, through its opinion in *US v. Alaska*, weakened states' rights. The high court decided a multi-decade dispute between the US Government and the State of Alaska concerning ownership of submerged lands offshore and within ANWR. It held that coastal lagoons in the northeast belonged to ANWR rather than to the State of Alaska.

This court decision was significant since federally controlled lands could be leased for energy exploration only by a future act of Congress. Such action would have to pass through network decision makers who protected the status quo. A contrary holding would have limited congressional options for protecting the area because Alaska would have controlled some subsurface resources at the refuge.[34]

During the next two years of the Clinton Administration, the Monica Lewinsky scandal and presidential electoral politics took center-stage, and ANWR and other important policy issues were subsequently sidelined. At any rate, pro-drilling interests during this period did not seem to pose much of a threat to the subsystem, perhaps due to victory by network actors on the budget reconciliation bill in 1995 and the cohesive position on ANWR presented by President Clinton and his allies.

Jamie Rappaport Clark contended in early 2003 that the decision-making structure for ANWR policy at the USFWS was "very different" during the Clinton Administration compared to the George W. Bush Administration. She asserted that the Clinton team was much more environmentally friendly and did "not get into message spinning." Instead, she and her colleagues "applied the science" to the debate. President Clinton and DOI Secretary Babbitt offered "terrific support" on the ANWR issue and "always said, 'so goes ANWR, so goes the whole ecosystem.'"

Clark also added that there was more delegation to the USFWS Director during the Clinton years than in the early Bush years. From the perspective of former Clinton Administration officials, by the time he had taken office, President Bush had drawn ANWR as a "line in the sand as a campaign issue [with] facts [not] matter[ing] any more on oil or caribou." ANWR became a "political rallying cry." In all, President Bush lifted ANWR out of the decision-making process and the USFWS was not involved in making policy.[35] Clark's assertion will be analyzed shortly.

ANWR-Related Developments during the Early Bush Years

In 2001, several events transpired that could potentially affect the ANWR coastal plain. In January, President-elect George W. Bush vowed "to fight a 'huge energy crisis' by analyzing all federal lands for oil exploration, enlisting Mexico's help and rejecting calls to breach hydroelectric dams."[36] The incoming president spoke as Californians faced an energy crisis (i.e., largely due to unconventional deregulation of electricity prices in that state), making energy policy a more salient issue.

During this same period, just before leaving office, President Clinton declared millions of acres of federal forest and other multiple-use public lands national monuments and roadless areas.[37] The 1002 Area was not declared a national monument at that time, according to former DOI Secretary Cecil Andrus, because ANILCA precluded President Clinton from doing so.[38] The next few sections analyze ANWR-related developments in both political branches of government during the Bush years.

The Bush Energy Plan

On May 16, 2001, Vice President Dick Cheney and the Energy Policy Development Group presented the Bush Administration's National Energy Policy (NEP) at a Cabinet meeting.[39] The plan included at least three provisions that directly concerned ANWR. First, it would authorize exploration and development of the 1002 Area, or coastal plain. This provision urged Congress to require use of the best available technologies so that development activities result in no significant environmental impact. Second, the plan would earmark oil and gas royalties from ANWR to a new Royalties Conservation Fund aimed at expediting the backlog of maintenance on public lands. The third provision would direct the Secretaries of the Interior and Energy to use some funds from ANWR leases to support research into various alternative and renewable energy sources.[40] Eight days later, Senator Jim Jeffords of Vermont officially abandoned the Republican Party, thus shifting control of the Senate to the Democrats and threatening President Bush's hopes of opening the 1002 Area for oil and natural gas leasing.[41]

House Action in 2001

On August 1, the most significant policy development in the 25-year history of the ANWR-environmental subsystem took place.[42] The US House of Representatives passed a variant of President Bush's energy plan (HR 4; 240-189). The bill included a provision to open a portion of the 1002 Area for energy development.[43] Subsystem actors in and outside of government were shocked by this occurrence.

This vote suggested that the center of opposition to the ANWR-environmental subsystem was now in the White House, just as the core of the subsystem had been in the White House less than one year earlier under President Clinton. This was a dramatic change by any account. Proponents of drilling had been pushing for two decades for congressional approval of a drilling provision for the coastal plain. The Bush Administration, according to most pundits, was proactive on this matter. Other factors, though, may also have contributed to this turn of events.

Debate on the bill included adoption of two critical amendments and rejection of another prior to the vote on final passage. Republican Congressman John Sununu (NH) offered the two provisions that were adopted. The first would split new oil and gas revenues between the State of Alaska and the national government; it would require the federal share to be used for research on renewable energy sources and maintenance of federal lands. The second provision would limit the surface area that would be opened to drilling to 2,000 acres (i.e., of the 1.5-million-acre coastal plain). Congressman Sununu's second amendment was aimed at broadening appeal of the bill to moderates, and it especially stunned the environmental community because of its substance and unexpected timing.[44]

The hand of the Bush White House was felt strongly in the US House of Representatives that day in 2001. Andrew Lundquist of the Bush Administration's energy task force, a veteran of energy-environmental battles as a staffer on the Senate Energy and Natural Resources Committee devised this approach.[45] Environmentalists were especially concerned that these 2000 acres would not be contiguous and that it would require a massive infrastructure to connect the plots of land.[46]

Congressman Edward Markey (D-MA) offered a critical amendment to HR 4 that was rejected by the full House. It would have gutted the bill's ANWR drilling provision. These and other ANWR-related votes in Congress will be analyzed further in chapter 4.

Senate Action in 2002

The year 2002 was an election year. In April, Senate Majority Leader Tom Daschle (D-SD) finally decided to give the Bush Administration its long-desired vote on an energy package (S. 517). Permitting a floor vote would free the Democrats and the Senate from being blamed for legislative gridlock. Similarly, Daschle could opt to kill the bill in conference committee should a compromise bill with the House fail to satisfy Senate Democrats. Evidence exists to support this alleged strategy as follows.

The bill passed the Senate in April 2002, and Daschle said that the bill met Democrats' goals in "a number of places," but "fell short" in some other areas. It may be that Senate Democrats had little intention of compromising with the GOP-led house.

According to Jeff Bingaman (D-NM), the Chairman of the Energy and Natural Resources Committee, Democrats did not "plan to split the difference" on critical issues such as ANWR. Adding to this evidence about the Democratic strategy in the Senate was their apparent concern that pro-environment constituents (e.g., the League of Conservation Voters) were dissatisfied with the pro-development amendments that were accepted on the floor.[47]

The critical vote was taken on April 18th when the Senate fell 14 votes shy of the 60 votes necessary under the "cloture" procedure to end a filibuster of an amendment that would have limited to 2000 acres the amount of land surface that could be impacted by drilling. The amendment also would have designated an additional 1.5 million acres of ANWR as wilderness in exchange for developing the 1.5-million-acre coastal plain.

Two competing political entrepreneurs took center stage that day: Senator Frank Murkowski (R-AK) who offered the amendment, and Senate Majority Leader Tom Daschle (D-SD) who defended the subsystem's position on ANWR. Daschle's version of the energy plan ultimately passed the Senate by a wide margin (88-11) on April 20.

A generic subsystem includes actors like Senator Daschle. Here's how. Bryner (1993) notes that "those who profit from the status quo will continue to lead the fight against change; they have considerable resources and incentives to block new approaches and inhibit new research."[48] The status quo policy ultimately prevailed for ANWR in 2002 because, after a filibuster of the pro-drilling energy bill and passage of an anti-drilling one, a conference committee ended talks on October 3 without reaching an agreement.

Senate Action in 2003

By early 2003, rumors were rife in Washington that pro-drilling forces would attempt to resurrect the budget battle of 1995 by attaching a drilling provision to the FY 2004 budget reconciliation bill (which cannot be filibustered under Senate rules). When a veteran of that earlier debate, former OMB Director Alice Rivlin, was asked if she had any predictions about how things might develop in 2003 she responded, "I don't know but there is a danger from an environmental standpoint."[49]

By the same token, former USFWS Director Jamie Rappaport Clark said, "If it gets in the package, it's gone." Opponents of drilling conceded that the Bush Administration pursued a brilliant political strategy.[50]

On the other side of the 2003 budget debate stood Becky Gay, an Alaskan, who epitomized the pro-drilling position. Gay worked on this issue in the Office of the Governor of Alaska, helped to establish Arctic Power, and later became a GOP candidate for the state legislature in 2002. In late 2002 she said that changing the status quo "would take unusual circumstances (i.e., a budget reconciliation bill) because [drilling was] held back [by unusual political tactics of the opposition]."[51]

On March 19, 2003, the Senate passed the Boxer (D-CA) Amendment to the budget resolution by a vote of 52-48 (S.Con.Res.23). This provision reinvigorated the issue network since it stripped the ANWR drilling provision from the budget bill. Environmentalists and their political allies were elated. This measure would be repeated in 2005, when energy interests would almost succeed, as we will see in chapter 4.

The Structure of the ANWR-Environmental Subsystem and Its Opposition under Bush

This section investigates some of the key actors in the subsystem operating both inside and outside government, and their opposition. It should become evident that the subsystem had been weakened significantly by an opposing network by the time of the House vote for drilling in August 2001. Yet, political entrepreneurs in the Senate managed to maintain a variant of the pro-environment decision structure. Government actors remained critical in the decision-making process for ANWR policy because the ANILCA law of 1980 required a statutory change to permit drilling along the coastal plain.

Governmental Actors: The Executive Branch

Looking back, pro-environment interest groups and lawmakers benefited by having the Clinton White House carry their proverbial water for protection of the 1002 Area. This high-level support evaporated in 2001. When George W. Bush became president he continued to set the agenda for ANWR, an agenda that contrasted starkly with the one set by the prior administration.

The Bush Administration centralized the decision-making process and did not trust some civil servants at the USFWS (i.e., those who rose through the ranks during the Clinton years). This shift had a weakening effect on the ANWR-environmental issue network. It was now up to Senate Democratic Leader, Tom Daschle and the usual cast of environmental groups (the Sierra Club, National Wildlife Federation, Friends of the Earth, and the National Audubon Society to name a few) to preserve network dominance over ANWR policy.

Prior to 2001, the Executive Branch created a new decision-making venue for network opponents, namely, the inter-agency energy task force headed by Vice President Cheney and his chief assistant, Andrew Lundquist. The panel was comprised of 14 Executive Branch officials, including the Secretaries of State, Interior, Treasury, Agriculture, Commerce, Energy, and Transportation, together with high-ranking administration officials such as the heads of the EPA, FEMA, OMB, and a few additional personal advisors to President Bush.[52]

It is difficult to ascertain who influenced President Bush more on ANWR policy and broader energy-environment issues: the USFWS director or other Executive Branch actors. When asked what agency representatives on the energy task force exerted the most influence on the president's policy agenda, Mr. Lundquist responded that he was "not comfortable divulging [that] to anybody." He further asserted that President Bush, as a matter of principle and precedent, decided to preserve the decision-making operations of the chief executive.[53] Others might call this another example of "secret governance" that would come to characterize the Bush era, especially after 9/11.

In contrast, more clarity seems to exist regarding earlier presidential delegation of authority on ANWR policy. One key subsystem actor during the Clinton Administration argues that the USFWS had primary managerial authority over the refuge system, and that it later ceded some of that authority during ANWR debates in the Bush Administration.

For instance, the USFWS was ordered by Bush Administration officials to remove data from its website because some of it would undermine the administration's arguments for drilling. Who played politics with ANWR and science? As for the National Park Service and the US Forest Service, they have had nothing to do with ANWR policy. The USGS has played the role of "the science guys," and the BLM has had some "tangential" dealings with the issue.[54] The latter agency manages, among other entities, the National Petroleum Reserve-Alaska (NPR-A).

Governmental Actors: Congress

The Democratic-controlled US Senate was compelled to lead the pro-environment subsystem in 2001 since mostly Republicans who opposed their ANWR policy ran the House and the White House. Senator Daschle, whether he liked it or not, had become the new "champion" for protection of the coastal plain. His capacity to steer the agenda in the Senate, coupled with pressure from rank-and-file Democrats, who largely opposed drilling, led him to "carry the water" for the pro-environment position just as President Clinton had done. As a subsystem leader, he continued to face opposition on ANWR from Congressman Young (R-AK), Senator Stevens (R-AK), and others.

Another change in this network occurred among congressional staff, according to Don Barry, Assistant Secretary for Fish, Wildlife and Parks during the Clinton Administration. Mr. Barry worked in government on both sides of the ANWR issue for a quarter century. He contends that since the enactment of ANILCA, there has been a wholesale change in Senate staff that handles ANWR issues and a corresponding loss of institutional memory. Further, very few highly informed staffers remain in the House. This situation undermines environmental policy making in the Congress today.[55]

Governmental Actors: Alaska State and Local Government

State officials in Juneau have remained influential in ANWR policy formulation. The State of Alaska and members from both political parties have been strong advocates for drilling at ANWR, at least since the 1970s when the state legislature appropriated 5 million dollars for a lobbying and advertising campaign against the pro-environment Alaska lands bill, HR 39. That measure was being considered by the national legislature thousands of miles from Juneau.[56]

This political and financial support continued through the end of the century and beyond. For instance, in February 1997 the Alaska State House and Senate overwhelmingly approved a Senate Joint Resolution urging the US Congress to open the coastal plain to oil and gas exploration, development, and production.

The following month, a delegation hand-delivered this resolution to the Alaska Congressional Delegation in Washington, DC. The core argument of pro-development forces was that opening ANWR would create over 38,000 new jobs by 2005.[57] Another example of state activism occurred in 2001 when the legislature appropriated more money to lobby in Washington, DC, for ANWR drilling that it had during past legislative cycles.

The Office of the Governor has taken the lead on state lobbying efforts by working closely with state legislators to fund Arctic Power (which was funded originally by oil companies exclusively). These actors have made their collective support for development of the 1002 Area known at the national level.

For instance, in December 2001 Alaska Governor Tony Knowles criticized his fellow Democrats, Senators Tom Daschle (SD) and Jeff Bingaman (NM), for their party's national energy plan, a measure that excluded development of a small portion of ANWR. Specifically, the governor noted that the bill was drafted without consulting with Alaskan environmental, indigenous, business, and civic leaders.[58]

The involvement of local officials in the drive to promote drilling at the 1002 Area likewise has had some impact on subsystem decision makers, at least indirectly. For instance, Arctic Power asserts that it has the grassroots support of 17 Alaskan mayors, cities, and boroughs. Another 17 community organizations[59] in the state support the goals of Arctic Power.[60] Further, while nationwide grassroots support for drilling at ANWR may have been elusive, (for instance, a Gallup Poll on April 24, 2002, revealed a 56-35 percent majority opposed to drilling), state and local polls tended to be evenly divided or favored oil exploration. As an example, a city survey of residents of Kaktovik, which is located along the coastal plain, showed that 78 percent of residents support development.[61]

Skeptics of this pro-drilling activism have alleged that state and local officials are motivated primarily by the political benefits that increased oil revenues would afford to incumbents (e.g., lower tax rates for constituents coupled with increased revenues for spending). Becky Gay, who supports states' rights and economic development, concedes that the money-motive accusation has some merit. She calls energy development on the coastal plain "taxable stuff" and acknowledges that monetary "bonuses" are "part of the [political] game."[62]

Numerous environmentalists and political observers have suggested that interest in filling state and local coffers has trumped environmental protection, and some data exists to support these claims. Two examples will be analyzed here—revenue distribution for oil leases and the relative tax burden on Alaska residents.

The Alaska Statehood Act mandated payment to Alaska of 90 percent of mineral (e.g., oil) lease revenue collected from federally owned lands located there; the remaining 10 percent would be used to manage federal lands in Alaska. Critics of this generous arrangement to Alaska (e.g., other states typically received 38 to 50 percent of mineral lease revenues) should note three counterpoints.

First, the federal government approved this provision.[63] Second, Alaska does not receive the 60/40 allocations for hydroelectric projects afforded to other states due to the Statehood Act and thus needs revenue.[64] Third, there is not necessarily a correlation between a state's revenue levels and its degree of environmental protection. Becky Gay added that drilling at ANWR would afford the aforementioned 10 percent oil-revenue benefit to the federal government, unlike, say, the revenue distribution pattern from leases at Prudhoe Bay. The land there is owned by the State of Alaska, not by the federal government, and revenues are shared among the state, oil producers, and the North Slope Borough.[65]

The State of Alaska was pro-drilling and appeared to have financial/fiscal incentives for their position. In 1998, Alaskans paid the lowest percentage of their personal income in combined state and local taxes, 6.1 percent, versus the national average of 11.4 percent.[66] At the same time, numerous environmental groups have documented and criticized the environmental record of oil producers at nearby Prudhoe Bay. Implicit here is that state officials, residents, and oil companies each contribute to the lowering of environmental standards since they have financial incentives to permit drilling.

The Alaska Permanent Fund directly relates to the tax burden issue. The fund provides over 1500 dollars annually to every state resident, but has nothing to do with oil revenues, according to Becky Gay. The key state windfall if ANWR were to be developed would be a reduction in property taxes on infrastructure rather than an impact on this per-capita payment. Currently, property taxes are used to fund Alaska's general fund.[67] Thus, development at ANWR would bolster the state's general fund and lower property taxes on infrastructure, according to this argument.

However, historian Stephen Haycox (2002) disputes this position. He notes that "25 percent of petroleum lease bonuses, royalties, and rentals" are deposited into the Alaska Permanent Fund, which was established when voters amended the state constitution at the urging of Governor Hammond in 1976. As an incentive for residents to vote for creation of the fund, the state legislature repealed the state income tax. Six years later, the legislature passed a statute that provided for distribution of the growing surplus in the Fund to state residents. Alaska has never had a sales tax.[68]

Finally, political culture is a facet of states' rights that deserves some attention. In many ways, the perspective provided by Alaska Republican and House Majority Leader Jeannette James exemplifies the perspective of pro-drilling Alaskans. James contends that most Alaskans live within a 450-mile "rail belt" that the federal government built in 1916, and that the failure to expand this area of human activity has constrained the people. People now want jobs and development of their natural resources.

Further, James, who is originally from Oregon, believes that non-Alaskans want to preclude Alaskans from experiencing the growing pains typically associated with a state's economic development. In other words, Alaska became a state in 1959 and its people remain relatively "behind the curve" in development, but they should not be precluded from expanding their state's economy. She adds that the ANWR debate "really is not a state issue because the ANILCA law makes this a federal issue. [Alaskans] have to go to Washington, DC, and beg. [Alaskans] need federal legislation and federal approval [to drill]; therefore, it costs money to go to DC and make that case."[69]   Generally speaking, Westerners tend to view Washington as a group of "outsiders" who are trying to control them from afar.

Non-Governmental Actors: Environmental Groups

Within the original pro-environment subsystem, the usual cast of environmental groups (e.g., Sierra Club, National Wildlife Federation, Friends of the Earth, National Audubon Society, Natural Resources Defense Council, League of Conservation Voters, and the Alaska Coalition) continued to work with governmental actors to preserve their longstanding dominance over ANWR policy. The discussion below aims to elucidate the nature of this environmental decision structure beginning in 2001; however, chapter 5 provides a more detailed view of its actors, their opponents, and their issue definitions of ANWR.

The characteristics of the ANWR decision-making structure had changed in one way by the early Bush years, but had remained the same in another way since enactment of the ANILCA statute in 1980. A well-organized environmental movement influenced the policy-making process during both periods; that movement viewed ANWR protection as its "holy grail," said Andrew Lundquist, a longtime Senate committee staffer and advisor to President George W. Bush. At the same time, those groups became increasingly competitive for money as the pool of funding sources increased over time.[70]

The latter claim is shared by those both inside and outside of the subsystem, in both the public and non-governmental sectors, who have observed the decision-making process. Many observers contend that the organizational structure and tactics of environmental groups have been transformed, ironically, to a corporate-style, money-driven framework over the past quarter century. By 2003, the top 30 national environmental organizations had nearly 7.8 million members or supporters and raised over $2.1 billion.[71]

One implication for the issue network is that it arguably lost some of its credibility or effectiveness, at least among some observers in the media, in government, and with the public.[72] This may have undermined its ability to maintain protection as evidenced by the House vote for drilling in 2001. House Members who voted for drilling were not especially concerned that environmental groups could mobilize constituencies effectively against them at the polls.

Besides, as one high-profile critic of today's environmental movement implied, internal dissension caused some groups to hope for a compromise on ANWR with pro-drilling forces so their respective organizations could proceed to other business, say, global warming and resurrection of the Kyoto Protocol against global warming.[73] Other critics of this increasingly corporate-type environmental movement noted that foundation moneys increasingly have funded pro-ANWR-protection forces and that this issue is one that largely has been "under the radar."[74]

On the policy front, some environmental groups have been willing to acknowledge that the technology of energy production has improved dramatically since oil production on state lands at Prudhoe Bay several decades ago. For example, on its website, the National Audubon Society discusses the involvement of BP and Phillips Petroleum as the two principal oil companies that operated in Alaska in 2001. This well-respected environmental interest group concedes that these two firms have made great strides toward protecting wildlife and its habitat, by, for example, shrinking the area needed at each oil production facility.

Despite this technological progress, however, environmental supporters (including the National Audubon Society) have emphasized that massive amounts of tankers, trucks, recording vehicles, an incinerator, and other equipment would be necessary just to look for oil at ANWR. Many fear that wildlife and the slow-growing vegetation would be despoiled through development.[75]

Regardless of any partial concessions to energy producers by environmental interests, former USFWS Director Jamie Rappaport Clark correctly noted the importance of ANWR policy to most environmental groups during the 2001-2002 congressional debates. ANWR, she said, is "huge" in the refuge system and the loss of ANWR to energy developers would create a "domino effect" in the system of 511 refuges across the US. Again, symbols matter in US politics.

The protection of the Porcupine Caribou Herd has long been a major rationale in favor of environmental protection. However, Clark concedes that the Caribou is not one of the five endangered species in Alaska.[76] Given the fact that oil and natural gas interests are not proposing to drill near the area inhabited by a currently endangered species, why would the environmental community not be willing to negotiate a solution to the impasse?

Perhaps, habitats are as equally important to environmentalists as species are. In a broader sense, evidently symbolic uses of politics on both sides, as discussed toward the beginning of this chapter, have supplanted the desire to formulate a consensus-based ANWR policy. The 1997 refuge reform law provides some evidence that finding common ground is possible.

Major environmental groups have remained unified, for the most part, in opposing development of the coastal plain at ANWR. The Alaska Coalition, for instance, has remained active, though it is now a looser coalition than it had been during the ANILCA debate of 1977-1980.[77] Its Director suggested in 2002 that the coalition's strategy of transcending the grassroots to deploy "grasstop" activists impacted the 2002 Senate debate by effectively lobbying Senator John McCain (R-AZ) and others to oppose drilling in the ANWR.[78]

One can plausibly argue that the environmental community remained cohesive against drilling even as it was weakened early in the Bush Administration. The evidence rests in the surprising House passage of an ANWR drilling provision as part of a broader energy bill in August 2001.

Despite the earlier critiques of the "corporatization" of the environmental movement, one thing is clear. Major players within the environmental movement have continued to remain fervently opposed to drilling at ANWR's coastal plain.

Some base their opposition on substantive/ecological arguments about ANWR, while others see ANWR as a critical part of a broader political battle aimed at preventing a pro-drilling administration from turning the proverbial clock back on thirty years of environmental gains. Most are willing to utilize symbols (e.g., the caribou, the Exxon Valdez spill, or the coastal plain as the "crown jewel" of the Arctic) and substantive policy arguments when making their case to the public and in Washington.

Environmental leaders corroborate these comments. The Porcupine Caribou are "skittish as hell" when it comes to their capacity to adapt to roads and pipelines, noted Don Barry of the Wilderness Society in an ecological argument. He claimed that the Bush plan for ANWR, unlike a drilling bill that was working its way through Congress during the Reagan years, has virtually no environmental safeguards, both a political and an ecological viewpoint.[79]

Dan Ritzman of the Alaska Coalition called the coastal plain "one of America's last great pieces of public lands." He also cited the importance of exchanging protection of the caribou and 129 species of birds for a six-month supply of oil.[80] Chuck Clusen of the National Resources Defense Council (NRDC), who served as chairman of the Alaska Coalition during the ANILCA debate of the late 1970s, said in 2002 that the ANWR issue remains the same today in the eyes of environmentalists; ANWR is an "icon of wilderness."[81]

Non-Governmental Actors: The Teamsters Union

On the other side of the debate, the Teamsters Union supports drilling, and has emerged as a prominent pro-development entity besides President Bush's inter-agency task force on energy. This union was inactive during the 1995 ANWR debate, but it became an important actor by 2001.

The role of organized labor in Alaskan oil and natural gas development is especially interesting, and longstanding. Many of the larger unions, including the AFL-CIO, the International Brotherhood of Teamsters, the International Union of Operating Engineers, and the maritime unions have been working in the majority of North Slope jobs and been closely aligned with oil companies.[82] This coopera-tive relationship has existed at least since the mid-1970s when the Teamsters Union in Fairbanks controlled most of the supplies and labor for construction of the Trans-Alaska Pipeline.[83]

Yet, several unions were members of the pro-environment Alaska Coalition in 1980 when the size of the Arctic Range was doubled. These groups included the United Automobile Workers of America, the United Electrical, Radio and Machine Workers, the United Mine Workers of America, and the United Steel Workers of America.[84]

The International Brotherhood of Teamsters, established in 1903, represented over 1.4 million workers in the US and Canada by 2002. The union had a significant impact on the passage of the pro-drilling bill (HR 4) in the House in 2001. After the House vote in August 2001 and prior to Senate floor action in April 2002, the Teamsters leadership worked to solidify its relationship with the Bush Administration.[85]

Early in October 2001, DOE Secretary Spencer Abraham and DOI Secretary Gale Norton met with the union's Special Assistant for Energy Policy, Jerry Hood, to discuss the prospects for Senate action on an energy plan that would include drilling at ANWR.[86] A month later, Hood participated (along with Republican Senators Murkowski (AK), Thomas (WY) and Craig (ID)) in a press conference advocating a Senate vote in favor of ANWR development. This influential union also joined in the unveiling of a list of more than 1,000 pro-development organizations that supported congressional action on ANWR as part of a comprehensive energy plan.[87]

This high degree of congruence between the Teamsters and the Executive Branch contrasts sharply with the rocky relationship that existed between the union and the DOJ during the late 1980s. Then, despite the union's earlier endorsements of presidential candidate Ronald Reagan, President Reagan's DOJ sought to control the union in 1987 for its alleged involvement with organized crime.[88]

Non-Governmental Actors: Indigenous Groups

Alaska's indigenous groups played interesting roles during and since the early 2000s congressional debates on ANWR.[89] Subsystem actors and their opponents have each claimed their support. Environmentalists claim the support of the Gwich'in Indians, and pro-drilling forces tout the backing of the Inupiat Eskimos, who are the only group that actually resides along the coastal plain at the Village of Kaktovik.

Both groups have increased their political influence in Washington since 1971. For instance, the Arctic Slope Regional Corporation (ASRC) is an Inupiat-run, pro-drilling organization that wields some influence over ANWR policy makers. Organized under Alaska law and the 1971 Alaska Native Claims Settlement Act passed by Congress, "ASRC is a private, for-profit Alaska Native-owned corporation representing the business interests of the Arctic Slope Inupiat [Eskimos]. ASRC is committed to preserving the Inupiat culture and traditions. ... [This corporation] represents eight villages above the Alaskan Arctic Circle"[90] One of those eight villages, Kaktovik, is located along the coastal plain of ANWR east of Prudhoe Bay.

The Inupiat Eskimos have been called the "first, best environmentalists" by pro-development groups such as Arctic Power, and by their political allies on Capitol Hill. The arguments offered by Inupiat leaders have been a factor in gaining votes in Congress, as we shall see. The following excerpt from the former mayor of the Inupiat people, Benjamin P. Nageak, appeared on Arctic Power's website in 2002:

> In 1969, when oil was first discovered on our lands, those fears were foremost in our minds as we fought for self-determination in order to be able to protect our resources. Since then, we have had over twenty years of working with the oil industry here. We enacted strict regulations to protect our land and the oil companies have consistently met the standards we imposed. ANWR holds resources that can be extracted safely with care and concern for the entire eco-system it encompasses. The Inupiat people, working through the North Slope Borough, will act in the same careful, caring and cautious manner we always have when dealing with our lands and the seas. We have the greatest stake possible that any and all development is done in such a way as to keep this land safe. Because it is our world. It is where we live. It holds the remains of our ancestors. It holds the future of our children.[91]

Two Republican Senate committee staffers, who were instrumental in shaping the Senate debate, especially during the 2001-2002 period, stated that the position of the Inupiat Eskimos favoring drilling prompted Hawaii's two Democratic senators to defect to the pro-drilling position by the time that the Senate voted on this issue in April 2002.[92]

Just as Inupiat Eskimo leaders have been the indigenous spokespersons for developing ANWR, the Gwich'in Indians of Alaska and Canada have been a point group for the environmental cause. However, pro-drilling forces have attempted to counter numerous press reports concerning Gwich'in opposition to drilling by noting that they live far to the south of the ANWR coastal plain.[93]

Becky Gay, who aided in the formation of Arctic Power, asserts, for instance, that Indians and Eskimos are very different culturally. Besides, millions of acres, plus the Brooks Mountain Range, provide a geographical separation of the coastal-dwelling Eskimos and the Indians who live in Alaska's interior. She also suggests that these communities oppose one another's position on ANWR because they are competing for "killing rights" to the Porcupine Caribou Herd. The claim that the Gwich'in want to protect the caribou is a "public relations game."[94]

To sum up, Alaskan indigenous groups have tended to align themselves with either subsystem actors or their opposition, with the Inupiat Eskimos siding with Arctic Power and other advocates of energy production, and the Gwich'in Indians tending to align with environmental interest groups and their political allies. Because the Inupiat, who overwhelmingly support drilling, live on the coastal plain at Kaktovik, their opinions have tended to carry greater weight with lawmakers.

Non-Governmental Actors: Oil Firms

Several large oil firms with interests in North Slope oil are arguably the most important set of actors opposing the ANWR-environmental subgovernment. A series of mergers has transformed the face of this industry since the late 1990s.

By 2002, both energy and environmental activists concurred that three firms dominated Alaskan production: BP Amoco-ARCO; Conoco-Phillips; and, Exxon-Mobil. According to an oil industry spokesperson on ANWR issues, Roger Herrera, who works for the advocacy group Arctic Power, British Petroleum (BP) was the top oil producer along Alaska's North Slope in 2002 with interests in development of the coastal plain.[95]

Looking back, these firms in their various iterations have had an interest in development of Alaskan oil and natural gas. Table 3.1 identifies these firms and their activities in Alaskan oil development and politics.

Table 3.1: Comparing Major Oil-Producing Firms on the North Slope

	BP Amoco-ARCO	Conoco-Phillips	Exxon-Mobil
Date of Merger	BP and Amoco merged in 1998; Acquired ARCO in April 2000; Also merged with Burma Castrol, and Vastar by 2001	Merger finalized by the FTC on 8/30/02; Acquired ARCO's AK business in April 2000	Merger completed on 11/30/99
North Slope Activity and other AK activity	Alaska's top private investor ($640 million in 2002)	Owns a major interest in the Prudhoe Bay field; Operates the Kuparuk and Alpine facilities on the North Slope	Largest resource owner at Prudhoe Bay (2003); Also operates Point Thomson gas-cycling project on the North Slope
Money Spent Lobbying in AK (1999), three firms listed in top ten	$300,000 (BP Exploration); 260,000 (ARCO)	(data unavailable)	$280,000 (Exxon)

Sources: bp.com; conocophillips.com; exxonmobil.com; Haycox 2002, pp. 11, 148, 165

Clearly, table 3.1 suggests that these three "big oil" firms, made even bigger by *environmentalist* President Bill Clinton's Federal Trade Commission (FTC) that approved these mergers, have a large stake in the form of investment in both hydrocarbon production and the political process. Yet, it is plausible to argue that "big oil" has not been the primary impetus for opening ANWR. Instead, it may be that non-indigenous Alaskans (i.e., 85 percent of the state's population) and their political allies in Washington have been the critical factor.

For example, during the 1998-1999 Alaska oil price crisis (when the price of Alaskan crude tumbled), the chairmen of the congressional committees with jurisdiction over ANWR, Senator Frank Murkowski and Congressman Don Young, both Alaska Republicans, made every effort to keep the possibility of opening ANWR for development in the public eye.[96] It seems that oil companies can drill in various places, but the State of Alaska has a more intense interest in drilling in their state.

At any rate, it is undeniable that major oil producers had an interest in events in Washington, DC. Their advocacy group, Arctic Power, conducted most or all of the political bidding for these companies in the capital during the early Bush years. The American Petroleum Institute, which represents 400 energy companies ranging from major firms to wildcat producers, is another organization that has advocated drilling at the 1002 Area, as is the American Alliance for Energy and Economic Growth.[97]

The major oil producers viewed ANWR as a political "hot potato" during the early Bush years. BP's website, for instance, does not include a single direct reference to ANWR.[98] Why? Interestingly, the former Director of the USFWS during the second Clinton Administration offered a plausible answer to this question. She asserted that BP withdrew from the ANWR debate by the end of 2002 because it realized that advocating drilling had become a "bad public relations move and they did not want to be on the losing side."[99]

Assuming her allegation is true, the question remains if BP also withdrew its financial support for Arctic Power. BP is not the only firm that has been largely silent on ANWR development. Efforts to contact a spokesperson for Exxon-Mobil, among other firms, have proven fruitless. Firms with an interest in developing the 1002 Area apparently have made a concerted effort to work through Arctic Power in their public relations game.

When asked why oil firms were largely silent about ANWR during the 2001-2002 debate, Arctic Power's Roger Herrera paused, and then replied: "That's a hard question to answer. No one is willing to take the lead on [ANWR] because of public relations perceptions. [Further, it is a] highly emotional issue [that is] partly controlled by environmentalists. [Oil-producing firms believe that] their water is being carried for them by Arctic Power and the Bush Administration."[100] Another subsystem opponent and advocate of development notes that Arctic Power was established with the help of the State of Alaska to "keep the fire burning" in favor of ANWR development during the "ebbs and flows when ANWR was not on the governmental agenda," and that the group has achieved this objective.[101]

This seems to imply that major oil firms may actually be concealing the true intensity of their preferences about development of the coastal plain. Industry sources and political actors have suggested, however, that many energy producers prefer to drill elsewhere, say, overseas, since this likely would involve less political opposition and lower production costs. Perhaps this question can only be resolved through energy lease offerings by the BLM in the wake of congressional action to open up the refuge. According to one longtime analyst who has worked for oil producing interests over the past four decades, firms viewed Alaska as a profitable place over the past 20 years but one that is becoming less profitable.[102]

Arctic Power's Roger Herrera asserts that oil companies in the US have three foci, namely, profit, their next quarterly report, and a three-year budget cycle rather than the ten-year cycle of years gone by. This combination suggests, according to Herrera, that large oil and natural gas firms have no slack to fund projects such as ANWR drilling over the short term.

This is not to say, however, that the "haves" that currently produce oil and natural gas in Alaska would balk at a leasing program within, say, two years of congressional approval. To be sure, they would "beg, borrow, or steal" to get the money to participate, but that effort would hurt some of their other enterprises. As for the so-called "have not" firms, such as Shell, they would view drilling as an opportunity to break into the Alaska market. They would "love to get into northern Alaska," said Herrera. If ANWR is opened for drilling in the future, oil companies "would come out of the woodwork," he continued. For instance, Total-Elf, a French energy producer, established a Washington, DC, office by late 2002 in order to position itself for a prospective congressional decision to lease at the 1002 Area.[103]

Implicit in all of this is the disparate interests among oil producing firms. Some have access to Alaska lands development. Some do not. Some would like to open ANWR for drilling. Others likely have other priorities—say, building political and economic ties between the US and oil-rich nations in order to facilitate corporate development there. In short, "big oil" may not be the monolithic entity that its opponents suggest it is.[104]

Instead, firms are natural competitors. For example, after confirming the magnitude of the Prudhoe Bay discovery, the State of Alaska in 1969 opened up that area of the North Slope to lease bids by oil firms. Aggressive, highly competitive bidding ensued *between companies*; by the end of the day, the state government collected over $900 million in lease revenue, more than triple the state budget at that time.[105]

Thus, we should consider alternative explanations for the push for ANWR development. Perhaps the political culture of Alaska is the driving force for development since hydrocarbon production would bring jobs, income, and infrastructure to the vast majority of Alaskans; people shape their environment more than it shapes them.[106]

Roger Herrera of Arctic Power supports the notion that forces other than corporate pressure on House and Senate Members have been the catalyst for change. A cleavage exists, he says, between congressional and corporate supporters of drilling. Major firms would prefer a longer-term timetable to begin drilling. But, Herrera comments, Members of Congress will not afford producers that luxury due to the importance of jobs to their constituents and national security for the nation.[107]

This discussion of non-governmental opponents of the ANWR-environmental subsystem indicates that similar forces were present during George W. Bush's Administration as were present during the Clinton Administration. Major oil companies and their chief lobbying group, Arctic Power, led these efforts but Alaskan interests were crucial as well. However, the Teamsters Union and other smaller unions were among the new, non-elite voices that were lobbying actively by 2001 for energy development.

Subsystem Maintenance in the Face of a Robust Threat

It is clear that an entity resembling a subgovernment began to arise when Arctic Power was established in late 1992: it began competing with the ANWR-environmental subsystem that was established in 1977. This new group of decision makers[108] was strengthened through the 1994 congressional elections, subsequent committee reorganization, and the election of Republican George W. Bush in 2000 coupled with a GOP majority in the US Senate in 2003. Certainly, this counter-weight to the ANWR subsystem demonstrated its power in August 2001 when the full House enacted an energy bill with a provision to permit drilling at ANWR.

This combination of developments forced Senate Democratic Leader Tom Daschle and environmental groups to bear a substantial burden in subsystem maintenance. Unlike the political entrepreneurs who established the subsystem in 1977 based partly on a statutory deadline (i.e., December 1978 for Congress to recommend Alaska lands to be set aside), these entrepreneurs relied largely on "political timing" to maintain the ANWR subgovernment just as their pro-drilling opponents have had to time opportunities to advance their cause.[109]

The pro-environment subsystem demonstrated its resilience in the wake of a defeat in the House in 2001 with legislative victories in the Senate in 2002 and 2003 respectively (the previously discussed filibuster of the Murkowski Amendment to the energy bill and passage of the Boxer Amendment to the FY2004 Senate Budget Resolution). I will analyze these and other critical ANWR-related votes in detail in the next chapter, especially as they concern alleged partisan voting. A primary aim of this chapter has been to analyze the shift of the subsystem's core from the House to the White House by 1993 and from the White House to the Senate by 2001. One Bush Administration insider characterized the House of Representatives as an "interesting creature" when it comes to making ANWR or other policy. It must be worked more intensively than the Senate since the House is a larger body that requires more Executive Branch lobbying in order to gain votes to pass legislation. Further, it does not afford members an opportunity to filibuster. These two dynamics suggest that, during the 2001-2002 ANWR debate, the Bush Administration was largely concerned with gaining "yea" votes for drilling in the House and tempering "nay" votes opposed to drilling in the Senate. President George W. Bush consequently focused more of his attention on the House during that period.[110]

In addition, prominent environmental lobbyist Adam Kolton in Washington, DC, reports that chairmen of the relevant committees in both chambers afforded few opportunities to the pro-environment side to present even a single witness during committee testimony. Mr. Kolton has been involved with ANWR matters and the Alaska Coalition since at least 1991.[111] This point demonstrates the potential influence of subsystem opponents in both the House and Senate by 2002.

In the Senate, pro-environment forces benefited from institutional rules and a sympathetic Democratic Party leader as evidenced by maintenance of the status quo ANWR policy in 2002. Senator Daschle and his allies managed to fend off the impending threat of a pro-drilling measure in April; eight months after the House passed an energy package that would have opened the 1002 Area to energy exploration.

According to Dan Kish and Christine Drager, Republican staffers on the Senate Committee on Energy and Natural Resources, a critical factor in the environmentalists' success was Senator Daschle's circumvention of Senate norms. The senator precluded the committee from marking up an energy bill during the 107th Congress. In other words, Senator Daschle discharged the committee because it had enough votes to pass an energy bill with an accompanying provision to permit drilling at ANWR. Many opponents of the senator's action believe that it had the effect of altering Democratic votes that would have supported a pro-drilling amendment in committee but those Democrats then were pressured to vote against a cloture motion on the Senate floor.[112]

Not surprisingly, environmental supporters do not concur with this assessment. Jack Hession of the Sierra Club, for instance, asserts that circumvention of the committee process was fair since pro-drilling senators were afforded a vote on the Senate floor by April 2002.[113]

However, one might critique this position by noting that the floor vote was on a motion to invoke cloture (i.e., requiring a 60-vote supermajority to end a filibuster); it was not an up-or-down vote on a drilling provision. So, there may have been an increased likelihood of defeat for environmental forces had the full committee been permitted to vote on drilling.

Subsystem forces eventually prevailed when, on April 18, 2002, the Senate failed to invoke cloture on an energy plan (S. 517; 46-54), thus precluding a vote on Senator Murkowski's (R-AK) pro-ANWR-drilling amendment. Two days later, on April 20th, the Senate passed an energy bill (88-11), absent the drilling provision. In short, Senate leaders maintained the anti-drilling subsystem in 2002 on energy legislation following the threat posed to ANWR by the House in 2001.

By early 2003, a second major threat to the ANWR-environmental subsystem in as many years was developing: namely prospective attachment of a rider to the FY 2004 budget reconciliation bill (which is insulated from any filibuster just as another budget blueprint was during the 1995 debate). In 2003, a Bush Administration official reflected on that earlier debate by calling the budget reconciliation strategy George W. Bush's "best but by no means easy" tactic to secure drilling at ANWR.[114] True, success through this process would not come easily, but, as one longtime subsystem operative conceded in 2002, President Bush is "going to give it his all," regardless of the obstacles that he faces.[115]

But the key battle aimed at destroying ANWR's pro-environment monopoly in 2005 on a series of budget votes and a related defense spending bill. Drilling at ANWR very nearly became law. Both chambers of Congress passed a pro-drilling budget resolution in April and the debate shifted to a defense-spending bill with similar language in December 2005. After the battle, the House ceded to the Senate's status quo position. The ANWR issue network, or subgovernment, survived once again and would become even stronger in 2006 and 2007 under Democratic majorities who tended to oppose drilling.

Summary

In all, after the passage of the ANILCA statute in 1980 and through the 1994 congressional elections, political entrepreneurs in the Democratic-run Congress and the Clinton Administration had little problem maintaining the ANWR-environmental subsystem. This subsystem, or issue network, promoted continuation of the ban on energy exploration along the coastal plain (a policy outcome with a perceived distributional impact of diffuse environmental benefits to the public and narrow costs for energy producers).

However, it became evident that, since the GOP gained control of the Congress in 1994 and the White House in 2000, a competing, somewhat elitist decision-making structure challenged the existing order and promoted a very different ANWR policy favoring drilling. This increasingly strong opposing structure shocked the old decision framework in the US House of Representatives in August 2001 by gaining passage of an energy bill that permitted drilling.

Therefore, this new structure affords a different perception of policy costs and benefits.

Bush ally Andrew Lundquist perhaps best characterized the ability of actors in the ANWR subsystem to sustain a high level of influence over policy. He suggested that maintenance is contingent upon "ebbs and flows." That is, the power of this largely pro-environment subsystem diminishes whenever issues such as oil shortages and Mideast political instability become salient. These situations prompt people to become more sensitive to energy issues and thus weaken the environmentalists' arguments and their political base.[116] The previous discussion of the ANWR drilling agenda in 1991 and 2001 supports this view since the Gulf War and California energy crisis respectively contributed to increased attention to America's energy needs and arguably placed environmental groups on the defensive.

Clearly, the ANWR-environmental subsystem has faced serious challenges from those who would open the coastal plain to energy exploration. Reflecting on the relative strength of this coalition, a 30-year environmental activist and Alaska resident said that during the 1977-1980 period, ANWR-protection forces "enjoyed the backing of President Carter and Democrats in the Senate." By 1991-1992, the coalition "still had considerable clout with a sympathetic [Congress] until 1994." Unlike some of his colleagues in the environmental community, this subsystem actor described the House vote in 2001 as "not that overwhelming" in support of drilling at ANWR. Over the long term, this activist feels that the subsystem has maintained its power. The evidence is that it was "able to fend off the other side"[117] through at least 2007.

It is worth noting that influential and activist Members of Congress often play critical roles in subsystem maintenance by lobbying colleagues on behalf of subsystem interests and shielding subsystem benefits from criticism. In the ANWR case, Congressmen Seiberling (D-OH) and Vento (D-MN) maintained the subsystem during the 1980s.

Senator Wirth (D-CO) did likewise in 1991, and Senator Tom Daschle (D-SD) served as the chief political entrepreneur in thwarting pro-development interests in 2002. This is not to say that actors outside of the Legislative Branch have not been effective in maintaining subsystem policy influence. President Clinton in 1995 is a clear example of the varied types of actors who have sustained the issue network and thus have preserved the status quo against drilling.

The last two chapters have examined how the ANWR-environmental subgovernment was established and maintained in the face of growing opposition. The next two chapters will test the roles of partisan voting and the so-called "life cycle" explanations for changing policy stances on ANWR and other contemporary debates. I will also analyze critical votes taken in Congress in 2005 that left environmentalists on the brink of defeat on ANWR.

Notes

1.   Telephone interview with Don Barry, 6 January 2003; Robert Cahn, *The Fight to Save Wild Alaska* (Washington, DC: National Audubon Society, 1982) 21.

2.   Sandra Suarez, *Does Business Learn? Tax Breaks, Uncertainty, and Political Strategies* (Ann Arbor, MI: The University of Michigan Press, 2000), 12-13; Frank R. Baumgartner and Bryan D. Jones, *Agendas and Instability in American Politics* (Chicago: The University of Chicago Press, 1993), chapter 10.

3.   See Murray Edelman, *The Symbolic Uses of Politics* (Urbana, IL: University of Illinois Press, 1995); and, James E. Anderson, *Public Policymaking* (Boston: Houghton Mifflin Company, 1994), 15-17.

4.   "Arctic National Wildlife Refuge: TimeLine," DOI, USFWS, 1997.

5.   Barry interview.

6.   David Vogel, "Representing Diffuse Interests in Environmental Policymaking," in *Do Institutions Matter? Government Capabilities in the United States and Abroad*, ed. R. Kent Weaver and Bert A. Rockman (Washington, DC: The Brookings Institution, 1993), 262.

7.   Vogel, "Representing Diffuse Interests," 261.

8.   United States Department of the Interior. *Arctic National Wildlife Refuge, Alaska, Coastal Plain Resource Assessment: Report and Recommendation to the Congress of the United States and Final Legislative Environmental Impact Statement*, 21 April 1987, vii.

9.   Barry interview; Telephone interview with Chuck Clusen, NRDC (former Chairman of the AK Coalition), 1 November 2002.

10.   "A History of the Arctic National Wildlife Refuge," Alaska Wilderness League website (29 Aug. 2002).

11.   Vogel, "Representing Diffuse Interests," 266.

12.   "ANWR Drilling Kills Energy Bill," *CQ Almanac*, 1991: 207.

13.   Alaska state lobbying in favor of ANWR development was transformed beginning in 1993. According to Becky Gay, who coordinated the governor's lobbying efforts from 1991 to 1992 and subsequently helped in the formation of Arctic Power, the center of the lobbying machinery shifted from the governor's office to the non-profit sector by 1993. One rationale for this modification was the ability of non-governmental actors (e.g., Arctic Power) to mobilize more volunteers than the governor's office. It was during this period that the organization received significant funding from the State of Alaska, about $3 million between 1991-1992, plus more in future years. Ms. Gay initiated the idea for state officials to lobby with local officials from other states in order gain grassroots support. They employed various media-related lobbying methods and approached groups such as chambers of commerce for support (Telephone interview with Becky Gay, 20 December 2002 and 14 July 2003.

14.   Gay interview.

15.   Mr. Murkowski served as senator until his election as governor in 2002 and was defeated for reelection in 2006.

16.   "The Players: Arctic Power, ANWR.org <www.anwr.org/features/players/apower.htm> (3 Dec. 2002); Telephone interview with Roger Herrera, 3 December 2002.

17.   Heclo (1978) may have popularized the phrase *issue network* more than any other scholar. He describes these structures by noting that, "[w]ith more public policies, more groups are being mobilized and there are more complex relationships among them. ... [Issue

networks involve] a play of influence that is many-stranded and loose. Iron triangles or other clear shapes may embrace some of the participants, but the larger picture in any policy area is likely to be one involving many other policy specialists. More than ever, policy making is becoming an intramural activity among expert issue-watchers, their networks, and their networks of networks. In this situation any neat distinction between the governmental structure and its environment tends to break down" (see Hugh Heclo, "Issue Networks and the Executive Establishment," in *The New American Political System,* ed. Anthony King (Washington, DC: American Enterprise Institute, 1978), 97, 105-106). My study has uncovered evidence that both sides in the ANWR debate have formed loosely connected groups that have added participants and mobilized when ANWR has resurfaced on the governmental agenda. One piece of supportive data is the aforementioned discussion about Arctic Power's capacity to mobilize. Another is the addition of the Teamsters Union, also to the pro-development organizational structure by 2001. On the pro-environment side, the Alaska Wilderness League, which was established in 1993, has demonstrated its longevity. One former, long-time lobbyist for the League noted that environmentalists created it to work on an "ongoing basis" on ANWR issues because "threats [to drill at the Refuge] often resurface" (Telephone interview with Adam Kolton, National Wildlife Federation (formerly with Alaska Wilderness League), 12 September 2002.

18. "ANWR Development Gains Momentum: Poll Shows Americans favor ANWR Development," ANWR.org <www.anwr.org/features/poll-anwr-2-6-02htm> (3 October 2002).

19. Bill Clinton and Al Gore, *Putting People First: How We Can All Change America* (New York: Times Books, 1992), 92.

20. My contention that the center of power for the ANWR-environmental subsystem shifted from the House Interior Committee and/or key environmental groups to the Executive Branch seems to have been confirmed by President Clinton's former USFWS Director, Jamie Rappaport Clark. She said that the dominant interest groups in ANWR policy making during the late 1990s, namely the Alaska Coalition, the Wilderness Society, the Alaska Wilderness League, another Alaskan conservation group, and, to a lesser extent, Defenders of Wildlife and the National Wildlife Federation, were not critical to maintaining the status of the 1002 Area. Why? The Clinton Administration was unified on this issue. The environmental community was merely a "left flank" that was "not as necessary" as it was during other periods. Ms. Clark noted that environmental groups "relaxed a lot" during the Clinton Administration and were not as potent as they would become by 2003 (Telephone interview with USFWS Director Jamie Rappaport Clark, Ret., 2 January 2003).

21. Gay interview.

22. Face-to-face interviews with Christopher Fluhr, House Resources Committee, Republican staff, 22 July 2002; Face-to-face interview with John Rishel, House Resources Committee, Subcommittee on Energy and Mineral Resources, Republican staff, 22 July 2002.

23. Barry interview.

24. *CQ Weekly Report,* 27 May 1995; 1536, 3416; Kolton interview.

25. H. Josef Hebert, "Senate GOP Renews Arctic Drilling Push," Associated Press, 1 January 2003.

26. Telephone interview with OMB Director Alice Rivlin, Ret., 20 December 2002.

27. Prior to joining the Bush Administration in early 2001, Andrew Lundquist had worked 16 years in government, all of them dealing with the ANWR issue. After joining the

Bush-Cheney team, Mr. Lundquist, an attorney, first held the title, *Executive Director of the National Energy Policy Group,* and subsequently became *Director of Energy Policy.* In both positions he reported to Vice President Dick Cheney (Telephone interview with Andrew Lundquist, The Lundquist Group (formerly with the George W. Bush Administration), 6 January 2003).

28. Lundquist interview.

29. Rivlin interview.

30. "Hunting and Fishing on Refuges," *CQ Almanac,* 1996: 4/22; "Balancing Conservation, Recreation," *CQ Almanac,* 1997: 4/16.

31. *CQ Almanac,* 1997.

32. This bill was passed under suspension of the rules; two-thirds of those present are required to pass these typically non-controversial bills.

33. "House Passes New Standards for Use of Wildlife Refuges," *CQ Weekly Report,* 7 June 1997: 1313.

34. Department of the Interior, "ANWR: TimeLine;" Lynne M. Corn and Bernard Gelb, "The Arctic National Wildlife Refuge: The Next Chapter," Congressional Research Service, 2 April 2001 (15).

35. Clark interview.

36. Yereth Rosen, "Alaska to Lobby for Oil Drilling," Reuters News Service, 18 March 2001.

37. "The Political Arena," Arctic Power website, <www.anwr.org> (3 October 2002).

38. Telephone interview with DOI Secretary Cecil Andrus, Ret., 16 December 2002 and 24 July 2003. Mr. Andrus added that President Carter did not make ANWR a national monument because President Eisenhower had protected the area as a refuge.

39. "Remarks by the President on National Energy Policy in Photo Opportunity with Cabinet Members," White House website, <http://www.whitehouse.gov/news/releases/2001/05/20010516-7.html> (16 May 2001).

40. "Analysis of the Bush Energy Plan," Friends of the Earth website (18 May 2001).

41. Howard Kurtz, "Republican Right Rips Jeffords," *Washington Post Online,* 24 May 2001.

42. Clark interview; Face-to-face interview with Daniel Lavery, Sierra Club, 23 July 2002.

43. A significant irony exists here. Senator Paul Tsongas (D-MA) and his subsystem allies shocked pro-development forces in July 1980 by comfortably winning five protection-oriented amendments to HR 39. This prompted Senate leaders to withdraw the environmentally friendly Alaska lands bill from consideration for six weeks (Clusen interview). Ironically, the shock of a pro-drilling bill passing the House in August 2001 and prospective passage of a similar measure in the Senate in April 2002 prompted Senate leadership to withdraw a bill that would have been friendly toward development rather than environmental interests. All of this implies that a competing subsystem was arising to potentially supplant the ANWR subgovernment.

44. *CQ Weekly Report,* 4 August 2001: 1946; Lundquist interview.

45. Lundquist interview.

46. Telephone interview with Dan Ritzman, National Outreach Director, Alaska Coalition, 16 September 2002.

47. Rebecca Adams and John Godfrey, "Nobody Expects to Get What They Want as Energy Bill Heads to Conference," *CQ Weekly Report,* 27 April 2002: 1090-92.

48. Gary Bryner, *Blue Skies, Green Politics: The Clean Air Act of 1990* (Washington, DC: CQ Press, 1993), preface.

49. Rivlin interview.

50. Clark interview.

51. Gay interview.

52. Lundquist interview.

53. This answer is not surprising given that Mr. Lundquist reported directly to the Vice President (Lundquist interview); Another subsystem opponent, who works outside of government, was more forthright in his reply. Roger Herrera has headed Arctic Power since 1993 and previously worked for the BP Corporation for 33 years. He said that the DOI and DOE under President Bush have played a "much more forceful and forward role" in advancing the drilling cause vis-à-vis prior administrations (Herrera interview).

54. Clark interview.

55. Barry interview.

56. Cahn, *The Fight to Save*, 19.

57. "State of Alaska: ANWR Resolution Passes Legislature," Arctic Power website, <www.anwr.org> (3 October 2002).

58. "Knowles Slams Senate Democrat's Energy Bill," Arctic Power website, <www.anwr.org> (3 October 2002); Herrera interview; Telephone interview with Alaska State Representative & Majority Leader Jeannette James (R), 12 December 2002; Telephone interview with Michael Tubman, Washington, DC, Office of Alaska Governor Tony Knowles, 16 December 2002.

59. These organizations include the Alaska State Chamber of Commerce; the Anchorage Chamber of Commerce; Alaska Women in Timber; the Alaska Federation of Natives; the Arctic Slope Regional Corporation; Doyon Limited; the Alaska Oil & Gas Association; the Alaska Support Industry Alliance; the Alaska AFL-CIO; Alaska Teamsters Local 959; the Anchorage Central Labor Council; the Alaska Miners Association; the Resource Development Council; the Alaska Forest Association; the Anchorage Convention & Visitors Bureau; the Alaska Railroad Corporation; and, the Alaska Trucking Association.

60. "State of Alaska: ANWR Resolution Passes Legislature" and "The Players: Alaska Residents," Arctic Power website, <www.anwr.org> (3 October 2002).

61. The Gallup Organization; Ben Spiess, "Arctic Oil Drilling Debate Escalates," *Anchorage Daily News*, 7 May 2001.

62. Gay interview.

63. Stephen Haycox, *Frigid Embrace: Politics, Economics and Environment in Alaska* (Corvallis, OR: Oregon State University Press, 2002), 82.

64. Gay interview.

65. Gay interview.

66. Cahn, *The Fight to* Save, 32; Ann Bowman and Richard C. Kearney, *State and Local Government: TheEssentials* (Boston: Houghton Mifflin Company, 2000), 276.

67. Gay interview.

68. Haycox, *Frigid Embrace*, 126-27.

69. James interview.

70. Lundquist interview; see Christopher J. Bosso, *Environment, Inc. From Grassroots to Beltway*, (Lawrence, KS: University of Kansas Press, 2005).

71. Bosso, *Environment, Inc.*, 7.

72. Journalists and members of the Clinton Administration are among those who have made these assertions. For instance, Pulitzer Prize-winning reporter, Tom Knudson, wrote

a five-part series on the changing structure of the environmental movement for the *Sacramento Bee* in 2001. Knudson traveled to 12 states over a 16-month period and conducted over 200 interviews in his investigation of the condition of environmentalism today. In the introductory article, Knudson characterizes the environmental movement as one that is "estranged from its past, one that has come to resemble the corporate world it often seeks to reform. Competition for money and members is keen. Litigation is a blood sport. Crisis, real or not, is a commodity. And slogans and sound bites masquerade as scientific fact" (Knudson, *Fat of the Land*). Many of the major environmental organizations that he cites are part of the ANWR subsystem. When asked to comment on Knudson's findings, former USFWS Director Jamie Rappaport Clark, who led the National Wildlife Federation (NWF) beginning in 2001, acknowledged, "Bureaucracy is not lost on the federal government. The environmental community is not a monolith. Some [organizations] are corporatized," she said. The NWF is a considered a "corporate giant," and is a "wieldy piece of machinery to run," but its mission is about the grassroots and links with Capitol Hill (Clark interview).

73. Lundquist interview.
74. Herrera interview.
75. <www.audubon.org>, 6 November 2002.
76. Clark interview.
77. Lavery interview.
78. Ritzman interview.
79. Barry interview.
80. Ritzman interview.
81. Clusen interview.
82. "Features: The Unions," Arctic Power website, <www.anwr.org> (3 October 2002). This website also indicated that additional union supporters of ANWR drilling included the American Maritime Officers, International Association of Bridge, Structural, Ornamental and Reinforcing Iron Workers, National Maritime Engineers' Beneficial Association, Seafarers International Union of North America, United Journeymen and Apprentices of the Plumbing and Pipe Fitting Industry of the US and Canada.
83. Haycox, *Frigid Embrace*, 107.
84. Cahn, *The Fight to Save*, 1.
85. The political approach of this union clearly shifted from one of apparent neutrality toward ANWR drilling in 1995 to a pro-development position by 2001. One high-ranking official from the George W. Bush Administration recounted that, during the 1995 debate on budget reconciliation, proponents of drilling "did not inspire [the Teamsters and other groups of laborers] early enough" in the debate to make a difference in the budget reconciliation process. Six years later, the attitude of the Teamsters had become "Wait a minute. We pony up to the Democrats every time. Where are they when it comes to jobs? We feel we have been taken for granted" (Lundquist interview).
86. "Cabinet Officials Join Union Leaders Calling for Responsible Energy Policy," Teamsters' Press Release, 3 October 2001.
87. "Hood Presses Senate Leaders for Energy Plan," Teamsters' Press Release, 2 November 2001.
88. Carol Matlack, "Taking on the Teamsters," *National Journal*, 7 November 1987: 2782-88.

89. Aleuts are a third Native group, but they are not critical for the purposes of this study. Many political observers, including Becky Gay, believe that Natives have the largest stake in ANWR development and that most of them support drilling. The Inupiats are Eskimos who live at the only permanent settlement along the coastal plain, Kaktovik. It took a while for them to get involved in the ANWR debate, but now they support onshore rather than offshore oil and natural gas drilling, primarily because any problems would be visible onshore and therefore rectifiable. Culturally, the Eskimos and Indians do not get along. Virtually 100 percent of Natives who live at or near ANWR favor "orderly development" of the 1002 Area. The Gwich'in Indians, who live in the southern area of the Brooks Range, are divided on whether ANWR should be developed. Their concern involves hunting and subsistence issues (Gay interview). This is to say, they are dependent upon the Porcupine Caribou Herd (James interview).

90. ASRC is one of 13 regional corporations created by the US Congress, 12 of which own land. Those 12 landholding regions span the entire state and are comprised of 227 tribes (ASRC.com. <www.asrc.com/page2.html> [3 October 2002]; James interview).

91. "Inupiat Eskimos First, Best Environmentalists" <www.anwr.org> 3 October 2002.

92. Face-to-face interview with Christine Drager and Daniel Kish, Senate Energy and Natural Resources Committee, Republican Staff, 23 July 2002.

93. For instance, Inupiat Mayor of the City of Kaktovik, population of 260 and located at the coastal plain, wrote a piece critical of the Gwich'in and their environmental allies. It was posted on Arctic Power's website:

When Sarah James, a Gwich'in spokesperson, signed the lease agreement years ago for oil and gas exploration within Gwich'in homelands, she said "we did not think to question the wisdom of her decision. It was their homelands to do with as they pleased. For the record, the Porcupine Caribou Herd calved again this year in Canada among the oil rigs Ottawa has set up there in what they like to call a national park. For the record, the herd is being devastated by hunters along the Dempster Highway under the watchful eye of the Canadian Wildlife Service. National environmental groups, their Gwich'in allies and members of the media have created a false reality of this issue, and those of us with any real knowledge of the coastal plain are left stunned, confused and defensive. We stand to be hopelessly defeated by ruthless liars. Now they want the entire coastal plain made wilderness. That is code for finally removing us from our homelands. That is code for genocide." "ANWR Reality Lies Far North of Gwich'in," <www.anwr.org> 3 October 2002.

94. Gay interview.

95. Herrera interview; Kolton interview.

96. Haycox, *Frigid Embrace*, 164.

97. Face-to-face interview with the Ken Leonard, American Petroleum Institute, 24 July 2002.

98. <www.bp.com> 8 October 2002.

99. Clark interview.

100. Herrera interview.

101. Lundquist interview; Applying the notion of "focusing events" to the latter point made by Andrew Lundquist, ANWR drilling surfaced on the congressional agenda when relevant national or international developments increased its saliency in Washington. However, "focusing events" for other issues or the failure to resolve the ANWR "problem" caused the issue to subside, but the drilling issue retained the capacity to resurface whenever energy, environmental, or budgetary "focusing events" or crises resurrected the issue.

Examples of events that have caught the attention of lawmakers and the public include the symbol of Saddam Hussein after his forces invaded Kuwait in 1990, and rolling brownouts in California a decade later (see John W. Kingdon, *Agendas, Alternatives, and Public Policies*, 2d ed. (New York: Harper Collins College Publishers, 1995), 94-100).

102. Herrera interview.

103. Herrera interview.

104. Lindblom's (1977) "privileged position of business" concept is relevant here insofar as a major critique of that notion is that business is not a monolithic entity. Instead, large and small businesses might compete with one another on policy questions and for a seat at the government decision-making table (Charles E. Lindblom, *Politics and Markets: The World's Political-Economic Systems* (Basic Books, 1977); also see Suarez, *Does Business Learn?*, 123-24, who bolsters this position by noting that similar types of firms sometimes oppose each other on the same policy (e.g., tax policy).

105. Haycox, *Frigid Embrace*, 122.

106. Haycox, *Frigid Embrace*, ix.

107. Herrera interview.

108. This competing subsystem, led by Arctic Power, was a new entity. It had little if anything to do with the pro-development CMAL coalition that fought against an Alaska lands bill during the ANILCA debate (1977-1980). That coalition "expired after ANILCA [was enacted]" (Gay interview).

109. Clark interview.

110. Lundquist interview.

111. Kolton interview.

112. Drager and Kish interview.

113. Telephone interview with Jack Hession, Sierra Club, 2 November 2002.

114. Lundquist interview.

115. Hession interview.

116. Lundquist interview.

117. Hession interview.

Chapter 4
"Civility" in Washington? Party Politics in Environmental-Energy Policy Making

> I have no stake in the bitter arguments of the last few years. I
> want to change the tone of Washington to one of civility and
> respect.—George W. Bush, 2000 Republican National Conven-
> tion, August 3, 2000

How did increased partisanship in Congress, especially since 1995, impact
environmentalists in their opposition to ANWR drilling? This chapter addresses
this question by using the Partisan Voting Model (PVM) as an explanation for
changing policy stances toward ANWR and other policies.

The PVM with its roll-call analyses helps explain the lack of ANWR policy
change toward drilling before 1995, and shifts by Congress in favor of drilling
since 1995. Subsequently, I use the model to analyze congressional partisanship
and its role in other environmental-energy policy outcomes, focusing on the cases
of drilling in the Eastern Gulf of Mexico (EGOM), in public lands in the West, and
offshore wind farming in Massachusetts.

Congressional Partisanship since 1995: Background

Cooper, Brady and Hurley (1979) are among the scholars that reported a decline
in congressional party voting from the early twentieth century until 1980. This
literature suggests that internal and external dimensions of congressional voting
(e.g., strength of the Speaker and regional representation respectively) triggered the
decline.[1]

As we saw in chapter 1, scholars have also documented an increase in
congressional partisanship since Republicans regained power in 1995. Broadly, the
polarization that started in the 1980s had an impact on policy through the 1990s.[2]
Barbara Sinclair (2000) has noted that the likelihood of a major bill becoming law

diminished compared with pre-1995 Congresses due to the filibuster and other constraints, and legislation was much more likely to gain House rather than Senate approval during the 104th and 105th Congresses shortly after the Republican takeover.[3]

Chris Bosso (2005) links this recent partisan polarization with environmental politics. He argues that although the two major political parties may have become more unified, or "responsible," these changes have afforded environmental activists little room to maneuver, since they now tend to be wedded to the Democratic Party. The recent polarization has, therefore, effectively narrowed environmentalists' tactical options in both chambers of Congress, thus excluding them from the inner circles of decision making through 2006.[4]

While environmentalists advocating protection of the coastal plain at ANWR may have faced exclusion from congressional decision making after 1994 during GOP control, they had more success preventing passage of pro-drilling legislation in the upper chamber of Congress, as we shall see. During the late 1990s, Senate Republicans faced a reasonably cohesive minority party in a highly polarized Senate, making it impossible for them to pass a pro-drilling law for ANWR.[5] The partisan voting approach helps to explain these and other ANWR-related policy decisions from 1977 through 2006.

Applying the PVM to the ANWR Case Study: The Findings

Congress enacted the Alaska National Interest Lands Conservation Act (ANILCA) in 1980, which doubled the size of the Arctic National Wildlife Refuge and made its coastal plain off-limits to development and oil exploration while the Department of Interior studied the issue. In 1995, Congress passed budget legislation that opened ANWR to drilling and President Clinton vetoed it.

In 2001, 2003, 2005, and 2006 the House passed pro-drilling energy legislation but the Senate precluded enactment of a pro-drilling law. It included a drilling provision in budget resolutions in 2005 and 2006 though.

The partisan framework explains congressional decisions on ANWR by focusing on key roll-call votes taken on budget and energy bills. This book used roll-call analysis to test this model.

The PVM is strong when a partisan voting pattern on congressional roll-call votes (i.e., majorities of each party's members voting differently) accompanies shifts toward pro-drilling policy outcomes during periods when Republicans held the majority. The partisan explanation is also compelling when partisan voting accompanies status quo, pro-environment policy outcomes when the Democratic Party controlled Congress.

The partisan explanation for ANWR policy decisions is indeterminate when partisan voting is present but the majority party fails to achieve its preferred outcome on ANWR due to defections by rank-and-file members of the majority party. Finally, this model is weak when lawmakers vote with bipartisanship.

Specifically, Rice's method of roll-call analysis helped determine levels of voting cohesion within and between the two parties on key ANWR votes in Congress since 1977. This tool does not shed light on why members voted as they did, but only on the presence and degree of partisanship (see the Methodological Appendix for a detailed discussion of how Rice's cohesion index is calculated and for how it is applied to ANWR).

First, it is important to recognize which party controlled each chamber when ANWR was high on the congressional agenda. Table 4.1 below identifies the periods of major legislative activity on ANWR in Congress, and it states which party held a majority during each voting period.

Table 4.1: Party Control of House and Senate
during ANWR Voting Periods

Voting Period	Party Control by Chamber	
	House	**Senate**
1977-1980	Democratic	Democratic
1991-1992	Democratic	Democratic
1995	Republican	Republican
2000	Republican	Republican
2001	Republican.	Republican / Democratic
2002	Republican	Democratic
2003	Republican	Republican
2005	Republican	Republican
2006	Republican	Republican

This book seeks to explain ANWR arena change toward drilling as well as change for other environmental-energy policies. Roll-call analysis for ANWR reveals that the partisan explanation is consistent with arena change or lack of it for two reasons.

First, most ANWR policy decisions made after 1980 were partisan and hindered passage of pro-drilling legislation when Democrats controlled Congress. Second, decisions were partisan and usually supported drilling when Republicans were in control.

Table 4.2: Policy Decisions on ANWR since 1977 in both Chambers of Congress and Power of the Partisan Voting Model

Key Bills Considered During Respective Voting Periods	Partisan Voting Model (Strong, Weak, or Indeterminate)	Vote/Decision Outcome in Each Chamber of Congress at End of Voting Period
ANILCA Debate in House and Senate (1977-1980)	Weak (very bipartisan voting)	House -- approved anti-drilling bill ** Senate -- approved anti-drilling bill **
Post-Gulf War Energy Bill in Senate (1991)	Strong (somewhat partisan voting)	House—no key votes on ANWR Senate—anti-drilling (filibuster of pro-drilling bill)
Budget Bill in House and Senate (1995)*	Strong (very partisan voting)	House—approved pro-drilling bill (vetoed) Senate—approved pro-drilling bill (vetoed)
Budget Bill in Senate (2000)*	Strong (very partisan voting)	House—no key votes on ANWR Senate—pro-drilling (defeated anti-drilling amendment)
Energy Bill in House (2001)*	Strong (very partisan voting)	House—approved pro-drilling bill Senate—no key votes on ANWR
Energy Bill in Senate (2002)	Strong (somewhat partisan voting)	House—no key votes on ANWR Senate—anti-drilling (filibuster of pro-drilling amendment)
Budget Bill in Senate (2003)	Indeterminate (very partisan voting)	House—no key votes on ANWR Senate—approved anti-drilling amendment to budget resolution

Key Bills Considered During Respective Voting Periods	Partisan Voting Model (Strong, Weak, or Indeterminate)	Vote/Decision Outcome in Each Chamber of Congress at End of Voting Period	
Energy Bill in House (2003)*	Strong (very partisan voting)	House—approved pro-drilling bill	Senate—no key votes on ANWR
Budget and Defense Spending Bills in House and Senate (2005)*	Strong (very partisan voting)	House—approved pro-drilling conference report on budget resolution; approved drilling in defense bill (bipartisan) but later ceded to Senate	Senate—defeated anti-drilling amendment; approved pro-drilling budget resolution and conference report; removed drilling from defense bill
Energy Bill in House (2005)*	Strong (very partisan voting)	House—approved pro-drilling bill	Senate—N/A
Energy and Budget Bills in House and Senate (2006)	Strong (very partisan voting)	House—approved pro-drilling jobs bill	Senate—approved budget resolution

* Indicates a shift in policy outcome either toward or adopting a pro-drilling position.

** The 1980 ANILCA law required DOI to study the hydrocarbon and environmental resources of the ANWR coastal plain.

There were three clear exceptions to this partisan voting pattern that included Republican defections opposing drilling. That is, two bipartisan votes in the House and Senate respectively on ANILCA (1977-1980), and partisan voting in the Senate in 2003 failed to shift the policy toward drilling. Table 4.2 summarizes the findings.

One can infer from this table that partisanship and the role of party offers at least a partial explanation for ANWR policy stances before and after 1995. On the one hand, policy decisions maintained the status quo before 1995 when the Democrats were the majority party. On the other hand, key decisions that favored drilling were made in both chambers in 1995, 2005, and 2006, in the Senate in 2000, and in the House in 2001, 2003, and 2005 when the Republicans were the majority party.

Federal lawmakers tended to vote for their party's expected position on ANWR when each party controlled Congress. In short, the partisan voting explanation for change is consistent with patterns of ANWR policy decisions.

The second finding is that Republican voting behavior was a key factor in this shift toward partisan voting on ANWR legislation. GOP defectors voted for the pro-environment ANILCA bill in 1979 and 1980 and thus promoted passage of bipartisan legislation, but the behavior of GOP legislators on future ANWR votes increased partisanship.

Table 4.2 summarizes the findings and demonstrates that legislators voted primarily along party lines on ANWR after 1980, and the section below details these changes in partisanship. However, it is important to realize that these findings do not answer why members did or did not vote for their party's expected position on ANWR (e.g., Republicans for drilling and Democrats against it). They do not explain why the PVM is weak or indeterminate during the 1977-1980 and 2003 voting periods respectively.

Below, I examine the reasons for defections on key votes in 1979, 1980, and 2003 in order to elucidate why arena change may or may not be present.[6] Region and constituency are found to offer possible explanations for Republican defections; voting for "good" public policy does not appear to explain those defections.

Changes in Partisanship in ANWR Voting

This section examines in detail changes in congressional partisanship by analyzing key floor votes from periods when ANWR was high on the congressional agenda. These periods include the 1977-1980 period of subsystem creation and subsequent passage of ANILCA, the 1991-1992 post–Gulf War legislative sessions, the 1995 presidential veto of a budget reconciliation bill that would have permitted drilling at ANWR, and the 2000-2006 timeframe. I examined them chronologically, but we may also conceptualize these four legislative periods as two—pre-1995 and 1995 onward—and assume that majority party control is critical to policy outcomes.[7]

The ultimate goal of detecting any rise or decline in party voting cohesion during these time frames is to explain why ANWR policy does or does not change due to partisan voting. The degree of partisanship for a given vote links party cohesion with policy change.

Partisanship is "high" if both parties vote cohesively on opposite sides of the issue. In this case study partisanship appears to have had a major impact on ANWR policy outcomes. Table 4.3 below clarifies the relationship between the level of party cohesion on roll-call votes and support for the partisan explanation when each party controlled Congress.

In table 4.3 the partisan explanation is strong only when the two parties possess high internal voting cohesion: that is, when most of the members of the parties are on the opposite side of a vote. In addition, we can regard a low cohesion level for each party's core position as indeterminate (i.e., neither weakens nor strengthens the partisan explanation) since this scenario is unlikely and the expected policy outcome is unknown.

In other words, majority party leadership in Congress rarely places legislation on the calendar if it expects to lose the vote. Even if the majority does this to place minority party legislators on the record before the next election, it is difficult to imagine a vote in which most of each party's rank-and-file defect from their leadership, thereby depriving the majority party of a policy victory. Overall, the cells in table 4.3 are consistent with Rice's definition of partisanship, namely high party cohesion on opposite sides of a vote.

One can think of the periods of Democratic and Republican majorities respectively as being consistent with the literature on so-called "conditional party government." Krehbiel (1998) provides a useful synopsis of that literature:

> This perspective is clearly intended to be descriptive—not normative. In conditional party government theory, the condition for party strength is stated in terms of legislators' preferences. If the parties' members have distinctly different preferences across parties but homogenous preferences within parties, then the majority party is predicted to be sufficiently strong to pass [its preferred legislation]. The majority party is cohesive, disciplined, and decisive [according to this theory].[8]

Table 4.3: Party Voting Cohesion: Inferred Impacts on the Partisan Voting Explanation for ANWR Arena Change

Dem Control	If	Dem Pro-Environmental Cohesion is (% of Vote)	&	GOP Pro-Development Cohesion is (% of Vote)	Then	Partisan Voting Model is
1977-1980 (House and Senate Votes)		Low Low High High		Low High Low High		— Weakened Weakened Strengthened
1991-1992 (Senate Vote)		Low Low High High		Low High Low High		— Weakened Weakened Strengthened
2002 (Senate Vote)		Low Low High High		Low High Low High		— Weakened Weakened Strengthened

GOP Control	If	Dem Pro-Environmental Cohesion is (% of Vote)		GOP Pro-Development Cohesion is (% of Vote)		Partisan Voting Model is
1995 (Senate Vote)		Low Low High High		Low High Low High		— Weakened Weakened Strengthened
2000 (Senate Vote)		Low Low High High		Low High Low High		— Weakened Weakened Strengthened
2001 (House Vote)		Low Low High High		Low High Low High		— Weakened Weakened Strengthened
2003 (House and Senate Votes)		Low Low High High		Low High Low High		— Weakened Weakened Strengthened
2005 (House and Senate Votes)		Low Low High High		Low High Low High		— Weakened Weakened Strengthened
2006 (House and Senate Votes)		Low Low High High		Low High Low High		— Weakened Weakened Strengthened

Table 4.4 shows the broad relationship between Democratic and Republican voting cohesion at a more micro level. This table helps us analyze roll-call votes by examining degrees of partisanship rather than the mere existence or absence of the partisan explanation. It does so by distinguishing between percentages of majorities voting a certain way and each party's respective Rice Index Value.

Table 4.4: Degrees of Partisanship[9]

		Large Majorities of Dems and Reps (Support/Oppose) One Another on a Vote	Dem and Rep Rice Index Values are Relatively
Partisan Voting Model Most Powerful	Very Partisan	Oppose	High (both above 40)
^ ^ ^	Somewhat Partisan	Oppose	Low (one or both below 40)
^ ^ ^	Somewhat Bipartisan	Support	Low (one or both below 40)
Partisan Voting Model Least Powerful	Very Bipartisan	Support	High (both above 40)

The Rice Index of Cohesion is a research tool that facilitates evaluation of voting cohesion within each party in order to compare levels of cohesion across parties, ultimately identifying degrees of partisan voting on ANWR and other public policies. This tool helps to evaluate key votes chronologically below, and this research specifies when Democrats and Republicans held a majority in Congress.

The Methodological Appendix presents the calculation for the Rice Index on each vote from 1978 to 2006 and indicates that there was a bipartisan voting pattern in Congress on ANWR through passage of the ANILCA statute in 1980. Yet, this analysis also reveals that a partisan voting pattern emerged after 1980 as Democratic majorities in Congress prevented drilling at the coastal plain through 1994 and Republican majorities subsequently increased the likelihood of drilling on several occasions since 1995.

The appendix clarifies these votes from a different vantage point by analyzing several facets of voting cohesion. These include average party voting cohesion across similar types of votes; that is, procedural votes; amendments and votes on final passage in a given chamber; and, average party voting cohesion across all types of votes in the same chamber during voting periods when at least two votes on ANWR were cast.

Democratic Majority Control during the ANILCA Debate, 1977-1980 (8 key votes)

Although no floor votes transpired in the House or Senate on a comprehensive Alaska lands bill in 1977, the House Subcommittee on General Oversight and Alaska Lands (i.e., the core of the original pro-environment ANWR subsystem) discussed an unnumbered draft bill that could be used later as a vehicle for legislative action. This draft helped set the stage for House committee action in 1978.

On March 21, 1978, the House Interior Committee approved the Alaska Lands Protection Bill, HR 39 (32-13). It rejected (20-24) an amendment to cut wilderness acreage in half. On May 4, the House Merchant Marine and Fisheries Committee reported its version of the bill and, 12 days later, the Rules Committee adopted a broad rule (11-5). The full House subsequently voted on the three motions in 1978 and two key motions in 1979. The Senate cast three key votes in 1980.[10] The outcome for ANWR in each case was pro-environment through mostly bipartisan voting in each chamber.

In short, bipartisan House and Senate voting on the ANILCA bill does not support the partisan explanation for policy change in this period. Despite a Democratic President and Democratic-controlled Congress, partisan politics did not drive ANWR toward policy outcomes during the 1977-1980 voting period as one might have anticipated if the PVM predicted correctly. Yet, it is clear that the Democratic majorities in both chambers voted more consistently with the policy position of the pro-environment subsystem than Republicans did with their pro-development opposition.

Democratic Majority Control during the Post–Gulf War Debate on President Bush'sNational Energy Policy, 1991-1992 (1 key vote)[11]

The House did not vote on any ANWR-specific motions in 1991 and leaders of the Democratic majority were not amenable to drilling at ANWR in the wake of the Gulf War. However, the Senate conducted a key vote on cloture for a pro-drilling energy bill. The Democratic majority successfully prevented a vote on final passage of the energy bill; Republican hopes of invoking cloture fell ten votes short of the 60 votes required to do so.

This 1991 Senate vote was the first floor vote taken in Congress concerning ANWR since the enactment of ANILCA in 1980. Based on table 4.4, the vote is a *somewhat partisan* one. Importantly, an initial increase in partisan voting on ANWR transpired by 1991.

This vote moderately strengthens the partisan explanation for ANWR policy making since, with a Democratic majority, we expect preservation of the status quo policy as this model, when strong, assumes the conditions of "conditional party government." In addition, the behavior of Republican senators was important because their cohesion had increased by 1991 compared with the ANILCA period, and Democratic voting cohesion had diminished.

After the defeat of this pro-drilling energy bill in 1991, the Democratic Congress overwhelmingly voted to enact the Energy Policy Act of 1992, a law that did not permit drilling at ANWR. We might speculate that since Energy Secretary James D. Watkins and the George H.W. Bush Administration endorsed the bill even without ANWR drilling, Republican senators set aside their policy preferences in order to support their party's leader in the White House.

Republican Majority Control during the 1995 Budget Reconciliation Debate (2 key votes)

By 1995, the budget process had become a means for Republican majorities in Congress to promote policy change on ANWR and a host of policy issues. The historic electoral victory by Republicans in 1994 set the stage for the new majority to send budgets with conservative-oriented provisions to the Democratic President. The Democrats' loss of control of the Congress prompted a major partisan battle as the Republicans viewed the years immediately after 1994 as crucial for consolidating their fledgling realignment.

The outcome of both Senate budget votes on ANWR in 1995 supports the partisan model used in this book, and GOP voting cohesion was marginally higher than that of the Democrats. According to the Congressional Research Service (CRS), only two recorded votes transpired from 1989 to 1999 that directly related to development at ANWR.[12]

Both votes took place in the Senate on a budget-related measure in 1995.[13] The outcome of each vote was *very partisan*, according to Rice's definition of partisanship (see table 4.4). I noted earlier that Senate rules preclude a filibuster on a budget resolution or reconciliation bill. A resolution is the budget blueprint that typically is voted on in the spring. Reconciliation is voted on later in the budget cycle.

Republican Majority Control during the 1997 Debate on a Broader Refuge Measure (no critical votes taken on ANWR)[14]

Non-controversial suspension votes that require two-thirds of House Members to gain passage in the House are sometimes important since this type of vote can inform us about the politics of an issue, especially in hindsight. For instance, the Patriot Act passed as a suspension bill 45 days after the attacks on 9/11/01, yet tensions soon arose between defense "hawks" and civil libertarians.

"Greasing the legislative wheel" by passing a supposedly non-controversial bill can sometimes mask underlying political tensions. The refuge bill in 1997 certainly was not in the same category as, say, a commemorative suspension bill that congressmen care little about. Instead, legislators reached a compromise on their longstanding differences concerning wildlife refuges.

On June 3, 1997 under the suspension of the rules procedure, the US House of Representatives approved HR 1420 by a 407-to-1 vote. This bill would define, legally and for the first time, the purpose of the nation's 511 wildlife refuges. The legal purpose was to protect both species and their habitats.

Clearly, this vote was *bipartisan*. The Senate later would amend the bill and pass it on a voice vote; it became public law (P.L. 105-57). Although this vote does not directly concern ANWR or the partisan approach, it is an interesting one nonetheless because it seems to define wildlife refuges as a bipartisan issue after six years of partisan voting on ANWR. This ostensible cooperation would, however, be short-lived.

Republican Majority Control during Debate on the 2000 Senate Budget Resolution (1 key vote)[15]

Like the Senate debate in 1995, Congress tried again in 2000 to allow ANWR drilling by tying this issue with the federal budget. Senator Frank Murkowski (R-AK) and a large majority of Republicans wanted to define ANWR development as a revenue-generating issue for the United States Treasury. An overwhelming majority of Democrats opposed this position.

A *very partisan* vote outcome assumed that oil exploration at ANWR would generate $1.2 billion in revenue, and it continued the emerging pattern of partisanship. The vote strengthens the PVM since the vote was partisan and the majority party won. Finally, voting cohesion was high for both parties, but it was slightly higher for the Democrats.

This analysis focuses on the key budget votes in 1995, 2000, 2003, 2005, and 2006 since the budget-making process can potentially lead to drilling at ANWR and completion of its life cycle. It is also worth noting that lawmakers from either party could defect on a budget vote for a variety of reasons, including proposed changes in government spending, the impact of the vote on one or more policy programs, changes in tax rates, or any of the three variables used later in this chapter.

As we shall see, critical GOP members may have defected on three key votes, including a budget vote in 2003, because of the region that they represent, their concern about the reaction of a particular constituency, or simply because the vote represented good public policy from their perspective. These three variables are important dimensions of defector votes in the literature.

Republican Majority Control during the 2001 House Debate on the Bush Energy Plan (5 key votes)[16]

Both the House and Senate took committee action in 2001 that potentially could have affected ANWR; however, legislation was brought to the floor for consideration only in the House. Surprisingly, it passed. In July 2001, the House Resources Committee approved an ANWR development bill (26-17). The panel defeated an amendment to remove the ANWR drilling section of the bill (19-30) and rejected a Democratic alternative (21-30) that did not include drilling.

In the upper chamber, the Senate Energy and Natural Resources Committee approved a draft section of the ANWR development bill (S. 597) by voice vote on August 2. House Members cast five key votes on ANWR in 2001, all of them partisan, as part of President Bush's pro-ANWR-drilling energy plan (HR 4). The partisan voting explanation for policy making is strong and the ANWR subsystem became destabilized as drilling became more likely. GOP voting cohesion surpassed Democratic unity too. Such voting cohesion is expected when the majority is narrow.[17]

Democratic Majority Control during the 2002 Senate Debate on the Bush Energy Plan (4 key votes)[18]

As we saw earlier, the House stunned the environmental community in August 2001 when it approved an energy package that included a provision to drill at ANWR's 1002 Area along the coast. In the Senate, Republican Senator Jim Jeffords of Vermont abandoned the Republican Party in 2001, and his action transferred control of that body to the Democrats. The Senate failed to act by the end of the year but Senate Democratic Leader Tom Daschle finally brought the measure to the floor in April 2002, before the congressional elections.

Alaskan Republican Senators Stevens and Murkowski failed to amend the bill to include drilling as senators cast four key floor votes (see Methodological Appendix). The first two cloture votes are critical to ANWR policy change and therefore strengthen the PVM since the votes were partisan and the Democratic majority won.

Clearly, by 2002, Senate Republicans had demonstrated a strong yet limited preference for drilling because they tended to vote for pro-drilling provisions but subsequently accepted an energy package absent the drilling provision. Perhaps they were hoping for inclusion of a drilling provision in a future conference report (if so, such a package never emerged).

The roll-call analysis (see appendix) suggests that the PVM is strong if one considers procedural votes, but arguably weak if final passage is included. This paradox suggests that increased partisanship in ANWR voting over time may not have been as deep as first suspected, at least not in the Senate.

The evidence is that nearly three-quarters of Republican senators supported the pro-environment ANILCA bill in 1980. They likewise tended to support an energy package in a partisan era (2002) that prohibited drilling at ANWR. We might have expected otherwise.

Republican Majority Control during the 2003 Debate on the FY 2004 Budget Resolution (3 key votes)[19]

After regaining majority status in the Senate because of the 2002 congressional elections, the GOP set its sights on ANWR drilling in 2003 through a budgetary measure, just as it did in 1995. I analyzed three votes: two in the Senate and one in the House, but the first Senate vote on the Boxer Amendment is the most important since the outcome prevented drilling.

This vote is especially interesting because the majority party lost on this partisan vote. The continued partisan voting pattern on ANWR fails to strengthen the partisan voting explanation for arena change. Instead, the PVM is indeterminate due to the failure of the Republican majority party to promote its desired policy.

Considering each vote individually, the first vote is the most critical vote. This *very partisan* vote on the Boxer Amendment, to strip the ANWR drilling provision from the bill, is indeterminate in inferring that partisan voting explains arena change. This vote occurred when the GOP held a majority in the Senate; yet, it did not result in an increased likelihood of drilling at the coastal plain of ANWR due to minority power in the Senate. The votes on final passage of the budget resolution in the Senate and House respectively likewise were partisan but failed to promote ANWR arena change since they subsequently failed to reinstate a drilling provision.[20]

Republican Majority Control during the 2003 Debate on Energy Legislation (3 key votes)

In the wake of the Senate's failure in 2003 to gain approval of a drilling provision as part of a budget resolution, pro-drilling forces quickly took action in the House and gained passage of an energy package (HR 6) that included a provision to permit drilling at the ANWR coastal plain. A similar bill passed the House in 2001.

This analysis includes two amendments and the vote on final passage using the Rice Index of Cohesion. The data indicates a continuation of the partisan pattern of voting on ANWR-related measures, a pattern that began to emerge on floor votes in 1991. In addition, GOP voting cohesion was higher than Democratic cohesion. The partisan explanation for policy shifts is strong.

In the upper chamber lawmakers ultimately adopted the same legislation in 2003 that they did in 2002. This research does not analyze the vote in 2002 because that bill omitted a drilling provision for ANWR. Furthermore, the conference report omitted that provision and the Senate filibustered the bill in November 2003.

Republican Majority Control during the 2005 Debate on the FY 2006 Budget Resolution and Defense Appropriations Bill (6 key votes)

The most important set of votes analyzed in this case study of ANWR policy includes three key Senate votes and two House votes on the non-binding budget resolution and conference report for FY 2006. The post-1994 partisan voting pattern continued, and this time the subsystem's pro-drilling competitors were nearly victorious as they capitalized on GOP gains in the Senate due to the 2004 elections (i.e., a pickup of three seats, all pro-drilling candidates).

First, they killed environmentalists' efforts to repeat their 2003 success when they stripped a drilling provision from the Senate budget resolution. The Senate passed the resolution with the drilling language included, the House omitted it (but included language in an energy bill, as we shall see), and both chambers passed the pro-drilling conference report on April 28, 2005. The final vote was partisan in each chamber.

Supporters of drilling later cleared the budget hurdle in the House but not in the Senate on a defense spending bill conference report in December 2005. A somewhat *bipartisan* vote in the House occurred probably because Members realized they had to pass the bill and knew that the Senate would fail to end debate on a filibuster, thus preventing drilling. The Senate acted as expected and the ANWR drilling initiative died.

It is interesting that Republican majorities in both chambers voted with less unity than the Democrats did on all five partisan votes. They could afford to do so since Republican majorities had grown in both bodies since 1995, thus rendering any defections less significant than prior years.

Republican Majority Control during the 2005 Debate on Energy Legislation (2 key votes)

In a repeat of the 2001 and 2003 House debates on an energy plan, the full House rejected an amendment offered by Congressman Edward Markey (D-MA) to strip the energy bill of its provision to drill at ANWR, and then the majority approved an energy plan. These votes strengthen the partisan explanation for ANWR policy making since the vote was partisan and the pro-drilling majority won the vote.

The Final Year of Republican Majority Control during the 2006 Debates on the Budget and Energy Measures (2 key votes)

In the final year of GOP control of both chambers of Congress, the House passed a measure (HR 5429) in May 2006 that would have directed the Secretary of the DOI to establish and execute a drilling plan for ANWR's coastal plain. The Senate failed to act on the bill, even though it had passed a budget resolution earlier in March that would have assumed revenue collection from an ANWR drilling program.

This last gasp, for now, by drilling proponents ended on Election Day when voters overturned the Republican revolution of 1994 by electing House and Senate Democratic majorities for the first time in a dozen years. The partisanship that had marked congressional debates and votes since at least the 1980s continued, not only on environmental-energy legislation, but also on a plethora of important issues facing the American people. Would it ever end?

The Role of Partisan Voting in Drilling in the Gulf of Mexico and on Public Lands, and in Promoting Wind Power

To help analyze policy and subsystem shifts for environmental-energy policies besides ANWR, I also evaluated other House and Senate roll-call votes. Drilling in the Eastern Gulf of Mexico seemed to offer the most roll-call votes for analysis, followed by legislative actions on the Cape Wind proposal in Nantucket Sound, followed by mostly regulatory rather than legislative action on expanded drilling on Western public lands. Those decisions tend to be made administratively in the form of drilling leases offered by the BLM.

The story of Congress's recent role in potentially oil-rich Eastern Gulf of Mexico (EGOM) drilling began for our purposes in 1969 off the coast of Santa Barbara, California when a disastrous spill led to a congressional moratorium, annually renewed, that has prohibited exploration on 85 percent of the Outer

Continental Shelf. That area stretches from three to 200 miles offshore where international waters begin. Presidents George H.W. Bush and Clinton signed directives providing further protection.[21]

The current Bush Administration, on the contrary, supports expanded drilling in the Gulf. The area approved for drilling by a Democratic-controlled Congress in late 2006 is thought to contain 1.2 billion barrels of oil and 5.8 trillion cubic feet of natural gas.[22] Yet, developing this area will have little impact on energy prices for several reasons, including high US demand and the global pricing of oil and regional pricing of natural gas that tend to mitigate domestic oil finds and their price impacts.

Major legislative activity on EGOM drilling occurred first in June 2006 when the House passed a bill permitting widespread drilling off US coasts as close as 50 miles offshore (providing some flexibility to states), thereby ending the longstanding federal ban on coastal drilling. The critical vote on final passage was very partisan and thus consistent with congressional roll-call voting generally and on environmental-energy debates specifically since the 1980s.[23]

In the Senate, lawmakers cast a surprisingly bipartisan vote in July, breaking a filibuster and permitting an up-or-down vote on the Gulf drilling bill in early August 2006. That vote was somewhat partisan. Final action took place in December with the House yielding to the upper chamber's narrower drilling bill as the Senate overwhelmingly passed the measure (79-9). Drilling was approved.

Why did Congress support drilling in the Eastern Gulf of Mexico in 2006 but not, ultimately, at ANWR? There are several plausible explanations. First, high energy prices may have prodded lawmakers to demonstrate that they cared about the average American's plight, so the less contentious Gulf vote with few if any environmental icons could help ease voter pressure on incumbents regardless of the fact that it was unlikely to impact gas prices. Second, all ten Gulf-state senators voted for drilling probably because the bill contained economic benefits for their states since Florida agreed to share drilling royalties in exchange for buffer zones to protect its beaches.[24] Overall, regionalism and economic factors seemed to trump partisan politics in the Gulf drilling case.

And what role did congressional partisanship play in policy decisions on the Cape Wind project for Massachusetts's Nantucket Sound? This would not be the world's first offshore wind farm. European democracies have built them in places such as Britain's Great Yarmouth coastline. Why has the world's greatest economic power and consumer of energy failed to respond in kind?

The Cape Wind proposal has moved forward in Congress in recent years with bipartisan support in the face of elite opposition and regulatory hurdles. Since the proposal began winding its way through the state and federal regulatory processes in 2001, it has faced opposition from then Governor Mitt Romney (R) and Senator Ted Kennedy (D) among other political elites. Yet, the plan to build 130 wind turbines on the Sound has survived.

Perhaps the main reason for its viability has been the backing of key environmental groups (e.g., the NRDC and Sierra Club), plus the bipartisan team of Senators Jeff Bingaman (D) and Pete Domenici (R), both of New Mexico. In 2006, those lawmakers, who are highly regarded for their expertise on energy issues, managed to defeat a project-killing amendment by threatening a filibuster on a Coast Guard bill in 2006. They negotiated a deal to give the Coast Guard Commandant and other federal agencies a voice in this decision rather than giving the governor veto power.

The key congressional vote on Cape Wind took place in June 2006 in the House. It was a unanimous vote in which language similar to the Senate's was approved. Keeping Cape Wind alive was a bipartisan effort in both chambers driven by interest groups and editorial protests against killing the project.[25] Perhaps this case study can serve as a model for cooperation on other environmental-energy projects across the country.

In the case of the debate over expanded drilling on public lands in Western states, most observers recognize that drilling for hydrocarbons increased during the Clinton Administration, but even more so under President George W. Bush, especially near environmentally sensitive areas. I do not analyze roll-call votes in this case since these decisions tend to be made administratively by the Bureau of Land Management (BLM) rather than by Congress. In fact, the BLM controls roughly one-eighth of all the land in the United States and sells leases to energy companies exploring and developing domestic energy resources. Yet, partisanship does underlie these decisions as, for example, when environmental interest groups sued the national government for issuing leases in a dozen areas of the Rocky Mountain States.[26]

Summary of Rice Index Analyses (1977-2006)

In this chapter I focus on Rice Index analyses to test the hypothesis that "partisan" voting in Congress explains ANWR policy shifts after passage of the pro-environment ANILCA law in 1980. In the ANWR case study, I find that partisanship has more explanatory power in recent years.

Clearly, federal lawmakers have tended to vote for their party's expected position on ANWR since 1991. Partisan voting was prevalent in every voting period except the 1977-1980 period (i.e., in 1991-1992, 1995, 2000-2006) on both budgetary and energy legislation concerning ANWR. Hence partisan congressional voting offers at least a partial explanation for pro-drilling decisions when Republicans were in control.

The partisan approach is supported as an explanation for changing ANWR policy stances, based on voting data from both chambers in 1995, 2005, and 2006, in the Senate in 2000, and in the House in 2001, 2003, and 2005. This model also helps explain the lack of ANWR policy shifts in Congress when Democrats were the majority party in at least one chamber (e.g., in 1991-1992 and 2002). The lack of shifts toward drilling has continued since 2007 under Democratic control of both chambers.

These findings are consistent with Cox and McCubbins's (1993) notion that the majority party serves as a structuring coalition for its members. Clearly, the Speaker of the House has a role to play in the voting behavior of majority party members. To paraphrase the late Speaker, Thomas "Tip" O'Neill, the scheduling power of the Speaker is critical to policy outcomes.[27]

Scholars also argue that party is more important than individual legislators' behavior (i.e., the rational choice argument) for determining voting in the House. Party protects self-serving legislators from external electoral effects:

> The picture of the postwar House is one in which the majority party acts as a structuring coalition, stacking the deck in its own favor, both on the floor and in committee, to create a kind of "legislative cartel" that dominates the legislative agenda. The majority party promotes its agenda-setting advantage in two basic ways: by giving its members greater power to veto legislative initiatives; and by giving its members greater power to push legislative initiatives onto the floor.[28]

The finding that partisan voting on ANWR legislation has been the norm since the 1980s also is consistent with a series of papers written by David Rohde in 1988, 1989, and 1990. Rohde found a significant increase in the frequency of party votes from the mid-1970s through the 1980s, accompanied by strong party cohesion.[29]

In a more speculative vein, it may be that the trend toward partisanship on ANWR after 1980 had to do partly with a backlash by congressional party leaders against the decentralizing reforms of the 1970s. On the other hand, polarization in Congress during the Reagan years after 1981 may have played a role.

Another challenge is to determine whether this presence of partisanship increased the likelihood of policy change toward drilling. The clear answer is affirmative when Republicans held a majority. Their near victory for drilling in 2005 supports this. Yet, subsystem actors during the 1990s, including President Clinton and Senate Democratic Leader Tom Daschle (D-SD), thwarted policy change when the Democrats controlled Congress and in one instance when they did not (2003).

The role of partisan voting in the three additional cases of environmental-energy policy making, interestingly, seems to deviate from the partisan pattern for ANWR as listed in table 4.5 below.

Table 4.5: Partisanship on Roll-calls for Case Studies

Case Study	Partisan Voting
ANWR	**Yes, since 1980**
Drilling in the Eastern Gulf of Mexico (EGOM)	No
Drilling on Public Lands in the West	N/A since decisions tend to be made administratively
Wind Power / Cape Wind Project	No

Bipartisan support was a precondition for enacting a pro-drilling law for the Eastern Gulf of Mexico in 2006. Other forces may have been at work though, as we shall in the next chapter.

As for the case of Cape Wind, this has been a conflictive issue, but the primary conflict has not been between Republicans and Democrats. Rather, this issue has pitted environmental interest groups and bipartisan congressional elites against the likes of Massachusetts Senator Ted Kennedy, former Governor Mitt Romney, and others who arguably did not want the wind farm in their own backyards. The key House vote in Congress was bipartisan, and it kept the project alive. The majority of Americans, or at least their representatives in Congress and in the media, as indicated in the next chapter, define this issue with a pro-environment tone.

So, the Gulf drilling and Cape Wind project seem to reveal some cracks in the longstanding partisanship in Congress on environmental-energy policies. Perhaps high gas prices are translating into political pressure for Congress to act. The case of drilling on public lands does not fit this pattern: rather, administrative action has largely driven policy decisions in this instance.

Deviations from the Partisan Voting Model (1979, 1980, 2003): Tthe Role of Defectors in ANWR Voting

The discussion thus far has focused on identifying the presence or absence of partisan voting as an explanation for stances on ANWR and other policies. Next, we turn to an examination of why a group of moderate Republican defectors voted with pro-environment legislators against ANWR development on three votes in 1979, 1980, and 2003.

These votes clearly deviate from either the partisan voting pattern or the expected policy outcome. Key votes in 1979-1980 made it possible to have a bipartisan policy on ANWR, and in 2003 congressional voting helped to delay drilling. Establishing the reasons for defections may clarify alternative reasons for why we observe arena change (or the lack of it). Before summarizing these findings, it is worth examining where this analysis fits in with related scholarship, understanding why these three votes are worthy of investigation, and addressing the reasons for emphasizing Republican rather than Democratic defections.

First, how do ANWR defection votes relate to political science? Davidson and Oleszek (1998) note that "House and Senate floor votes are crude channels for registering Members' views."[30] Scholars have written that Members cast their votes for one or a combination of reasons.

Some vote primarily based on their party affiliation or party leadership pressures. Others cast their votes due to the influence of constituencies, or constituencies through interest group pressure. Some may vote a certain way due to presidential influence, the influence of like-minded Members of Congress, the state delegation, or region (see chapter 1 for a summary of relevant literature on determinants of congressional voting).

The first part of this chapter examined party as a determinant of congressional voting on ANWR policy. Here we investigate three additional determinants of voting for GOP defectors in 1979, 1980, and 2003. The unit of analysis in both parts of the chapter is the roll-call vote.

Like Kingdon's (1989) work, this portion of the chapter "portrays legislators as individuals, deciding largely on their own rather than as integral members of voting blocs or other groups. [Yet] they do consult one another and band together for strategic reasons, but they are mostly autonomous actors."[31]

Also like Kingdon's (1989) study, this segment on defector voting aims to measure actor influence on congressional decisions. However, I examine roll-call votes rather than other types of policy decisions and employ a somewhat different methodology. The approach for studying ANWR defector voting behavior discussed in the appendix is an exploratory one that begins to help us understand why legislators voted as they did. Its chief benefit likely is a heuristic one (i.e., future researchers should be able to formulate and test new propositions).

Second, why are these three defection votes studied? It is not surprising that congressmen defected from their respective parties on ANWR votes, especially during the late 1970s. Congressional reorganization arguably led to a rise in staff influence, a proliferation in single-issue interest groups, increased autonomy of subcommittees, and the rise of junior legislators at the expense of the seniority system, all of which diminished the role of party in roll-call voting. These changes weakened the parties in government as power became further fragmented.[32]

Although one might expect Democrats to support the pro-environment position and Republicans to oppose, this does not always occur. Why did some Republicans defect on the votes they cast in 1979, 1980, and 2003? One reason why Republican moderates were able to influence policy outcomes at all was that the size of the Republican majority during the 2003 Senate vote was so small that even a few defectors could undermine the agenda of the majority leadership.[33]

The behavior of those legislators during those debates either weakens the partisan explanation for ANWR policy making or makes the model indeterminate (i.e., neither weakens nor strengthens the partisan explanation). So, these votes are worth investigating.

Specifically, votes taken on ANILCA in the House and Senate in 1979 and 1980 and the vote on the Boxer Amendment to the Senate budget measure in 2003 are anomalies since the former two bipartisan votes weaken rather than strengthen the PVM while the partisan vote in 2003 makes it indeterminate. In all, this relatively sophisticated analysis transcends simple detection of partisanship.

Third, why evaluate Republican rather than Democratic defections on ANWR votes? It is true that on some highly partisan votes, Democratic rather than Republican defectors were decisive in the outcome (see table 4.6 below), but I do not analyze these because those votes strengthen the partisan model. In other words, the Republican majority party advanced ANWR arena change. No anomaly was present because the majority neither lost nor was the vote bipartisan.

However, this study acknowledges the larger theoretical point that although the PVM helps to explain continuity and policy change for ANWR, party voting alone did not always determine arena change. Table 4.6 below lists the votes when Democratic defectors influenced policy outcomes.

Table 4-6: Cases of a Strong PVM with Democratic Defections Driving ANWR Arena Change

Chamber and Voting Period	Voting Decision
Senate, 1995	Domenici (R-NM) Motion
Senate, 2000	Murkowski (R-AK) Motion
House, 2001	Sununu (R-NH) Amendment #1
House, 2001	Sununu (R-NH) Amendment #2
House, 2001	Markey (D-MA) Amendment
House, 2001	Final Passage of Energy Bill
House, 2003	Wilson (R-NM) Amendment
House, 2003	Markey (D-MA) Amendment
House, 2003	Final Passage of Energy Bill
Senate, 2005	Cantwell (D-WA) Motion
House, 2005	Markey (D-MA) Amendment
House, 2005	Final Passage of Energy and Defense Spending Bills

More importantly, this study borrows three variables or determinants of voting behavior from the literature to study Republican defections—*good public policy, environmental constituency,* and *regional variables.* Again, these defections either weaken the PVM or make the model indeterminate.

This research operationalized these variables and transformed their data into a data set to facilitate rudimentary statistical analysis using both Excel and SPSS. The table below lists the findings for these factors.

Table 4.7: Determinants of GOP Defector Voting on Three ANWR-Related Anomalies—Summary of Significant Variables

Variable (i.e., explanation)	House Vote on ANILCA (1979)	Senate Vote on ANILCA (1980)	Boxer Amendment in Senate (2003)
Environmental Constituency	Not Confirmed	Confirmed	Confirmed
Good Public Policy	Not Confirmed	Not Confirmed	Not Confirmed
Region	Confirmed: a voting pattern is present	Confirmed: a voting pattern is present	Confirmed: a voting pattern is present

The approach used here contends that some combination of these factors is thought to explain Republican defector votes that favored environmental protection on the ANILCA vote (in the House and Senate in 1979 and 1980) and on the Boxer Amendment to the Senate budget measure in 2003. These votes are counterintuitive.

The goal is to facilitate data collection and the drawing of inferences concerning the partisan explanation for ANWR voting. The Methodological Appendix details procedures for operationalizing, or measuring the three independent variables or explanations.

Significance of the Findings on Defections

Democrats did not always support the pro-environment position on ANWR and Republicans did not always oppose it. These defections, one can argue, are consistent with the Madisonian view that the Senate functions with more "coolness, with more system, and with more wisdom, than the popular branch"[34] since they represent broader constituencies than House members and therefore often need to balance those varied interests, conventional wisdom suggests.

One explanation for GOP legislators voting for environmental protection and weakening the partisan explanation for outcomes is their desire to please *environmental constituencies* in their districts or states. This factor is confirmed when explaining GOP Senate defections in 1980 and 2003, but it is not confirmed when explaining House defections in 1979.

In addition, the sample size for GOP Senate defectors was small in both 1980 and in 2003—28 and 8 defectors respectively. This suggests that this portion of the research may be less reliable than the study of House GOP defector behavior.

This book also finds that the *good public policy* variable offers an unlikely explanation for GOP defectors' voting behavior in the House in 1979 and in the Senate in 1980 and 2003. The findings do not support the argument that enacting *good public policy* was important in explaining GOP defectors' behavior and deviations from partisanship. Instead, those defectors tended to have a voting pattern that was more conservative than the liberal-leaning votes they cast against drilling in 1979, 1980, and 2003.

Region is the third explanation for GOP defector voting and deviation from the partisan voting pattern. The Middle Atlantic and East North Central regions[35] are critical in explaining deviations from the partisan explanation. On two of three defector votes analyzed here a significant percentage of representatives or senators came from those regions.

Specifically, legislators from the Middle Atlantic States influenced the outcome of the pro-environment ANILCA bill in the House in 1979 and in the Senate in 1980; legislators from the East North Central (i.e., Midwestern) States affected the outcome of the ANILCA bill in the House in 1979 and the Boxer Amendment in the Senate in 2003.

By most accounts, environmental protection has become an important issue in the electorate. The birth of the modern environmental movement in 1970 and its aftermath have influenced voters in the Northeast and Midwest over time; suburban voters in those regions have tended to vote Democratic. These two regions at the Arctic National Wildlife Refuge.

In all, I analyzed key votes in 1979-1980 and 2003 that were driven by defecting Republicans. Votes mattered in the earlier period since they undermine the partisan model through bipartisan voting on ANWR. The vote on the Boxer Amendment in 2003 makes the PVM indeterminate because the policy outcome delayed drilling. Finally and importantly, these findings scratch the surface in the quest to identify factors driving votes on ANWR policy. Other researchers might formulate and test additional hypotheses using advanced, multivariate statistical analysis.

Conclusions

Broadly, the goal of this chapter has been to predict or explain why ANWR policy has or has not changed in one or both chambers of Congress since creation of the pro-environment subsystem in 1977. Other than Republican defections in 1979, 1980, and 2003, the voting pattern in Congress tended toward partisanship on

ANWR votes cast since the late 1970s. Party explains how the issue has been resurrected periodically on the congressional agenda, so partisan majorities seem to be a necessary condition for changing policy outcomes of ANWR.

On the other hand, partisanship may not be the only political force driving arena change. If it were, Republican majorities would have enacted a law sometime after 1994 providing for drilling at the coastal plain. Instead, their efforts were thwarted during the Clinton Administration and during George W. Bush's tenure.

In the other cases studied here, I found that partisan voting was less prevalent and therefore inferred to be less important in the law enacted to expand drilling in the Eastern Gulf of Mexico and the incremental changes that have put the Cape Wind project on the brink of success in 2007. The case of expanded drilling on public lands in the West was found to be more a case of administrative lawmaking with President George W. Bush using the BLM to advance drilling there.

The findings for ANWR are not surprising since American politics involves complex relationships between a variety of actors whose values are often in conflict. Conventional wisdom suggests that direct causation is difficult if not impossible to prove in this field of study. In the next chapter we will explore three additional explanations for changing ANWR policy stances to help solve this puzzle by testing the more sophisticated Life Cycle Model in all four environmental-energy case studies.

Notes

1.   David W. Rohde, *Parties and Leaders in the Postreform House* (Chicago: The University of Chicago Press, 1991), 9-10.

2.   See John H. Aldrich, *Why Parties? The Origin and Transformation of Political Parties in America* (Chicago: The University of Chicago Press, 1995); Keith T. Poole and Howard Rosenthal, *Congress: A Political-Economic Theory of Roll-call Voting* (Oxford University Press, 1997); Barbara Sinclair, *Legislators, Leaders, and Lawmaking: The US House of Representatives in the Postreform Era* (Baltimore: The Johns Hopkins University Press, 1995); Rohde, *Parties and Leaders.*

3.   Barbara Sinclair, "The New World of US Senators," in *Congress Reconsidered* (7 ed.), ed. Lawrence E. Dodd and Bruce I. Oppenheimer (Washington, DC: CQ Press, 2001), 13-14.

4.   Christopher J. Bosso, *Environment, Inc. From Grassroots to Beltway* (Lawrence, KS: University of Kansas Press, 2005), 127,132-33.

5.   Steven S. Smith and Gerald Gamm, "The Dynamics of Party Government in Congress," in *Congress Reconsidered* (7 ed.), ed. Lawrence E. Dodd and Bruce I. Oppenheimer (Washington, DC: CQ Press, 2001), 265.

6.   Scholars often try to explain deviations from patterns of empirically observed phenomena. These deviations are called "anomalies."

7.   See Gary W. Cox and Mathew D. McCubbins, *Legislative Leviathan: Party Government in the House* (Los Angeles: University of California Press, 1993).

8.   See Keith Krehbiel, *Pivotal Politics: A Theory of US Lawmaking* (Chicago: The University of Chicago Press, 1998), 9. He references scholarly works by Rohde (1991), Aldrich (1995), and Aldrich and Rohde (2000) in that analysis.

9.   The boundary between high and low Rice Index Values (i.e., the value 40) admittedly is somewhat arbitrary. However, the key point is that a *very partisan* or *very bipartisan* vote requires both parties' Rice Index Values to be high. Otherwise, the degree of partisanship or bipartisanship is less.

10.   More details may be found in the following: *1977 CQ Almanac*, 673; *1978 CQ Almanac*,724-742; *1979 CQ Almanac*, 663-677; *1980 CQ Almanac*, 575-584; *CQ Weekly Report* for 20 May 1978, 1281-83 & 27 May 1978, 1362-63 & 19 May 1979, 986-87 & 23 August 1980, 2552-53; *1980 US Code*, 5057-5059.

11.   The *1991 CQ Almanac*, 195-209 provides more details concerning this vote.

12.   Apparently CRS discounts the importance of the cloture vote in 1991 on a broader energy package.

13.   Lynne M. Corn and Bernard Gelb, "Arctic National Wildlife Refuge: Legislative Issues," Congressional Research Service, 14 May 2002, 5.

14.   This analysis is based on the 1997 *CQ Almanac*, 4-15, 4-16 and the *CQ Weekly Report*, 7 June 1997, 1313, 1334-1335.

15.   This discussion is based on *CQ Weekly Report*, 8 April 2000, 822.

16.   Data from this section can be found in: *CQ Weekly Report*, 21 July 2001, 1769,1771; *CQ Weekly Report*, 4 August 2001, 1916-1917,1944-1948; and, *CQ Weekly Report*, 22 December 2001, 3037+.

17.   Sinclair, *The New World*, 12.

18.   This section uses data found in *CQ Weekly Report*, 20 April 2002, 1048 & 27 April 2002, 1118; Corn and Gelb, "Arctic;" Patricia A. Hurley and Rick K. Wilson, "Partisan Voting Patterns in the US Senate," *Legislative Studies Quarterly*, 14 (May 1989): 225-250.

19.   The Library of Congress website (www.thomas.loc.gov/) provides information on all key votes in 2003 on the budget resolution and energy legislation, and in 2005 that were analyzed here.

20.   This analysis omits the conference report for the FY 2004 budget resolution. Like the Senate and House votes on final passage, the conference report did not include a provision to open the 1002 Area for energy development.

21.   Steven Mufson, "The New Drilling Battle; High Energy Prices Spur Fresh Debate on Offshore Moratorium," *Washington Post*, 15 June 2006, 01(D).

22.   Richard Simon and Maura Reynolds, "The Nation; Senate OKs Bill to Expand Oil, Gas Drilling; Measure Opens a Section in the Gulf of Mexico but Must Be Reconciled with a House Version that Allows Production along the Pacific Coast," *LA Times*, 2 August 2006, 17(A).

23.   "Energy," *CQ Weekly Report*, 11 December 2006: 3289; http://library.cqpress. com, 8 March 2007.

24.   "Energy," *CQ Weekly Report*, 11 December 2006: 3289; http://library.cqpress. com, 8 March 2007.

25.   "Saving the Cape Wind Project," *Washington Times* editorial, 5 July 2006, 16(A).

26.   Timothy Egan, "Bush Administration Allows Oil Drilling Near Utah Parks," Common Dreams News Center, <http://www.commondreams.org/cgi-bin/print.cgi?file=headlines02/0208-03.htm> (8 February 2002).

27. Cox and McCubbins, *Legislative Leviathan*, 233,270.

28. Cox and McCubbins, *Legislative Leviathan*, 270.

29. Cox and McCubbins, *Legislative Leviathan*, 140.

30. Roger H. Davidson and Walter J. Oleszek, *Congress and its Members*, 6 ed. (Washington, DC: CQ Press, 1998), 258.

31. John W. Kingdon, John W, *Congressmen's Voting Decisions*, 3d ed. (Ann Arbor, MI: The University of Michigan Press, 1989), xvii.

32. Kingdon, *Congressmen's Voting*, preface.

33. Robin Kolodny, "Moderate Success: Majority Status and the Changing Nature of Factionalism in the House Republican Party," in *New Majority or Old Minority? The Impact of Republicans on Congress*, ed. Nicol C. Rae and Colton C. Campbell (New York: Rowman & Littlefield Publishers, Inc., 1999) 165.

34. Sarah A. Binder, *Minority Rights, Majority Rule: Partisanship and the Development of Congress*.Cambridge; New York: Cambridge University Press, 1997, 402.

35. The region variable is comprised of eight elements. (1) The Northeast includes: Maine, New Hampshire, Vermont, Connecticut, Rhode Island, and, Massachusetts. (2) The Middle Atlantic includes: New York, Pennsylvania, New Jersey, and, Delaware. (3) The East North Central includes: Ohio, Michigan, Indiana, Illinois, and, Wisconsin. (4) The West North Central includes: Minnesota, Iowa, North Dakota, South Dakota, Nebraska, and, Kansas. (5) The Mountain region includes: Montana, Wyoming, Colorado, New Mexico, Utah, Idaho, Nevada, and, Arizona. (6) The Pacific includes: California, Oregon, Washington, Alaska, and, Hawaii. (7) The Border region includes: Missouri, Kentucky, Tennessee, Oklahoma, Maryland, and, West Virginia. (8) The South includes: Virginia, North Carolina, South Carolina, Georgia, Florida, Alabama, Louisiana, Mississippi, Texas, and, Arkansas.

Chapter 5
Forces for Change: Political and Social Currents for ANWR, Western Lands, the Gulf of Mexico, and Cape Cod Wind Farms

In the last chapter, we saw that partisan voting in Congress is one influence driving environmental-energy policy change. But a second possible explanation exists for change in this category of policy decisions: a combination of political forces that comprises the Life Cycle Model (LCM).

The LCM offers a more sophisticated analysis of changes in policy stances. Its three independent variables or explanations include: a shifting issue definition, changes in public opinion; and entry of new actors into the decision-making process. These three critical elements of the model may lead to changes in the respective decision-making structures of this book's four case studies and their policy outcomes.

In this chapter, I test several hypotheses that represent three separate variables in the LCM. In the main case, ANWR, data were collected for these variables using several sources including congressional committee and subcommittee hearing documents, news and editorial accounts in the *New York Times* and the *Readers' Guide to Periodical Literature*, opinion polls, and interviews with subsystem actors (see Methodological Appendix). The method used here is based on the approaches used by Baumgartner and Jones (1993) and Bosso (1987).

The inferential power of the life cycle explanation of ANWR arena change is greatest when one or more conditions are met. In the LCM, the three influences can independently explain policy outcomes. However, they may also interact in complex ways to redefine the issues. For instance, the media's definition of a policy issue can affect public opinion and enable the emergence of new actors (the question of issue salience as a spur to new policy stakeholders).[1]

In order to support the LCM in the ANWR case, the following evidence must be present. First, we should observe a redefinition of the issue from a pro-environment to a pro-drilling position. If the issue began to be redefined before the

GOP takeover of Congress in 1995, then we have clearer evidence of the independent influence of the issue redefinition explanation for policy shifts. Second, there should be a shift in public opinion from a pro-refuge-protection position during the 1977-1980 period to a less environmentally friendly or pro-development one over time. Third, we should expect to find an expanded "scope of conflict" via identification of new or latent actors in the policy-making process, both public and private, as the subsystem is weakened and pro-drilling decisions are made.

Below, I present the findings relevant to each component of the Life Cycle Model: first for drilling at ANWR, then for drilling on public lands in the West and in the Eastern Gulf of Mexico (EGOM), and the unique case of environmentalists contesting each other on whether to build an offshore wind farm at Cape Cod.

My analysis revealed that there is little evidence that the print media has helped to redefine the ANWR issue in favor of drilling. Data from the *New York Times* and the *Readers' Guide to Periodical Literature* indicate that the tone of articles favored the pro-environment position prior to the 1994 congressional elections. Although the tone shifted slightly toward the pro-development position after 1994 in the *New York Times* articles, the overall tone of those articles continued to oppose drilling at ANWR. These data do not support the life cycle explanation for policy making.

On the other hand, issue redefinition *in congressional hearings* likely affected ANWR policy decisions in the House and Senate since ANWR was defined as a pro-development issue in both chambers prior to a shift in party control of Congress in 1995. Committee and subcommittee chairs tended to invite more pro-development witnesses to testify at hearings regardless of which party controlled Congress. These data are consistent with the life cycle perspective mainly because the committees in question tended to favor resource extraction to attract members from states with large extractive industry sectors.

I also found that there was no upsurge in popular sentiment in favor of drilling after the passage of the pro-development ANILCA law in 1980. Polls conducted in 1991 reveal a mix of support and opposition to development of ANWR. Later, between 1995 and 2005, public opinion clearly opposed drilling in 9 out of 11 major polls. These data weaken the life cycle argument.

Finally, new or formerly inactive pro-drilling actors became involved in the arena after 1994. Specifically, these were the Teamsters Union, Arctic Power, and Vice President Cheney's National Energy Policy Development Group (NEPDG). Involvement of these largely elite actors supports the LCM. Table 5.1 summarizes the chapter findings for the ANWR case study.

**Table 5-1: Life Cycle Forces and Their Impacts on
ANWR Pro-Drilling Decisions**

Independent Variable/ Force	Issue Redefinition (Tone of Media Attention)	Issue Redefinition (Tone of Congressional Hearings)	Public Opinion	New Actors
Impact	Not Confirmed	Confirmed	Not Confirmed	Confirmed

The three sections that follow provide detailed findings and analyses, first addressing forces driving ANWR policy making followed by those driving policy change (or lack of it) in my three supplemental case studies.

Part I—Issue Redefinition

Most scholars agree that a shifting issue definition represents the heart of a life cycle analysis, and this analysis is consistent with that thinking. Broadly, the tone of ANWR-related media accounts and congressional hearings are two key data sources used to determine how this issue has been defined over time. Independent support for the LCM rests largely on finding that the issue was redefined in favor of drilling prior to a change in party control of Congress in 1995. If found, this would provide evidence that redefinition was independent of party changes in Congress. This section therefore tests this hypothesis:

> The tone and content of media coverage and of committee hearings shifted in favor of drilling, preceding favorable votes in Congress on permitting drilling in ANWR.

It should be noted that an absence of issue redefinition would not eliminate the LCM as an explanation for the weakening of the ANWR subsystem and passage of pro-drilling bills. Shifts in public opinion or involvement of new actors might have been necessary to propel subsystem change.

The next two sections present and analyze the findings based on the data collection method outlined in the Methodological Appendix. I subsequently analyze President George W. Bush's role in redefining ANWR in Congress since 2001and then evaluate the role of issue redefinition in other environmental-energy policies besides ANWR.

Defining ANWR through Media Attention

I collected and analyzed media accounts of the ANWR-environmental subsystem using a method similar to those of Spencer Weart (1988) and Baumgartner and Jones (1993), who documented the levels of attention surrounding a given policy. Baumgartner, Jones, and their staff of coders analyzed articles from both the *Readers' Guide to Periodical Literature* and the *New York Times Index*. For my analysis of ANWR media attention, I coded a large sample of articles and opinion pieces (i.e., editorials, letters to the editor, and op-eds) appearing in the *New York Times*, and a smaller sample from the *Readers' Guide*.

Some may question the use of the *Times* as representative of national print media coverage of public policy issues. But Siler's (2004) analysis of media content during the 2000 presidential election provides a logical rationale for using the *New York Times* in a content analysis. She writes:

> The *New York Times* is particularly suitable to represent newspapers in general because it is often considered the newspaper of record. Given the extent to which [its] content is distributed worldwide and made available to other editors, it is apparent that content in the *Times* could adequately represent national newspapers. With the general trend toward less diversity and more elitism in media outlets in many different genres, the *New York Times* is clearly elite. The high profile of the contributors to the *Times*, the reporters, editors and columnists, would easily qualify this paper as a form of elite communication.[2]

As fig. 5.1 shows, the general print media did follow the lead of the *New York Times* in its frequency of ANWR coverage. The volume of the *New York Times*'s coverage changed over time in ways that were consistent with the changes in coverage of the print media generally (i.e., as represented in the *Readers' Guide*) during roughly the same period (1977-2003). Clearly, media attention tended to rise and fall for each source as the issue ebbed and flowed on and off the national political agenda. Coverage peaked during the ANILCA debate (1980), release of the DOI study of ANWR (1987), after the Persian Gulf War (1990), after the GOP takeover of Congress (1995), and after the attacks on the US on September 11, 2001.

Of course, this figure does not say anything about whether the tone and content of coverage in the *Times* was similar to the print media generally. Sampling the *Times* alone might be problematic because it is arguably a "liberal" newspaper. The tone of the print media as a whole could have been more pro-drilling than the *New York Times* in the period before 1995. Thus, a smaller sample of articles was also coded (1990-1994) for the *Readers' Guide*. The two tables that follow present the findings for each data source.

Figure 5.1: Coverage of ANWR in the
Reader's Digest* and the *New York Times

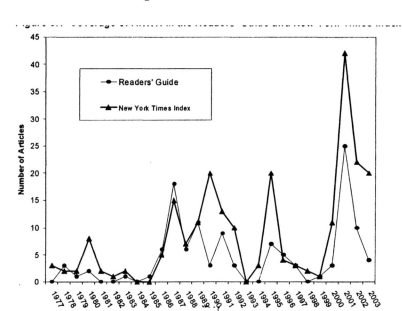

Baumgartner and Jones's (1993) general approach is used here to code both media attention and congressional hearings.[3] The Methodological Appendix details coding procedures and related terminology. In short, 229 articles were chosen for examination from the universe of 481 the *New York Times* articles on the subject.

Also coded were the issue definitions that appeared in all of the articles sampled. The relative frequency with which the various articles appeared was measured in two ways—as the percentage of articles in which the definition appears and as a definition's appearance as a percentage of all definitions in articles. Dominant issue definitions elucidate the tone of each article.

Similarly, this analysis also sampled 149 of 225 the *New York Times* opinion pieces (editorials and letters to the editor) that were found using the same databases. The appendix explains how the tone of articles and opinion pieces were measured using issue definitions. Table 5.2 below summarizes the findings for tone in the *New York Times* coverage.

Table 5-2: Summary of Media Coverage for ANWR:
Number and Tone of Articles and Opinion Pieces
Coded from the *New York Times*
(1977-1994; 1995-2003)

Years	Pro-Environ-ment Articles	Pro-Drilling Articles	Neutral/Uncodeable Articles	Mean Tone of Articles
1977-1994	44 (57.1%)	22 (28.6%)	11 / 27	4.5
1995-2003	26 (41.3%)	25 (39.7%)	12 / 62	4.3

Years	Pro-Environment Opinion Pieces	Pro-Drilling Opinion Pieces	Neutral/ Uncodeable Opinion Pieces	Mean Tone of Opinion Pieces
1977-1994	43 (71.7%)	14 (23.3%)	3 / 5	4.7
1995-2003	66 (86.8%)	10 (13.2%)	0 / 8	4.8

[Note: A mean tone of coded articles or opinion pieces above 4 indicates support for the pro-environment position. Those coded below 4 are found to support drilling. A score of 1 is the most pro-drilling and 7 is the most pro-environment. Percentages within the table are calculated based on codeable cases only.]

The table above indicates that the mean tone of both articles and opinion pieces favored the pro-environment position before and after 1995, the watershed year when party control of Congress changed. Opinion pieces favored environmental protection of ANWR more than articles did during both periods.

Interestingly, the *New York Times* news articles became less pro-environment after 1994, dropping from 57 to 41 percent of articles. At the same time, the percentage of pro-drilling articles increased from nearly 29 percent to roughly 40 percent after 1994. We can infer from these two shifts that pro-drilling forces were making inroads into the media after 1994. On the other hand, this dynamic may simply reflect that the GOP takeover in 1995 changed the policy agenda as the ANWR debate intensified. As for the tone of opinion pieces, it shifted from a pro-environment to a more intense pro-environment tone beginning in 1995, indicating that the editorial board and guest writers of the *New York Times* mostly opposed drilling on the coastal plain at ANWR.

The evidence also suggests that the print media in general were even more opposed to drilling than columnists and editors at the *New York Times*. I measured the tone of a 100 percent sample of *14 articles* that appeared in the general print media during the five years prior to change in party control of Congress (see table 5.3 that follows and the appendix for details on this sample).

Table 5.3: Summary of Media Coverage for ANWR: Number and Tone of Articles from the *Readers' Guide to Periodical Literature* (1990-1994)

Years	Pro-Environ-mental Articles	Pro-Drilling Articles	Neutral/ Uncode-able Articles	Mean Tone of Articles
1990-1994	11	1	2	5.1

[Note: A mean tone of coded articles or opinion pieces above 4 indicates support for the pro-environment position. Those coded below 4 are found to support drilling. A score of 1 is the most pro-drilling and 7 is the most pro-environment. Percentages within the table are calculated based on codeable cases only.]

In sum, tone is relatively insignificant in explaining ANWR arena change because supporters of drilling had failed in convincing writers for the elite and general print media that drilling was meritorious, especially prior to 1995. However, some evidence exists that pro-drilling forces were able to persuade more mainstream journalists (but not authors of opinion pieces) after 1994 that drilling had some merit as ANWR was put on the agenda by the GOP Congress.

Clearly, pro-environment issue definitions dominated both news articles and opinion pieces before and after Republicans won control of Congress in November 1994. The issue definition variable in media attention is weak due to the absence of a pro-drilling tone in the *New York Times* and *Readers' Guide* before 1995. The explanatory power of the LCM is weakened therefore.

Inter-coder reliability for accounts in the *Times* is estimated to be 78 percent for articles (N=9) and 80 percent for opinion pieces (N=10) since a second coder likewise measured tone. The tone of an article or opinion piece was considered reliable if coded within one point of the original measure on the scale (1-7) on the coding sheet (see Methodological Appendix).

Consider next the frequency of the top issue definitions for ANWR appearing in the *New York Times* articles.

Table 5.4: Summary of Media Coverage for ANWR: Dominant Issue Definitions for Articles Coded in *The New York Times* (1977-1994; 1995-2003)

Issue Definition: Pro-Environment	Percentage of Articles in which the Definition Appears (1977-1994; N=77)	Percentage of Articles in which the Definition Appears (1995-2003; N=63)	Definition's Appearance Once as a Percentage of all Definitions in Articles (1977-1994; N=272)	Definition's Appearance Once as a Percentage of all Definitions in Articles (1995-2003; N=142)
(Broadly defined) Pristine wilderness or "crown jewel" of the Arctic must be preserved for future generations; environmentally important/special area; protection consistent with our values	39%	32%	11%	14%
"Big oil" would benefit most from drilling	34%	11%	10%	5%
(Narrowly defined) Caribou and other species or habitats must be protected; ecosystem protection; pollution threat with drilling	65%	44%	18%	20%
Movement toward energy independence /prevent an energy crisis if drilling; replace oil supply from Prudhoe Bay	29%	17%	8%	8%
National security would be enhanced if drilling	22%	11%	6%	5%
Drilling leaves a small "footprint" on the environment; environmentally sound drilling is feasible; it's only a small	25%	24%	7%	11%

Issue Definition: Pro-Environment	Percentage of Articles in which the Definition Appears (1977-1994; N=77)	Percentage of Articles in which the Definition Appears (1995-2003; N=63)	Definition's Appearance Once as a Percentage of all Definitions in Articles (1977-1994; N=272)	Definition's Appearance Once as a Percentage of all Definitions in Articles (1995-2003; N=142)
portion of ANWR				
Drilling would create economic benefits (e.g., thousands of jobs; raises federal revenue; decreases the trade deficit; lowers gas prices); Alaskans support its economic benefits	21%	17%	6%	8%
The coastal plain has a huge oil and gas potential	43%	17%	12%	8%

[Note: Percentages within the table are calculated based on codeable cases only. Percentages are rounded. "Other" refers to issue definitions that individually appeared with less than 5% in all four frequency measures.]

Table 5.4 indicates that the environmental community was consistent over time in its support for coastal plain protection. Elite press coverage in the *New York Times* denotes that shifts in political control of the Congress and the White House did not deter environmentalists from consistently defining ANWR through the press as follows.

First, the press tended to report that the *Porcupine Caribou Herd*, along with other species and their habitats, and the entire ecosystem, deserved continued protection along the coastal plain. Second, the refuge was said to be a *pristine wilderness*. Third, and to a lesser extent, arguments against *big oil* influenced the debate, but mostly prior to 1995, perhaps because that period included the 1989 Exxon Valdez spill and its anti-big-oil aftermath. The *New York Times* articles also focused on the minimal amount of recoverable oil at ANWR after 1995 perhaps because oil prices reached a 25-year low in February 1999. This is an important point since estimates of "economically recoverable" oil increase as prices rise because oil-producing firms might spend more to extract oil and natural gas.

By contrast, it seems that advocates of drilling at ANWR attempted to redefine the issue in the press beginning in 1995. The dominant competing issue definition (i.e., among the pro-drilling community) prior to 1995 was the *huge oil and gas potential* in the area, and, to a lesser extent, ANWR's contribution to *energy independence*. The dominant definition after 1994 was the minimal impact of drilling on the environment. Perhaps the *small footprint* argument is buttressed in part by changes in technology and the ability to drill with less eco-disruption than in the past.

It is plausible to say that the pro-drilling coalition utilized the elite media to help neutralize the longstanding arguments by environmentalists that caribou and the ecosystem were in jeopardy. Apparently, they were attempting to broaden the coalition in favor of drilling by appealing to the latent masses and to labor unions.

In addition, job creation and economic development rose from the fifth to second most cited definition after 1994. Perhaps the entry of the Teamsters Union into the debate as an ally of the pro-drilling coalition helped shape the issue, since their high-profile campaign for drilling emphasized job creation. However, efforts to redefine ANWR by pro-drilling forces were insufficient counterweights to the pro-environment subsystem. The overall tone of articles during both periods favored the environmentalists' position against drilling.

Next, let us consider the dominant issue definitions in opinion pieces in table 5.5.

Table 5.5: Summary of Media Coverage for ANWR: Dominant Issue Definitions for Opinion Pieces Coded in the *New York Times* (1977-1994; 1995-2003)

Issue Definition: Pro-Environment	Percentage of Opinion Pieces in which the Definition Appears (1977-1994; N=60)	Percentage of Opinion Pieces in which the Definition Appears (1995-2003; N=76)	Definition's Appearance Once as a Percentage of all Definitions in Opinion Pieces (1977-1994; N=215)	Definition's Appearance Once as a Percentage of all Definitions in Opinion Pieces (1995-2003; N=204)
(Broadly defined) Pristine wilderness or "crown jewel" of the Arctic must be preserved for future generations; environmentally important/special area; protection consistent with our values	60%	30%	17%	11%
(Narrowly defined) Caribou and other species or habitats must be protected; ecosystem protection; pollution threat with drilling	52%	33%	14%	12%
Pro-Development				
Movement toward energy independence / prevent an energy crisis if drilling; replace oil supply from Prudhoe Bay	23%	21%	7%	8%
Drilling leaves a small "footprint" on the environment; environmentally sound drilling is feasible; it's only a small portion of ANWR	37%16%	10%6%		
The coastal plain has a huge oil and gas potential	23%	9%	7%	3%

[Note: Percentages within the table are calculated based on codeable cases only. Percentages are rounded. "Other" refers to issue definitions that individually appeared with less than 5% in all four frequency measures.]

The overall theme in both tables above indicates that the two dominant, pro-subsystem definitions were *wildlife protection* and the *pristine* nature of the refuge; they appeared consistently in both opinion pieces and articles across the two time periods emphasized in this analysis. Evidently, the pro-environment coalition was cohesive and consistent in its arguments against drilling.

As for pro-development definitions in opinion pieces, the dominant definition before 1995 was the capacity for *environmentally sound drilling*. ANWR's *huge oil potential* and the need for US *energy independence* were also emphasized, much as they were in articles during the same period. After 1994, opinion pieces emphasized the various economic benefits of drilling more than any other pro-development definition.

This finding is consistent with the findings for the *New York Times* articles during the same period relative to other pro-development definitions. Again, it appears that the increased role of the Teamsters Union in a broadened pro-drilling coalition helped to redefine drilling as *beneficial to the economy* in the press.

Finally, the top ANWR issue definitions found in the print media generally through the *Readers' Guide to Periodical Literature* are found in table 5.6.

Table 5-6 indicates that the two dominant pro-environment issue definitions in *Readers' Guide* articles before Republicans won back control of Congress were the pristine nature of the coastal plain and the need to protect wildlife. This finding is consistent with the dominant issue definitions found for articles and opinion pieces in the *New York Times*. Similarly, the general print media defined ANWR in pro-development pieces much as it did in similar pieces in the *New York Times*, that is, as having huge oil potential and that drilling would have minimal impact on the environment.

One can infer from all of this that political actors in the pro-environment ANWR subsystem chose not to shift their arguments in the media against drilling because these had been effective since the subsystem's creation in 1977. As the old adage says, "If it ain't broke, don't fix it." Conversely, drilling supporters tried to expand the scope of the conflict to broaden their coalition and therefore promote policy change since they were losing the fight.

Opinion pieces that once emphasized *environmentally sound drilling* redefined the issue in terms of its *economic benefits* and movement toward *energy independence*. Again, if one assumes that authors of opinion pieces write to gain a strategic advantage, then the more sophisticated readers of the *Times*'s editorial page might find the economic and energy independence arguments compelling and support drilling.

Table 5.6: Summary of Media Coverage for ANWR: Dominant Issue Definitions for Articles Coded in the *Readers' Guide* (1990-1994)

Issue Definition: Pro-Environment	Percentage of Articles in which the Definition Appears (1990-1994; N=12)	Definition's Appearance Once as a Percentage of all Definitions in Articles (1990-1994; N=80)
(Broadly Defined) Pristine wilderness or "crown jewel" of the Arctic must be preserved for future generations; environmentally important/special area; protection consistent with our values	67%	10%
(Narrowly Defined) Caribou and other species or habitats must be protected; ecosystem protection; pollution threat with drilling	83%	12.5%
Drilling would yield little recoverable oil; would add little energy security	50%	8%
Alaska Natives oppose drilling	58%	8.75%
Link drilling with Exxon Valdez spill	33%	5%
Alternatives to drilling are best	50%	7.5%
Pro-Development		
Movement toward energy independence/ prevent an energy crisis if drilling; replace oil supply from Prudhoe Bay	33%	5%
Drilling leaves a small "footprint" on the environment; environmentally sound drilling is feasible; it's only a small portion of ANWR	42%5%	
Drilling would create economic benefits (e.g., thousands of jobs; raises federal revenue; decreases the trade deficit; lowers gas prices); Alaskans support its economic benefits	33%	5%
Alaska Natives support drilling	33%	5%
The coastal plain has a huge oil and gas potential	58%	7.5%

[Note: Percentages within the table are calculated based on codeable cases only. Percentages are rounded. "Other" refers to issue definitions that individually appeared with less than 5% in both frequency measures.]

Redefining ANWR through Congressional Hearings

This analysis of congressional hearings identifies and measures factors that led to the weakening of the ANWR subsystem or decision-making structure and decisions to drill. It is consistent with the work of Baumgartner and Jones (1993), which hypothesized that several forces could weaken a subsystem including, a negative shift in tone (e.g., against the pro-environment position in the ANWR case), an increase in the number of congressional hearings, or an increase in the number of committees or subcommittees addressing the issue. I examine each of these underlying political forces below.

One can reasonably expect Democratic majorities in Congress to hold hearings that favored ANWR protection, despite the greater autonomy that committee and subcommittee chairs enjoyed before the Gingrich-led Congress. Likewise, Republican majorities after 1994 were likely to hold hearings that support drilling.

Thus, I hypothesize that the life cycle explanation for policy shifts is supported if major changes in the tone or definitions of ANWR occurred at hearings while the Democrats retained control of each chamber of Congress. Even if the tone of the hearings changed only with change in party control, there still might be evidence of life cycle change in other areas, as in *media coverage, public opinion,* or *entry of new subsystem actors* or competitors.

The procedures for coding the tone of congressional hearings on ANWR are more sophisticated than those used by Baumgartner and Jones (1993) in the following sense (see Methodological Appendix for a list of hearings and details of coding procedures). Those scholars coded the "title and description in the Congressional Information Service Abstracts,"[4] but this analysis of ANWR policy making codes the testimony of witnesses from hearings rather than their titles and descriptions. Titles can be misleading.

Furthermore, I examined the life cycle of ANWR according to committee activity in the House and Senate rather than grouping data from the two chambers as other scholars have done. This facilitates our understanding of the relative strength and weakness of the subsystem in each chamber of Congress.

Congressional redefinition of ANWR was found to be a significant factor in House and Senate policy making because the tone of hearings favored drilling at the coastal plain regardless of which party controlled Congress. The findings for hearings support the Life Cycle Model.

Fig. 5.2 illustrates the number and tone of House hearings held since Congress passed the pro-environment ANILCA bill in 1980, a law that doubled the size of ANWR and required the DOI to study wildlife and hydrocarbon resources along the coastal plain.

It is not surprising that the number of hearings on ANWR increased when the issue was high on the policy agenda (i.e., after the 1987 DOI study of ANWR, after the Gulf War, and during the 2000 Presidential campaign and its aftermath). This finding is consistent with Kingdon's[5] "policy windows" concept whereby an opportunity for policy change exists for a short time due to changing political events.

Figure 5.2: House Hearings on ANWR since Passage of ANILCA in 1980

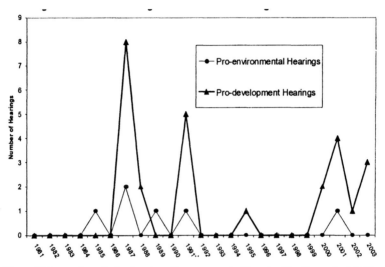

[Note: This graph excludes hearings that were coded "neutral" or "uncodeable".]

Importantly, the Democratic-controlled House of Representatives defined ANWR as a pro-drilling issue prior to a shift in party control in 1995 since most committee and subcommittee chairs invited a majority of pro-drilling witnesses to testify at hearings. This finding supports the life cycle explanation for arena change. This finding is somewhat surprising since both the literature on political parties and conventional wisdom suggest that the majority party leadership utilizes the structures of Congress to advance its party's preferences at the expense of the minority party (though divisions within the parties can sometimes sabotage legislative victories).

In the House, testimonies were coded for 124 witnesses (either pro-environment or pro-drilling) prior to the shift in partisan control of the chamber in 1995. Afterwards, 51 witnesses' testimonies were coded through 2003 (see Methodological Appendix for a list of committees and subcommittees).

The findings for Senate hearings are similar to House hearings, namely they are largely pro-drilling in tone. These findings also support the LCM due to the dominance of pro-drilling hearings during both periods: drilling was favored independently and prior to the Republican takeover in 1995 (see fig. 5.3 below).

In the Senate, testimonies were coded for 99 witnesses (either pro-environment or pro-drilling) prior to the GOP regaining control of the chamber in 1995. Also, 45 witness testimonies were coded from 1995 through 2003. Again, the total number of witnesses on each side was counted to determine the overall tone for the hearing. The subsystem is inferred to be weakened by the tone of hearings in both chambers. The data strengthen the LCM.

Figure 5.3: Senate Hearings on ANWR since Passage of ANILCA in 1980

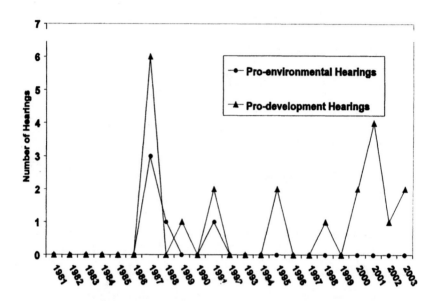

[Note: This graph excludes hearings coded "neutral" or "uncodeable".]

What may account for the pro-drilling tone at hearings in both chambers after the passage of ANILCA but prior to 1995? One possibility is that chairpersons of the relevant committees represented oil-producing states and so tended to invite pro-drilling witnesses to testify.

I found that two Democratic chairmen in the House (i.e., George Miller, CA and Gerry Studds, MA) convened over 75% of those (codeable) hearings, which overwhelmingly favored drilling. Congressman Studds was a big protector of fisheries and maritime industries so drilling issues always mattered to him, so his behavior is curious, and California has been one of the top five petroleum-producing states.[6] The hypothesis is only partially confirmed since one of two chairmen came from a top petroleum-producing state.

A staff member from Congressman George Miller's (D-CA) office who requested anonymity offered an alternative explanation for Democratic Party chairs presiding over pro-drilling hearings:

> There were a number of factors that might have tipped the numerical balance. For starters, many of the hearings were about specific industry practices and operations, so those primarily featured industry witnesses. The other factor, of course, was that in addition to the industry, both state and federal agencies supported development, meaning that hearings designed to get every position on

record would naturally feature more supporters than opponents. The bottom line is that Mr. Miller wanted to hold hearings that were scrupulously fair; like many others in Congress and across the country, though, the Exxon Valdez spill solidified my boss's opposition to opening the Arctic Refuge.[7]

The remaining four House chairpersons convened only one-quarter of the hearings on ANWR from 1981 to 1994. These hearings overwhelmingly opposed drilling, as measured by the number of pro-environment versus pro-drilling witnesses. None of those chairpersons represented a major oil-producing state, so this supports but does not confirm the hypothesis that committee and subcommittee chairs presided over pro-drilling hearings because they represented oil-rich states.

In the Senate, one Democratic chairman (J. Bennett Johnston, LA) convened nearly two-thirds of the (codeable) hearings from 1981 to 1994, which overwhelmingly favored drilling. He chaired the often pro-development Energy and Natural Resources Committee.

According to the DOE, Louisiana is one of the top five petroleum-producing states, primarily from offshore rigs. The three chairpersons who held the remaining hearings did not represent oil-rich states. The tone of those hearings was evenly divided between pro-drilling and pro-environment. The hypothesis is largely confirmed due to the behavior of Senator Johnston of Louisiana.

In this case, I also hypothesized that key members of Congress significantly affected the tone of congressional hearings through their oral and written testimonies (but not through questions) since they are perhaps more trusted or deferred to than other witnesses. I found that the tone of both committee/ subcommittee chairmen and ranking minority members was consistent with the overall tone of hearings 70 percent of the time in the House and 79 percent of the time in the Senate since 1980. In the minority of cases, the overall tone of hearings conflicted with the tone of one or both of these key committee members.

In short, both the majority and minority party leaders at hearings tended to support the pro-drilling tone that dominated hearings in both chambers. This finding, like the finding of a pro-drilling tone for non-leadership witnesses, suggests that the party in power (or at least key Democrats) supported hearings that were dominated by pro-drilling interests.

This was partly the result of seniority and self-selection of witnesses. J. Bennett Johnston is a prime example of both. The life cycle approach is supported by House and Senate hearings over time since the likelihood of ANWR drilling increased. Now consider ANWR's top issue definitions found in congressional hearings in table 5.7. These are closely related to tone as discussed above.

Table 5.7: Defining ANWR in Congressional Hearings after Passage of ANILCA (1981-2003)

Issue Definition: Pro-Environment	House Hearings: Percentage of Hearings in which the Definition Appears (1981-1994; N=20)	House Hearings: Percentage of Hearings in which the Definition Appears (1995-2003; N=12)	Senate Hearings: Percentage of Hearings in which the Definition Appears (1981-1994; N=14)	Senate Hearings: Percentage of Hearings in which the Definition Appears (1995-2003; N=12)
(Broadly Defined) Pristine wilderness or "crown jewel" of the Arctic must be preserved for future generations; environmentally important/special area; protection consistent with our values	65%	50%	71%	33%
"Big oil" would benefit most from drilling	40%	17%	43%	8%
(Narrowly Defined) Caribou and other species or habitats must be protected; ecosystem protection; pollution threat with drilling	85%	58%	86%	33%
Drilling would yield little recoverable oil; would add little energy security	25%	50%	29%	25%
Alternatives to drilling are Best	35%	50%	50%	17%
95% of North Slope is already open to development	10%	33%	71%	8%

Issue Definition: Pro-Environment	House Hearings: Percentage of Hearings in which the Definition Appears (1981-1994; N=20)	House Hearings: Percentage of Hearings in which the Definition Appears (1995-2003; N=12)	Senate Hearings: Percentage of Hearings in which the Definition Appears (1981-1994; N=14)	Senate Hearings: Percentage of Hearings in which the Definition Appears (1995-2003; N=12)
Requires a huge infrastructure; another Prudhoe Bay; would scar the land/leave large "footprint"	20%	33%	57%	17%
Pro-Development				
Movement toward energy independence/prevent an energy crisis if drilling; replace oil supply from Prudhoe Bay	75%	67%	79%	67%
National security would be enhanced if drilling	45%	58%	50%	17%
Drilling leaves a small "footprint" on the environment; environmentally sound drilling is feasible; it's only a small portion of ANWR	90%92%	100%92%		
Drilling would create economic benefits (e.g., thousands of jobs; raises federal revenue; decreases the trade deficit; lowers gas prices); Alaskans support its economic benefits	55%	67%	71%	42%

Issue Definition: Pro-Environment	House Hearings: Percentage of Hearings in which the Definition Appears (1981-1994; N=20)	House Hearings: Percentage of Hearings in which the Definition Appears (1995-2003; N=12)	Senate Hearings: Percentage of Hearings in which the Definition Appears (1981-1994; N=14)	Senate Hearings: Percentage of Hearings in which the Definition Appears (1995-2003; N=12)
Alaska Natives support drilling	20%	33%	36%	17%
The coastal plain has a huge oil and gas potential	55%	75%	86%	58%

[Note: Percentages within the table are calculated based on codeable cases only. Percentages are rounded. The "Other" refers to issue definitions that individually appeared with less than 5% in all four frequency measures.]

Table 5.7 tells us that pro-environment witnesses in House hearings consistently attempted to promote a policy image that the ANWR coastal plain must be preserved for wildlife and their habitats. Yet, beginning in 1995, these witnesses increasingly emphasized that ANWR would produce little oil and that the US should develop alternative energy sources instead.

Pro-drilling witnesses testified more frequently than environmentalists at House hearings during both periods. They consistently defined ANWR drilling as an *environmentally sound* enterprise. Yet, these actors increasingly emphasized ANWR's *huge oil potential*, its *economic* and *national security benefits, support for drilling by indigenous people*, and the *desolateness of the coastal plain* in House testimony since 1995. These shifts in definitions evidently were intended to broaden support for drilling by appealing to consumers, defense hawks, and other segments of civil society who could influence Congress.

In the Senate, pro-environment witnesses attempted to create a policy image or definition during both time periods that was similar to the one created by environmentalists in the House; namely the image of the *caribou* and other *species needing protection* from developers. Senate witnesses opposed to development also advanced the notion of ANWR being a *pristine area*, especially in hearings since 1995. On the other hand, pro-environment witnesses in the Senate placed less emphasis on the lack of recoverable oil at ANWR compared with House witnesses during the same period.

The pro-drilling witnesses that dominated Senate hearings over time defined ANWR drilling between 1981 and 1994 as an *environmentally sound* endeavor that would produce huge amounts of oil and promote American *energy independence*. After 1994, however, pro-drilling witnesses in the Senate tended to continue emphasizing environmentally responsible drilling while placing less emphasis on amounts of oil or energy independence.

Evidently, witnesses during House and Senate hearings consistently stated or implied that ANWR drilling would be environmentally sound since new technologies would leave a small "footprint" on the habitat used by caribou and other species, or that only a small portion of the refuge would be drilled. They probably had to go this route since the *Achilles heel* of the pro-drilling argument was its environmental impact.

Furthermore, since the tone of hearings in both chambers tended to favor development, it makes sense that witnesses tended to maintain pro-drilling momentum and neutralize the arguments of environmentalists who consistently argued that the Porcupine Caribou herd and the entire Arctic ecosystem would be jeopardized by drilling. Each chamber tinkered with other possible definitions at the committee and subcommittee levels, and attempted to broaden the appeal of drilling, but the debate largely centered on environmental protection versus environmentally sound drilling (see Methodological Appendix for procedures that were used to identify issue definitions in congressional hearings).

Numbers of Hearings and Jurisdictional Shifts

Next, I analyzed the number of hearings, jurisdictional shifts across committees, and their role in arena change. I counted the number of hearings held when the Democrats were a majority and compared them with the number when the GOP was the majority party in Congress.

In the House, 20 codeable hearings were held after the passage of the ANILCA law in 1980 and prior to 1995, and 12 hearings were held from 1995 to 2003. In the Senate, 14 codeable hearings were held prior to 1995 and 12 were held after the 1994 elections through 2003.

All of this supports the life cycle argument because committee and subcommittee attention to ANWR was high and favored drilling prior to a shift in party control in 1995. However, this rise in attention was not strong enough to produce policy change favoring drilling. The LCM is supported to an extent since ANWR's decision structure was weakened but not destroyed through hearings.

I also hypothesized that a shift in tone of hearings is related to a shift in venues in Congress.[8] The data show that for two reasons this factor had little to do with change in the policy arena (see Methodological Appendix).

First, pro-development hearings were the norm both prior to and after the 1994 congressional elections, so the tone of hearings did not shift in either chamber. Second, the same (or renamed) committees and subcommittees tended to hold those hearings, so venue shifts were negligible.

In the House, the first sets of hearings during the late 1970s were held in the Interior Committee (later renamed the Committee on Resources) and Merchant Marine and Fisheries Committee. It is likely that those hearings were pro-environment since the two committee chairmen reached a consensus on protecting 120 million acres of land in Alaska, an enormous amount, in March 1978. This set the stage for votes in the full House in 1978 and 1979 that designated the ANWR coastal plain "wilderness," the highest level of environmental protection possible.

Those two committees likewise held the majority of hearings on ANWR during the 1980s and afterwards, but House hearings after 1980 tended to support drilling. Even if I had studied House hearings prior to 1980, the tone of hearings would have been found to shift later within the same committees to favor drilling. In short, the introduction of new venues in the House was not a factor in ANWR arena change and the life cycle approach with its multi-faceted explanations for policy shifts is not supported by House-related data.

The Senate held no hearings on ANWR during the ANILCA era of the late 1970s and it tended to hold pro-development hearings from 1980 to 2003. Senate data on venue shifts do not support the life cycle perspective either. The ANWR subsystem that opposed drilling weakened due to reasons other than jurisdictional shifts in Congress. However, it is undeniable that Vice President Cheney's energy task force represented an alternative, non-legislative venue at which pro-development definitions of ANWR were advanced since their report called for ANWR development.

President George W. Bush and ANWR Issue Definition

What role did President George W. Bush play in redefining the ANWR issue? As detailed in the section above, I found that both the House and Senate redefined ANWR as a pro-drilling issue *prior* to the election of Presidents George W. Bush and Bill Clinton. We can hypothesize that President Bush continued to build on the arena change that was underway in Congress by increasing the issue's salience[9] and by possibly redefining the issue from one pro-drilling definition to another. So, this section tests the following hypothesis:

> President George W. Bush's leadership on ANWR helped to redefine ANWR as a pro-drilling policy.

To measure "leadership," I coded the oral and written congressional testimonies of Bush Administration officials from 2001 to 2003 and compared them with the dominant issue definitions from the pre-1995 and post-1994 periods. If the Bush Administration's primary definition of ANWR is found to differ from the definition that dominated Congress prior to 1995 (i.e., environmentally sound drilling), then perhaps President Bush attempted to shift problem salience in order to gain support for drilling.

Also, if the administration's primary or secondary definition of ANWR is found to differ from the primary definition that was advanced by the Republican majority in Congress (i.e., environmentally sound drilling), then we can surmise that the president may have attempted to sway moderate Republicans to support his definition of drilling. This action could help to gain passage of pro-drilling legislation.

As listed in the appendix, I discovered that the Bush Administration's primary definition of ANWR in the House and Senate (i.e., environmentally sound drilling) was consistent with the congressional definition prior to 1995. This is no surprise given the cohesiveness of congressional issue definition on environmental and energy issues, especially in the Bush years.

There was tremendous coordination on "talking points" on ANWR coming out of the White House. Witnesses from the Bush Administration emphasized the following issue definitions in descending order of importance: *environmentally responsible drilling*, the *huge oil potential* of the coastal plain, a *minimal amount of surface* area that would be developed, and that oil revenues from ANWR would be used to promote *energy conservation*.

House and Senate hearings stressed these definitions. In 88 percent of House hearings (N=8) and 100 percent of Senate hearings (N=4) held between 2001 and

2003, administration witnesses defined ANWR drilling as an activity that could be conducted in an environmentally sound manner, leaving a "small footprint" on the Arctic tundra. Likewise, in 63 percent of House hearings and 75 percent of Senate hearings, President Bush's representatives defined the ANWR coastal plain as having huge oil and gas potential. Administration officials also underscored using ANWR-generated revenue for energy conservation in their Senate testimony.

Apparently, the George W. Bush Administration's testimonies at congressional committee hearings reinforced a longstanding and underlying support for ANWR drilling by Congress at that level. Both chambers and President Bush tended to define ANWR drilling as an environmentally sound enterprise.

President Bush evidently was trying to shape the debate and to shore up support from a group of moderates and conservatives in both chambers of Congress. The administration's secondary definitions (e.g., the huge oil potential of the coastal plain and generation of revenue to help promote energy conservation) suggest he was also targeting lawmakers who were concerned more about diminishing oil supplies and/or energy demand.

In short, he likely aimed to provide politicians with "political cover" when facing their constituents should they decide to vote for drilling. Such issues could appeal to congressmen who represented swing congressional districts in areas such as suburban Philadelphia where Republicans are vulnerable.

Issue Redefinition for Other Environmental-Energy Policies

This chapter so far has found that Congress but not the media was an important force in redefining ANWR as a pro-drilling issue, thus helping to drive policy shifts over time. But what role has issue redefinition by the media and Congress played in other contemporary environmental-energy debates? Tables 5.8, 5.9 (see below) and subsequent analyses aim to answer this question in the cases of expanded drilling in the Eastern Gulf of Mexico (EGOM) and on public lands in the West, and in the case of proposed offshore wind farming in Massachusetts' Nantucket Sound.

First, consider the role of the media, or at least the *New York Times*, in setting the tone for each of these public policy issues as a pro-environment or pro-development (or drilling) issue. We already saw that the *Times* influences other print media and therefore can be used as something of a proxy here. Again, 1995 is the cutoff year to provide a window into activities when each party controlled Congress. I used pre-1995 and post-1995 data.

Table 5.8: Summary of Media Coverage for Eastern Gulf of Mexico Drilling, Public Lands Drilling, and Wind Power Cases: Tone of Articles and Opinion Pieces Coded from the *New York Times* (1990-1994; 2001-2007)

Case Study	Tone of Articles (1990-1994)	Tone of Opinion Pieces (1990-1994)	Tone of Articles (2001-2007)	Tone of Opinion Pieces (2001-2007)
Drilling in the Eastern Gulf of Mexico (EGOM)	Pro-drilling	N/A	Pro-drilling	Pro-drilling
Drilling on Public Lands in the West	Pro-environment	Pro-environment	Pro-environment	Pro-environment
Wind Power/ Cape Wind Project	Pro-development	N/A	Pro-development	Pro-development

Next, examine the tone of congressional hearings in defining these issues on one side of the debate or the other.

Table 5.9: Summary of Congressional Hearings for Eastern Gulf of Mexico Drilling, Public Lands Drilling, and Wind Power Cases: Tone of Hearings (1990-1994; 2001-2007)

Case Study	Tone of Hearings (1990-1994)	Tone of Hearings (2001-2007)
Drilling in the Eastern Gulf of Mexico (EGOM)	Pro-drilling	Pro-drilling
Drilling on Public Lands in the West	Pro-drilling	Pro-drilling
Wind Power/Cape Wind Project	Pro-development	Pro-development

Take each case in order. The EGOM is similar to ANWR since in both cases subsystem actors managed to prevent drilling for many years. The costs of these policies also were perceived to be narrowly imposed on energy producers and widely distributed to the public in the form of environmental protection at the coastal plain of ANWR and in the Eastern Gulf of Mexico because of the anti-drilling votes.

The Gulf of Mexico drilling issue had been a contentious one for many years. Congress has precluded drilling on most of the outer continental shelf extending 3 to 200 miles from America's coasts, except in a portion of the Gulf of Mexico.

Former Florida Governor Jeb Bush and his predecessor, Lawton Chiles, along with President Clinton, fought to keep drilling beyond the state's 100-mile mark. Ultimately, Congress approved drilling in the EGOM and President Bush signed the Gulf of Mexico Security Act in December 2006. Leases subsequently were negotiated or renegotiated through the Minerals Management Service (MMS), a part of the DOI. Perhaps the plum area for development is the "Sale 181 Area," located mostly outside the 100-mile range, a New Jersey-size tract with enormous oil potential.

On the contrary, ANWR has remained off limits to development, though its decision-making structure weakened on numerous occasions when one or both houses passed a drilling provision. Clearly, a policy shift favoring expanded Gulf drilling occurred. But what political forces underlie these changes? Were the media and Congress catalysts for redefining the EGOM as a pro-drilling issue, or not? Perhaps the existence of offshore production elsewhere in the Gulf undercut the potency of the pristine wilderness theme?

Table 5.8 shows that the elite media helped to define the EGOM as a pro-drilling issue even before the Republican Party won back control of Congress in the 1994 landslide and that this pro-drilling consensus-setting by the *New York Times* continued into the George W. Bush Administration. Supporters of drilling helped convince writers for this influential newspaper that drilling in the Eastern Gulf was a good idea, although this portion of my book does not define how this was done, and only examines the tone of media accounts for or against drilling. We can contrast this finding with the ANWR case where the media failed to generate support for drilling before and after the GOP won control of Congress in late 1994.

This raises the question, though, of why pro-environment interests manage to sway the media in protecting ANWR but not the EGOM. Perhaps the EGOM lacked emotive pro-environment symbols like the Porcupine Caribou. Public support for Gulf drilling, industry's experience in Gulf drilling, the political clout for Gulf state members, and the drilling bill's energy tax breaks provided enough impetus for Congress to support drilling (see chapter 4 for key votes).

Both the media and congressional hearings defined the EGOM as a pro-drilling issue both before and after the change in party control of Congress in 1995. There was a pro-drilling tone in Congress on both ANWR and the EGOM.

In the next case, expansion of drilling on public lands in Western states, one can plausibly argue that the perceived distributional impact of this policy resembled a traditional subsystem since energy producers tended to defeat pro-environment interests, especially in the 1990s and even more so in the 2000s.

By July 2006, the US had opened 85 percent of federal oil and gas reserves in the Rocky Mountains' five major energy basins to drilling as demand and energy costs increased. Though President Clinton increased lease sales to drill on public lands, the Bush Administration dwarfed those numbers by issuing over 7,000 drilling permits in 2005, about twice as many as President Clinton approved in 2000, and without opposition from the GOP-controlled Congress whose members tended to support such drilling.[10]

The Bureau of Land Management (BLM), part of the DOI, and the US Forest Service, an offshoot of the Agriculture Department, are the two biggest landlords in Western states, a responsibility that often puts them at odds with a region with a rich history of independence and individualism. To begin with, many Westerners resent that the national government owns about 48% of the land in the 11 westernmost states combined.[11]

The two tables above suggest that, like in the ANWR case, elite actors in Congress at congressional hearings rather than the broader media forces helped propel expansion of drilling on public lands during the Clinton and George W. Bush years. We may consider those two presidents as new actors who built on the pro-drilling tone in Congress generally.

Finally, the unique case of offshore wind power in Massachusetts pits environmentalist against environmentalist. I say *unique* because conventional wisdom suggests that environmentalists are ordinarily united. Looking closely, though, lots of evidence exists that the environmental community is *not* monolithic.

Supporters of the Cape Wind project think wind is a clean source of energy that will supply three-quarters of the Cape Cod area's electricity while lowering electric bills, creating new jobs, reducing dependence on foreign oil, and tackling global warming.[12] The print media, represented by the newspaper of record, the *New York Times*, is among these supporters of wind power and Cape Wind.

Affluent Cape residents including Senator Ted Kennedy, longtime news anchor and legend Walter Cronkite, and historian David McCullough have led the opposing coalition. This group has called for deepwater wind development instead for numerous reasons including a potential threat to birds, shipping lanes, and the Air Force's PAVE PAWS phased array radar system that aids in missile defense and space surveillance. However, the media and others generally have accused these Cape elites of the NIMBY, or not-in-my-backyard syndrome.[13]

Here I found that the Kennedy/Cronkite argument is *inconsistent* with the longstanding tone in media accounts and at congressional hearings that wind power projects should be pursued. The Congress and the elite print media have consistently defined wind power as beneficial, so affluent owners of beachfront property are facing some tough hurdles against a very well organized pro-wind coalition in their quest to retain the status quo. At any rate, both sides claim a wide distribution of environmental protection to the public. I will have more to say about how these cases relate to ANWR later.

Part II—Shift in Public Opinion

Public opinion is a second possible explanation for policy shifts (or lack of them) when using the life cycle concept. Let's first revisit the ANWR case and the role that public opinion played there and then compare those findings with other environmental-energy debates.

The life cycle approach is bolstered if public opinion opposed drilling at the Arctic "Range" when the pro-environment subsystem was created during the late 1970s.[14] More importantly, this approach provides a more potent explanation for the policy-making dynamic if public opinion later shifted against the environmentalists' view because life-cycle theorists assert that public opinion changes as the issue is redefined or supplanted by other issues on the political agenda.

These changes tend to weaken or destroy policy-making structures, in this case the ANWR subsystem. This is the so-called Schattschneider mobilization thesis. In short, this part of the book tests the following hypothesis:

Public opinion favored the environmental position prior to creation of the ANWR subsystem, but it shifted against the environmentalists' view later.

The critical juncture for measuring public opinion is 1995, just as it was in analyzing issue definitions in the media and in hearings. The power of the LCM increases if public sentiment shifts toward the pro-drilling position, especially before party control of Congress changed.

Yet, it is important to note that measurement techniques used here are not systematic. Baumgartner and Jones (1993)[15] and other scholars recognize that polling questions typically are not comparable over time and that the systematic study of policy issues can be elusive.

It is difficult to measure public opinion on a given policy issue for several reasons. First, pollsters do not necessarily pose questions regarding specific issues, say, drilling at ANWR. They might instead ask about general environmental or energy-related questions.

In addition, when pollsters ask questions about the same policy over time the questions are frequently worded differently and therefore are not necessarily comparable. Notwithstanding, Baumgartner and Jones (1993) explain how public opinion, imprecise as it is, may be used to explain the creation or destruction of policy monopolies. This analysis largely follows those guidelines.[16]

Also, many of the polls that addressed the issue of ANWR drilling are seemingly contradictory. This is a problem other scholars have encountered.[17] Combinations of pro-drilling and anti-drilling data may represent sensible public responses to different wording in different polls rather than a contradictory public.

Six nationwide polls taken by two well-regarded polling organizations in 1991 revealed apparent contradictions among the public over the future of ANWR. Three polls indicated that most Americans supported developing the ANWR or North Slope oil fields while three polls found that a majority opposed such development. Variation in question wording may have skewed the results.

A review of these polls since 1995 was taken with eight reputable news or polling organizations (i.e., in one case a bipartisan group conducted the polling) that conducted at least 11 polls between 1995 and 2005. In 9 out of 11 polls, the American public opposed drilling at ANWR.[18] The Gallup Organization, CBS News/the *New York Times*, Zogby International, and *Newsweek* are several of the organizations that collected these data.

Although question wording varied across these 11 polls, a majority of Americans opposed development of the ANWR coastal plain in nine cases. In short, I found that this explanation in the life cycle framework does not appear to explain subsystem change prior to or since 1995.

In March 1991, a Roper Center poll found that when asked to choose between developing oil in the ANWR or increasing imports of foreign oil, 50 percent of Americans chose developing the ANWR while 35 percent chose increasing imports. Another poll taken by Roper that same month revealed that a majority (61 percent) of Americans felt that we could both permit energy development at ANWR and protect it from environmental damage. Similarly, a third Roper poll in March 1991 found that three-quarters of Americans believed that "it is possible to explore, produce, and transport oil and gas" in coastal waters and the Arctic North Slope of Alaska "in an environmentally safe manner." Different wording in the three poll questions may account for the varied support for drilling in the same month.

At the same time, three other polls taken in 1991 showed public opposition to drilling at ANWR. This evidence ostensibly contradicts data above that the public supported drilling. Two 1991 Roper polls indirectly bolstered public opposition to ANWR development since they found that a majority of Americans generally opposed "developing oil and natural gas reserves in publicly owned wilderness areas." A poll taken by Environmental Opinion Study Inc. likewise found that a majority of Americans opposed drilling at ANWR because "it is one of the nation's great wilderness areas," despite possibly helping to "reduce our dependence on foreign sources and help hold down the price of energy."

Intuitively, these data suggest that by 1991 it was unlikely that a new pro-drilling policy monopoly would supplant the pro-environment subsystem since no "wave of popular enthusiasm"[19] was present to facilitate construction of a new pro-drilling decision structure. However, it is plausible to argue that enough criticism of the status quo policy was present when the drilling issue emerged after the Persian Gulf War that dilution of support for the existing subsystem was possible.

It is also worth noting that these findings are consistent with the argument that public opinion often reflects media coverage. Since the media can influence the public (or vice versa), there tends to be a positive correlation between the two.

The evidence is twofold. As discussed, media coverage in both the *New York Times* and the *Readers' Guide to Periodical Literature* mostly remained pro-environment throughout the entire period studied. Here, public opinion is also consistently pro-environment after 1995 and at least neutral prior to that.

Next, consider the importance of polling data on ANWR after the GOP sweep in the 1994 congressional elections. Again, if the life cycle approach is confirmed then we expect public support for protecting the coastal plain to drop sometime after passage of the ANILCA law in 1980. The model would be stronger if public opinion was found to shift before 1995, but a later shift also would bolster the LCM.

However, most polls taken by major polling organizations or media firms do not support the LCM since the public tended to oppose drilling. Why? GOP efforts to push the issue may have galvanized public opposition to drilling. Polls taken by other organizations were excluded here due to their potential bias either for or against drilling (e.g., The Mellman Group, Arctic Power, and the Wilderness Society). This admittedly quasi-scientific approach suggests that it is unlikely that public sentiment shifted against environmental protection, which we expect to find if the LCM is valid. In all, the public opinion explanation for ANWR policy shifts is unconvincing since no new wave of popular support for drilling was present.

Public Opinion and Other Environmental-Energy Policies

Results from the ANWR case study, this book's primary focus, arguably undermine the standard argument by life-cycle theorists that shifts in public opinion are critical to changing policy-making structures and outcomes. The ANWR decision structure and resultant policy shifted toward a pro-drilling position on numerous votes since 1995 (see chapter 5), despite the absence of public support. On the other hand, drilling did not become law probably because the critical forces of public opinion and media issue definition opposed it, so these forces matter, those theorists might counter.

What role did public opinion play in other cases of environmental-energy policies examined in this book? Table 5.10 below elucidates this political force and its role in policy change.

Table 5.10: Summary of Polling Data for Eastern Gulf of Mexico Drilling, Public Lands Drilling, and Wind Power Cases (1990-1994; 2001-2007)

Case Study	Sample of Polls (1990-1994)	Sample of Polls (2001-2007)
Drilling in the Eastern Gulf of Mexico (EGOM)	Pro-environment	Pro-drilling
Drilling on Public Lands in the West	Pro-development	Pro-environment
Wind Power/ Cape Wind Project	Pro-development	Pro-development

Consider each case in order. Although the EGOM and ANWR cases had pro-environment outcomes initially, a pro-Gulf drilling bill became law with the aid of a shift in public support, while in the ANWR case drilling failed as the public continued to oppose it.

We can infer from these findings that broad-based political forces in the media and the public helped to tip congressional support for drilling for oil and gas in the Eastern Gulf of Mexico by 2006. These two factors bolster the life-cycle argument in this case.

The next case, the so-called "war for the West," as we saw, is most like ANWR when it comes to its lack of support for drilling in media accounts coupled with support for drilling in congressional hearings. However, ANWR drilling may have failed to become law, in part, due to the lack of public support for drilling.

Table 5.10 on the one hand indicates that drilling in the Gulf also lacked public support since 2001, yet drilling on public lands expanded dramatically. Why? Perhaps President Clinton's expansion of drilling with public support helped set the stage for further expansion under President Bush's tenure. Both of these actors were able to utilize the *low saliency* administrative apparatus in the BLM and promote domestic hydrocarbon development to varying degrees, notwithstanding President Clinton's record of protecting public lands from development.

The story of the Cape Wind project in Nantucket Sound is a simple one when it comes to the life-cycle explanation of forces driving decision making. Tables 5.8, 5.9, 5.10 show that the media, Congress, and the public have consistently defined wind power and the Cape Wind project as a pro-development issue. The data fly in the face of the Kennedy clan and some environmentalists who were concerned about the scope of the wind farm, the size of the turbines, and the location.

Part III—New Interests/Subsystem Actors

Life-cycle scholars have found that the entry of new or latent governmental or non-governmental actors can have a weakening effect on subsystems. This result may be achieved through administrative action or a shift in supporters of a policy coalition. In either case, these actors sometimes try to redefine the issue to gain support for their particular policy stance.

In my core case, ANWR, I hypothesize that the following three political actors increased their presence at congressional hearings or at other venues and necessarily challenged the dominance of subsystem actors: the Teamsters Union, Arctic Power, and the National Energy Policy Development Group (NEPDG) headed by Vice President Cheney. Each of these actors was identified in more detail in chapter 3. In short, this section tests the hypothesis that was first stated in chapter 1:

> The weakening of the ANWR subsystem and policy decisions in favor of drilling are associated with pro-drilling Executive Branch agencies and interest groups formerly not involved in the issue.

If the data support the LCM, we should find that a federal agency or interest group served as a catalyst for ANWR arena change by expanding the scope of the debate (see Schattschneider 1960). Generally, this book aims to identify the role of these actors in the policy-making process and whether they were critical in advancing drilling.

Specifically, we must find that representatives from the Teamsters Union or Arctic Power favored drilling and testified at hearings more frequently when pro-drilling legislation passed one or both chambers of Congress (e.g., in 1995, 2000, 2001, 2003, etc.). I wondered not only whether new actors were mobilizing their constituencies and shaping public discourse, but also whether they tried to impact Congress's views at the committee or subcommittee level.

First, consider the role of the pro-development interest group, Arctic Power. This group was established in 1992 after pro-drilling forces had failed to break a Senate filibuster on an energy bill in 1991. It is a single-issue advocacy group devoted to persuading Congress to open the coastal plain of ANWR to hydrocarbon development. Like pro-environment organizations, this pro-development organization seems to have found its policy niche.[20] Major oil companies funded it originally (and still provide the bulk of its funding), but Arctic Power quickly gained financial support from the Alaska State Legislature, and it has continued to find support from the Alaska congressional delegation.

Jamie Clark is former Director of the USFWS during the Clinton Administration. She noted that Arctic Power had a "great cheerleader" in the "triumvirate" of Alaska Congressman Don Young and Senators Ted Stevens and Frank Murkowski during the 1990s, and that Arctic Power now has more supporters in Congress.[21]

Arctic Power vowed to maintain a presence in the Congress even during periods when ANWR drilling was not on the congressional agenda, an example of what Bosso calls "presence politics."[22] As pro-drilling legislation arose on the congressional agenda, Arctic Power mobilized support from union workers and other members to lobby lawmakers from swing congressional districts and states. Drilling at ANWR would create thousands of jobs in the oil industry and related industries, they argued.

Alaskan Becky Gay, who was instrumental in founding Arctic Power, said that the organization "did help centralize efforts among many groups, and served to focus those efforts more effectively as resources diminished.[23] In short, Arctic Power has contributed to the ANWR policy-making process by keeping hopes for drilling alive in Congress since the end of the Persian Gulf War in 1991.

The International Brotherhood of Teamsters was another pro-drilling actor, although a less elitist one, that entered the ANWR arena during the 1990s and maintained its presence on Capitol Hill. Adam Kolton of the National Wildlife Federation claimed that the Teamsters and Arctic Power were part of a "huge industry coalition" supporting drilling at the coastal plain of ANWR.[24]

Historically, the Teamsters Union has tended to favor both Republicans and energy development since the Kennedy Administration "went after [Teamsters President Jimmy] Hoffa."[25] However, the union was not seen as an impetus for drilling until after the 1995 budget reconciliation debate as Alice Rivlin, President Clinton's former OMB Director noted in 2002.[26]

This union became an important actor by 2001 and helped to push for passage of the pro-drilling energy bill (HR 4) in the US House of Representatives that year by sending the union's energy lobbyist, Gerry Hood, to meet with Bush Administration officials and Members of Congress. Interestingly, Hood left his position with the Teamsters to establish his own lobbying firm in Washington, DC, Gerald Hood & Associates, in 2005. He continues to lobby on energy and transportation issues in a small office formerly occupied by Arctic Power.[27]

Representatives from both the Teamsters Union and Arctic Power testified on five occasions in three of four years (i.e. 1995, 2000, and 2001) when pro-drilling legislation passed in at least one chamber in Congress. These interest groups did not testify in 2003 or in years when drilling bills failed or were not considered in Congress. Importantly, these two actors may be characterized as economic interest groups that seek monetary benefits for their membership, and, importantly, have the capacity to mobilize constituencies who could influence Members of Congress. Necessarily, they have tended to define ANWR development as fostering job creation and economic development.

Evidently, their entry into ANWR debates in Congress helped to redefine this issue in Congress, as we saw previously. The new actors increased the *salience* of drilling. Their impact apparently was greater on Congress than in the elite print media since the media continued defining ANWR as a pro-environment issue while Congress voted on several occasions to develop the coastal plain. It appears that the *new actors* variable in the LCM is partially confirmed. In short, participation of these two interest groups in a broadened pro-drilling coalition after 1994 is a necessary but insufficient condition for ANWR arena change to drill.

The Vice President's inter-agency energy task force, or National Energy Policy Development Group (NEPDG), was a new government actor on the scene in 2001 that entered the political arena to formulate and propose recommendations for a national energy policy. It opposed the anti-drilling policies of the ANWR subsystem. I hypothesized that the task force built upon the pro-drilling momentum that had already been created prior to the Bush era: that is, if the NEPDG were found to hold hearings outside congressional jurisdiction then this likely would strengthen momentum for drilling. This factor is potentially important according to scholars:

> Dramatic changes in policy outcomes are often the result of changes in the institutions that exert control.[28]

According to Karen Knutson, Deputy Assistant to the Vice President (Cheney) for Domestic Policy, a DOE employee who worked on the task force in 2001 and 2002, the NEPDG met 12 times in Washington, DC, between January and July 2001. President Bush appointed a variety of federal officers including the Vice President, Secretary of the Treasury, DOI Secretary, Secretary of Agriculture, Secretary of Commerce, Secretary of Transportation, DOE Secretary, FEMA Director, EPA Director, Assistant to the President and Deputy Chief of Staff, Assistant to the President for Economic Policy, and the Assistant to the President for Intergovernmental Affairs.[29]

The composition of this task force undoubtedly enabled the Executive Branch to exert influence on Congress as it debated the merits of drilling at ANWR. News accounts reported that Congress incorporated the NEPDG's recommendations from May 2001 into an energy bill.

In addition, the head of the NEPDG, Andrew Lundquist, a Capitol Hill veteran staff member, stated that he worked with members of the House of Representatives in 2001 as Congressman John Sununu (R-NH) utilized his idea to define ANWR drilling as a policy that would limit the "footprint" on the tundra to 2000 acres.[30] The House soon afterward approved drilling at ANWR as part of a broader energy bill in 2001.

Clearly, the reach of President Bush and Vice President Cheney influenced Capitol Hill, and perhaps the public through the NEPDG. In short, the NEPDG entered the ANWR policy-making arena in 2001, confirmed and clarified Congress' existing definition of drilling (i.e., environmentally sound), thereby expanding the scope of the energy debate as Congress adopted its drilling proposal. The "new actors" variable in the Life Cycle Model is supported therefore.

New Actors and Other Environmental-Energy Policies

This book provides hard, empirical data to help analyze policy and subsystem shifts for four environmental-energy policies, and it includes congressional hearings data on the pro-drilling effects of three new actors on ANWR policy decisions as we saw. Yet, the following section is admittedly more speculative in examining whether entry of new decision makers affected policy outcomes for drilling in the Eastern Gulf of Mexico and on Western public lands, and whether new actors influenced decisions on the proposed 420-megawatt offshore wind farm in Nantucket Sound.

According to chapter 1 for the data to support the life cycle approach we should find that a federal agency, interest group(s), or political entrepreneur served as a catalyst for arena change by expanding the scope of the debate. I posit from media accounts that the "new actors" explanation for policy arena change was important in the cases of expanded drilling on Western public lands and the Cape Wind project, and less important in EGOM drilling.

Since the BLM controls roughly one-eighth of all land in the United States, and since the President of the United States appoints the BLM chief, which is a critical position in terms of selling leases for oil and gas development, it is plausible to argue that Presidents Clinton and Bush were key administrative actors in recent expansion of drilling on those lands. The progressive web site <CommonDreams.org> notes that

> during the Clinton years, oil and gas leasing increased considerably over previous administrations.

But areas considered wilderness and areas near national parks were usually off-limits.[31]

An example of expanded leasing during the Clinton years occurred in 1998. Then DOI Secretary Bruce Babbitt opened 4 million acres of the NPR-A in Alaska to drilling, roughly 87 percent of the reserve's northeast sector. However, over one-half million acres were off limits since they were considered critical wetlands habitat.[32]

Perhaps President Clinton's expansion of drilling during an era of public support helped set the stage for further expansion under President Bush's tenure. Both of these actors were able to manipulate the machinery of *administrative* lawmaking to their advantage. The Clinton Administration tended to balance its agenda more, however, to the dismay of many hard core environmental activists.

In the case of Cape Wind, it seems likely that support by key environmental interest groups and political entrepreneurs in Congress has helped build momentum for the project. Greenpeace, the Sierra Club, the Union of Concerned Scientists and the Natural Resources Defense Council all support the wind farm proposal.

Likewise, Senators Bingaman (D-NM) and Domenici (R-NM) of the Natural Resources Committee used their influence to kill an amendment in 2006 that would have given then Massachusetts Governor Mitt Romney veto power over the proposal. This plan has so far survived five years of regulatory scrutiny at the state and federal levels.[33]

The Eastern Gulf of Mexico case and its pro-drilling outcome seem less influenced by the entry of new actors into the subsystem because the issue had a pro-drilling tone in the media, in congressional hearings, and among the public largely before and after party change in Congress in 1995. This seemed to be a potent combination with high demand for gasoline and natural gas and increasing prices at the pump.

Summarizing the Life Cycle Model

This analysis finds that the life-cycle approach offers a partial explanation for ANWR arena change or lack of it in both chambers of Congress since the passage of the ANILCA law in 1980. That law doubled the size of the refuge and required congressional approval for drilling.

Two of the three major political explanations that comprise the LCM were confirmed or partly confirmed—namely issue redefinition in congressional hearings (but not in the media) and the entry of new actors that competed with and undermined the ANWR subsystem. The public opinion variable was not confirmed. The results are mixed, therefore, in this case study.

Naturally, I devoted much of the discussion above to the issue redefinition variable since earlier scholarship said it represents the heart of the life cycle understanding of public policies. The congressional hearings show that the issue was being redefined in Congress prior to the GOP takeover, but the evidence from the mass media shows no major shift from defining the issue as environmental protection and in favor of drilling.

Specifically, I partly confirmed the redefinition explanation since the number and tone of congressional hearings redefined ANWR as a pro-development issue in the House and Senate from 1987 through 2003, but beginning before 1995. Despite some shifts in the policy image, ANWR was not redefined in the elite or general print media because the *New York Times* and publications in the *Readers' Guide to Periodical Literature* continued to define ANWR as a pro-environment issue in the tone of its articles and opinion pieces before and after 1995.

The second explanatory variable confirmed in the ANWR case is the entry of new actors that challenged subsystem decision makers and expanded the pro-drilling coalition. The Teamsters Union and the pro-industry group, Arctic Power, influenced ANWR policy decisions as they testified in favor of drilling in three out of four years (1995, 2000, and 2001) when pro-drilling legislation passed in at least one chamber of Congress, but not in 2003. Similarly, Vice President Cheney's NEPDG and President George W. Bush built upon the pro-drilling momentum in Congress that had already begun prior to their arrival on Pennsylvania Avenue.

Third, public opinion as a political force for change was not confirmed since there was no clear shift in American public opinion supporting drilling at the ANWR coastal plain. It is not surprising that public opinion and media attention were both found to be weak explanations for ANWR policy decisions because there tends to be a correlation between public opinion and media coverage. Neither favored drilling at ANWR in this case.

In addition, some of the data support lesser factors in the LCM in the refuge case. The large number of pro-development hearings held in both chambers of Congress supports the life-cycle argument since congressional attention to ANWR was high, even prior to 1995 when Democrats were in charge. The data also support the LCM because committee and subcommittee chairmen in both chambers of Congress tended to define ANWR as a pro-development issue. However, the absence of shifts in committees holding hearings on ANWR does not support the life-cycle explanation.

In the supplemental case studies on expanded drilling on public lands and in the Eastern Gulf of Mexico, and the wind power case, the findings are as follows. The EGOM case largely bolsters the life-cycle explanation for a shift in policy favoring drilling since the media, public opinion, and issue definition in congressional hearings drove policy change—the more the merrier, as it were. However, entry of new actors into the decision-making process was unlikely to have shifted the debate.

The public lands drilling case shows that *gatekeeping elites* were more important in policy shifts than the broad-based forces of the media and public opinion. Elites in Congress helped define the issue as a pro-drilling one in congressional hearings and through the Clinton Presidency and its BLM appointees. However, media accounts were largely pro-environment. Public support for drilling may have provided President Clinton with political cover for issuing more drilling leases on public lands, but President Bush built on that momentum. This action may have simply reflected his priorities and a calculation that most Americans cared little about Western BLM lands.

Current evidence suggests that the Cape Wind project will likely be approved since all of the life-cycle variables are supportive. The issue has been defined as a pro-development one in the press and in Congress, and public support has followed a similar tone during the latest energy crisis. The high profile of the lynchpin pro-environment interest groups in recent years evidently has likewise bolstered chances for success.

These findings along with the importance of partisan voting on ANWR (see chapter 4) suggest that the ANWR policy-making process is highly complex. I found that the data support two factors in the LCM. Issue redefinition in congressional hearings helps to explain the weakening of the subsystem before 1995 (although partisan voting with Democratic majorities prevented subsystem collapse). I also found that entry of new pro-drilling actors since the 1990s coupled with partisan Republican majorities in Congress helps to explain ANWR arena change in recent years.

After testing the life-cycle framework in the ANWR case, it is clear that elites in Washington, DC, greatly influenced the decision-making process in this case because lawmakers in Washington, DC (including those from Alaska), the president, and oil companies advanced drilling rather than broad-based political influences. That is, given that Congress and President Bush very nearly approved ANWR drilling in 2005, these policy shifts occurred without changes in media attention or public opinion. Elite influences seemed strong, but perhaps broader forces in the media and public suggest how important it is to have these players on either side of a policy coalition. The concluding chapter tries to make sense of all of this by identifying patterns of decision making and their implications for environmental-energy policy making in general.

Notes

1. Benjamin I. Page, *Who Deliberates? Mass Media in Modern Democracy* (Chicago: The University of Chicago Press, 1996), 11-12.

2. Sonja Moore Siler, "Who Deliberates Better? A Comparative Analysis of Media Content During the 2000 US Presidential Election" (dissertation submitted to Temple University, Philadelphia, PA, January 2004), 80.

3. Frank R. Baumgartner and Bryan D. Jones, *Agendas and Instability in American Politics* (Chicago: The University of Chicago Press, 1993), 50,89-90.

4. Baumgartner and Jones, *Agendas*, 204.

5. John W. Kingdon, *Agendas, Alternatives, and Public Policies*, 2d ed. (New York: Harper Collins College Publishers, 1995), 166.

6. The Energy Information Administration at the US Department of Energy <www.eia.gov> is the source for this discussion concerning energy-producing states (27 April 2005).

7. Interview conducted on 11 May 2005.

8. Baumgartner and Jones, *Agendas*, 206.

9. This term represents the "degree to which people are aware of a problem and care about it." See Gary Mucciaroni, "Problem Definition and Special Interest Politics in Tax Policy and Agriculture," in *The Politics of Problem Definition*, ed. David A. Rochefort and Roger W. Cobb (Lawrence, KS: University of Kansas Press, 1994), 120.

10. Juliet Eilperin, "Growing Coalition Opposes Drilling; In NM Battle, Hunters Team with Environmentalists," *Washington Post*, 25 July 2006, 01(A).

11. Tom Kenworthy, "In War Over the West, Industry Gets an Edge," *USA Today*, 14 June 2002, 17(A).

12. <www.capewind.org> accessed 12 July 2007.

13. "Cape Wind Flies in Under the Radar," <www.renewableenergy access.com>accessed 21 June 2007; Mary Wiltenburg, "Who's Got the Power," *Christian Science Monitor*, 28 August 2003, 11.

14. Finding such data would be consistent with Downs' (1972) proposition that public interest peaks concerning an issue as its policy is institutionalized (see Baumgartner and Jones, *Agendas*, 86,87).

15. Baumgartner and Jones, *Agendas*, 53.

16. They note that issue definition determines positive or negative public images of an issue. Second, image is closely related to perceptions rather than facts. Third, public attitudes may be contradictory on a given subject. Fourth, media coverage appears to be the critical link in the process of publics shifting their attention from one group of consequences to another. Fifth, for technical issues, increases in media coverage, either positive or negative, tend to lead to decreases in public support for policies. Sixth, it only takes a short-term spurt of public attention to an issue to leave an institutional legacy (Baumgartner and Jones, *Agendas*, 61,87).

17. Baumgartner and Jones, *Agendas*, 61.

18. The nine pro-ANWR-protection polls were taken by: the Roper Center (September 1995, January 2001); CBS/*New York Times* (March 2001); the Gallup Organization (November 2001, April 2002); *Newsweek* (November 2002); CBS News (November 2002); Zogby International (December 2004); and, the bipartisan team of Bellweather Research & Lake, Snell, Perry and Associates (January 2005). The two pro-drilling polls taken after 1994 were administered by the *Los Angeles Times* (February 2003); and the Fox News Channel/Opinion Dynamics (April 2004).

19. Baumgartner and Jones, *Agendas*, 84.

20. Christopher J. Bosso, *Environment, Inc. From Grassroots to Beltway* (Lawrence, KS: University of Kansas Press, 2005), 123.

21. Telephone interview with USFWS Director Jamie Rappaport Clark, Ret., 2 January 2003.

22. Christopher J. Bosso, *Pesticides and Politics: The Life Cycle of a Public Issue* (Pittsburgh: University of Pittsburgh Press, 1987), 257.

23. Telephone interview with Becky Gay, 12/20/02

24. Telephone interview with Adam Kolton, National Wildlife Federation (formerly with Alaska Wilderness League), 12 September 2002.

25. Telephone interview with Jack Hession, Sierra Club, 12 November 2002.

26. Telephone interview with OMB Director Alice Rivlin, Ret., 20 December 2003.

27. Seth Linden, "Hood Takes New Role in Nation's Capital," NBC News, <http://www.ktuu.com/CMS/templates/master.asp?articleid=11441&zoneid=4> (2 Feb. 2005).

28. Baumgartner and Jones, *Agendas*, 33.

29. *Judicial Watch v. National Energy Policy Development Group and Sierra Club v. VicePresident Richard B. Cheney*, United States District Court for the District of Columbia, Declaration by Karen Y. Knutson, Deputy Assistant to the Vice President for Domestic Policy, 3 September 2002.

30.   Telephone interview with Andrew Lundquist, The Lundquist Group (formerly with the George W. Bush Administration), 6 January 2003.

31.   Timothy Egan, "Bush Administration Allows Oil Drilling Near Utah Parks," <www.commondreams.org/cgi-bin/print.cgi?file=headlines02/0208-03.htm> (8 Feb. 2002).

32.   Felicity Barringer, "Bush's Record: New Priorities in Environment," *The New York Times*, 14 September 2004, 1(A).

33.   "Saving the Cape Wind Project," *Washington Times* editorial, 5 July 2006, 16(A).

Chapter 6
Patterns of Decisions Across the
Environmental-Energy Divide

> The more you read and observe about this politics thing, you got
> to admit that each party is worse than the other. The one that's
> out always looks the best.—Will Rogers

On August 2, 2007, the US House of Representatives erupted in chaos as
Democrats and Republicans bickered over a procedural vote on illegal immigration.
This led to name calling on both sides as Republicans walked out of the chamber
without voting, accusing the Democratic majority of maneuvering to reverse an
unfavorable outcome for their party.[1]

These actions symbolize the discord that has increasingly permeated Congress
since the early 1980s on issues ranging from immigration to environmental
protection and energy development. At another level, symbols have been used by
both parties to make emotive appeals and therefore define policies such as ANWR.

While this book speaks to the usefulness of policy-making models in studying
subsystem and policy change, we also know that public policies by definition are
supposed to serve the interests of the citizenry. We can ask, therefore, whether the
evolution of ANWR as a policy issue has served the masses in a tangible way since
1977, or whether it has been more of a symbolic issue (see Edelman 1995), caught
up in increasingly partisan politics in Washington.

I found evidence that actors on both sides of the issue have defined ANWR
symbolically and have tried to maintain or broaden their respective decision-
making structures. The debate largely centered on environmental protection versus
environmentally sound drilling (see chapter 5). Pro-environment witnesses at
hearings in both chambers of Congress consistently advanced the policy images of
the Porcupine Caribou Herd (which are not listed as endangered species) and the
coastal plain as a pristine wilderness or the "crown jewel" of wildlife sanctuaries.

Similarly, pro-drilling witnesses also defined ANWR symbolically in the House and Senate. Drilling, they argued, would leave a small "footprint" on the habitat used by Porcupine Caribou and other species. Or, they insisted that only a small portion of the refuge would be drilled. We can conclude that the House and Senate, despite their different procedures, treated ANWR symbolically and as a pro-drilling issue at committee hearings based on hard data.

But has this use of symbols on both sides of the ANWR debate served the public, or not? According to James Anderson,

> The material-symbolic typology is especially useful to keep in mind when analyzing effects of policy because it directs our attention beyond formal policy statements. It also alerts us to the symbol's important role in political behavior.[2]

Apparently the anti-drilling policy at the coastal plain has appealed to many Americans' personal values since passage of ANILCA in 1980. But the tangible benefits of this policy are difficult to define. It could be argued, for instance, that most citizens will never travel to ANWR in their lifetimes and therefore not receive benefits. Yet, protection of ANWR's pristine beauty probably affords some benefits to the national community as a whole.

Pro-drilling forces have touted the economic benefits of drilling in recent years, but they too have depended largely on symbols (e.g., a small "footprint" in the tundra and the goal of "energy independence"). The evidence therefore suggests that ANWR has been a largely symbolic issue since 1980: neither coalition has delivered substantive benefits to the public. The *1002 Area* is neither *wilderness* nor has it been drilled.

While both coalitions have maintained a presence in Washington DC (see Bosso 1987), Arctic Power, which has played a leading role in representing energy interests on Capitol Hill, has adopted a somewhat lower profile in recent years. In part, this is because there seems to be less confidence that a huge amount of economically recoverable oil will be found on the expensive-to-drill coastal plain.

Roger Herrera and others in the oil industry critique this argument by asserting energy interests have taken a lower profile on ANWR in recent years to avoid bad publicity, and that energy companies of various sizes would bid on leases for drilling once offered by the BLM. However, oil prices may continue to soar and make drilling more appealing and returns higher. The price of crude oil reached an all-time high of $80 per barrel in September 2007, for instance.

In short, both the environmental movement and the energy industry have maintained a presence in Washington, DC, and have used that presence to engage in symbolic politics in the ANWR debate. Failure to offer symbols might weaken their respective positions of influence on ANWR and other contentious policy issues.

The other case study with parallel impacts is drilling in the Eastern Gulf of Mexico (EGOM). Drilling has been conducted in vast areas of both Alaska and the Gulf of Mexico, yet narrow pieces of land (or water) have been off limits for years in both places. Then, why was drilling approved for the EGOM's contentious *181 Area* in 2006 but not in ANWR's *1002 Area*? This question piqued my interest. Perhaps the chief reason for this variation in policy outcomes is the lack of symbols in the EGOM case that might have been used to mobilize opposition to drilling. There aren't any caribou or especially pristine areas deep beneath the Gulf of Mexico, one might argue. Yet, other factors may have been in play driving environmental-energy policy decisions, as we shall see momentarily.

The fact is that symbols matter in politics as they help political entrepreneurs and others to define policy issues. Whether it is President Bush standing at ground zero after 911 with a huge flag draped from a building in the background representing his *war on terror*, or whether it is a collapsed bridge in Minneapolis defining America's inattention to its infrastructure, symbols help set political agendas in Washington, DC. They can cause issues to ebb and flow on or off the policy agenda just as the 1989 Exxon Valdez spill helped to delay a vote on ANWR drilling for six years. This raises all sorts of questions. What is the relationship between symbols and good public policy, for instance? Does the use of symbols detract from or contribute to sound public policy?

Summary of Approach, Findings, and their Implications

The aim of this book has been to answer two questions. First, what political and societal forces have shaped modern, contentious, environmental-energy debates in the US? While I have focused on the case of ANWR, I have extended the inquiry to other debates to see if broader explanatory patterns are present. Second, what do the findings reveal about the perceived distributional impacts of the way in which environmental-energy policies are made, about our institutions of government, and about the influences of the public versus elites in making policy?

I have described the policy evolution of the Arctic National Wildlife Refuge and three other contemporary environmental-energy policies using three approaches that generally have lacked emphasis from students in this branch of political science. My explanations are based on partisan voting and roll calls in Congress; the *life-cycle* forces including issue definition, public opinion, new actors, and media attention to issues; and, my own variant of policy subsystems that is based on pro-environment distributional impacts (i.e., policies' perceived costs and benefits favoring the environment rather than industry).

My key findings are summarized here.

1) Partisan voting in Congress has been a necessary (but insufficient) condition for policy shifts for ANWR since 1980, a case involving the regular use of symbols to define the issue for or against drilling; but partisanship in floor voting is less important in explaining outcomes for drilling in the EGOM, on Western public lands, and in the Massachusetts wind farm case where symbols were used less. We can learn some lessons or draw inferences from the data collected in these four cases. Let us focus on the core case, ANWR. Bipartisanship ended with passage of the Alaska lands bill in 1980, a law that protected some lands prior to distributing others to the state and to indigenous peoples. The rise in partisanship on this issue may have had more to do with institutional changes and broader forces in American politics rather than with policy content.

The broad challenge for scholars is how to construct systematic means to measure the relationship between partisan voting and policy outcomes.[3] Various explanations exist for the increased partisanship in Congress including greater influence of ideological constituencies, Democratic organization of Congress before 1995 (e.g., providing agenda-setting tools for a strong Speaker), regional divisions, and the ascent of disciplined parties. We can plausibly explain the rise of partisan voting for ANWR based on some of these larger political forces.

Bipartisan voting transpired on ANWR and environmental measures generally through the 1970s when Congress passed the National Environmental Policy Act, the Clean Air Act, the Endangered Species Act, the Surface Mining Control and Reclamation Act, and ANILCA. At the same time, this was a period of congressional reorganization leading to fragmented party power. Reforms empowered junior Members of Congress, staff, subcommittees, and interest groups at the same time that party influence waned in roll-call voting and other areas of the legislative process.

Broader political forces reacted against these institutional reforms and increased partisanship in Congress. The shift to divided government in 1980 likely contributed to congressional partisanship since lawmakers in the Democratic-controlled House viewed President Ronald Reagan as a divisive figure. Furthermore, the Democratic Party was fighting for its political life as the Republican Party also regained control of the Senate in 1980. These electoral forces seemed to have fostered increased partisan voting in Congress. Evidently ANWR became part of a larger political battle in environmental politics described by Rosenbaum (2002):

> The floodtide of environmental legislation originating in Washington, DC, during the 1970s was, in large part, the result of a broad, bipartisan environmental coalition in both chambers that strongly supported innovative environmental programs proposed or accepted by both Republican and Democratic presidents. The political climate for environmentalists darkened markedly with Reagan's election and has remained unsettled ever since. Even when the Republicans enjoyed a brief, tenuous Senate majority from 1980 through 1984, Democrats

controlling the major House environmental committees mounted a fierce campaign of investigations, budget reviews, and other forays against important Republicans in environmentally sensitive positions; this threw the Republicans on the defensive and turned much of the media and public opinion against Reagan's most ambitious attempts at regulatory relief. [By the same token, Reagan-Bush era appointees to the EPA, DOI and OMB helped promote inter-party divisions by] obstruct[ing] and revis[ing] many environmental regulations.[4]

Other scholars have found that environmental politics (and American politics as a whole) generally have remained polarized since the 1980s, especially since 1996 on environmental issues.[5]

In addition, partisanship likely increased because party leaders in the congressional duopoly wanted to regain influence over their members. Party leaders could protect Members of Congress from external electoral threats and offer them more influence over the agenda and other benefits. Lawmakers evidently went along with this strategy with good reason. For instance, reelection arguably became more lucrative as Congress continued to vote itself numerous pay raises, climbing to a salary of over $165,000 annually by 2006.

2) When seeking policy victories, issue networks or subsystems would be better off having both public support and the media defining the issues in their favor rather than relying primarily on political elites to do their bidding—unless the policy is made administratively rather than through legislation. This conclusion suggests that the public still matters to policy makers in our democratic republic, and it is based on findings from the ANWR, EGOM, and public lands drilling cases.

Despite having support from Washington-centered elites after 1980 (e.g., key Members of Congress, President Bush, a coalition of Alaskan political elites backed by in-state public opinion, oil companies and Arctic Power, as well as the Teamsters Union), the pro-drilling coalition for ANWR ultimately failed. They consistently lacked national public and media support (i.e., a filter for issues to the public). In contrast, in the EGOM case drilling became law in 2006 as public opinion had shifted to favor drilling, and the elite media had consistently defined the issue as a pro-drilling one, unlike ANWR. The assumption here is that public opinion matters to Members of Congress since people vote.

In both cases, Congress defined ANWR and the EGOM as pro-drilling in tone. Thus, congressional elites can be inferred to be less critical to policy outcomes since the policy shifted in both cases but the law changed toward drilling only in the EGOM. This inference does not seem to apply, however, to drilling on Western public lands since President Bush's BLM and US Forest Service increased oil and gas lease sales *administratively*, despite opposition in elite media coverage and in recent years by the public. Elite actors mattered most.

In these *administrative* decisions to drill on Western public lands, usually made by the BLM or the Forest Service on land (and by the MMS offshore), elites rather than broader forces tend to carry more weight. It seems important to have gatekeepers in Congress, since government agencies, the President, or private sector elites rather than the press or public push for drilling.

All of this supports the life-cycle explanation for policy change and elucidates the conditions under which components of that approach most influence change. It is worth noting though that the sample sizes for congressional hearings and media accounts are smaller in the non-ANWR cases (the core case study), so future research might expand the samples.

3) Based on data in the ANWR case, GOP lawmakers' home regions and their concern about their environmental constituencies likely explain why they voted with environmentalists on several critical votes. However, these defections probably are not explained as Republicans voting for their own conceptions of good public policy. All of this is detailed in chapter 4 and in the Methodological Appendix. Future research might apply these findings from ANWR to similar environmental-energy debates.

4) Another pattern of decision making suggests that the House and Senate had similar pro-drilling effects on policy outcomes at the committee level of analysis, but a somewhat different one when we examine floor voting for ANWR. The two chambers followed a similar pattern *within committees* for other cases. They defined Gulf of Mexico drilling (EGOM), public lands drilling, and building a wind farm as pro-development and therefore independent of the changes in party control of Congress since 1995. The EGOM case was the only other one evaluated with multiple-chamber *floor votes*, and those findings are similar to ANWR since the House favored drilling to a greater extent than the Senate in recent years.

Subsystems are decision-making structures that control the policy-making process for an issue and therefore tend to achieve their desired policy outcomes. But scholarship on this concept fails to differentiate between the roles of the House versus Senate within subsystems. This book makes that distinction to help shed light on the role of each chamber in designing environmental-energy policies.

Consider the ANWR case. We saw in chapter 5 that a majority of witnesses at committee and subcommittee hearings in both chambers consistently defined ANWR as a pro-drilling issue, one that could be conducted in an environmentally sound manner. These data support the life-cycle explanation for policy and subsystem changes on ANWR since pro-drilling momentum transpired independent of the changes in party control in 1995. Both chambers contributed to policy shifts at this level. On the other hand, neither chamber shifted its hearings to new committees or subcommittees, so venue changes do not help to explain the pro-drilling momentum in Congress (see Baumgartner and Jones 1993).

House and Senate differences shaped the ANWR issue differently on the floor. The Senate prevented drilling from being adopted, except in 1995 when President

Clinton vetoed a pro-drilling budget. Senate rules empower individual senators and the minority party through the filibuster. The upper chamber also played an important role in subsystem maintenance throughout the 1990s and into the early 2000s by working closely with the champion of ANWR protection, President Clinton, and by stripping drilling language from legislation backed by President Bush. Despite the Senate's inability to stop a determined Republican majority on a pro-drilling budget vote in April 2005, the Senate's 60-vote requirement to break a filibuster killed ANWR drilling in late 2006 as part of a defense spending measure.

The impact of the House was different. That chamber is more responsive to majority preferences and usually has more party discipline than the Senate. For instance, the House Rules Committee tends to structure floor legislation to favor majority policy preferences at the expense of the minority. The House party leadership likewise has more influence over its members since leaders distribute coveted committee posts. All of this suggests that the House is not only swifter in embracing policy change, but tends to embrace more extreme changes. In the ANWR case, the House produced legislation that was more pro-environment than the Senate in the late 1970s and more pro-development since 2000 during the period when drilling was adopted.

Overall, I found a pattern of environmental-energy policy making across the case studies as follows. Committee hearings defined these policies as pro-development, even with Democratic majorities. And the House tended to support stronger development bills than the Senate did.

5) The distributional impacts of a subsystem's preferred policies may not be as important in explaining policy outcomes as first hypothesized (see chapter 1). I say this because the ANWR case, unlike other life cycle cases such as pesticides and tobacco, finds that Washington-centered elites rather than broad-based forces (e.g., the media and public opinion) were forces for policy shifts and weakening of a policy subsystem. I also expected the Gulf of Mexico drilling case, which likewise had a pro-environment distributional impact, to show that gatekeeping elites were critical in shifting the policy toward drilling. Instead, I found broader forces at work too as public opinion and the media *supported* drilling, unlike in ANWR. Fortunately, it is permissible *not* to confirm hypotheses in scholarly research. My notion of an *anti*-industry subsystem admittedly is a heuristic device to spark further exploration by students of environmental politics and subsystems.

6) The finding that the elite print media opposed drilling before and after 1995 infers that they helped sway an undecided electorate to oppose drilling, or at least not to become involved in a broad-based movement to support it. This answers a question that students of the media and politics might ask: How much of the lack of support for drilling is a result of the lack of enthusiasm for drilling or "liberal bias" in the print media? Really, how much influence did the media have on

ANWR policy making? The likely explanation is somewhat complex, based on scholarship on the media and public opinion.

One school of thought regarding media effects on the public's policy preferences suggests that the media generally inform people which issues are important and deserve to be ranked on the public's agenda. They do this by cuing readers through headlines, placement of stories, and frequency of coverage. Necessarily, political systems need public support to maintain legitimacy and function smoothly.[6]

Mainstream scholars in political communication generally believe that the media, under certain conditions, can affect public opinion, strengthen or weaken subsystems, and impact the policy-making process (Paletz 1998). They also recognize that the media do not always influence the public agenda. For instance, it was widely reported that media exposure barely affected President Clinton's public approval ratings during the Monica Lewinsky scandal of the late 1990s. Moreover, the direction of causation can vary; public attention can prompt media coverage. Real-world events likewise can impact underlying political forces, making for complex interactions (Perloff 1998; McCombs and Shaw 1972).

In the ANWR case, perhaps the public was more likely to be swayed by the views of the national and international media when citizens lacked personal experience or familiarity with the issue. Why? The media tend to have less influence when citizens have already formed opinions based on their own experience and values.[7] We can plausibly say that most Americans will never travel to the ANWR coastal plain. It is unfamiliar and less immediate to them than Social Security or education, for instance. This raises the possibility that the media could have a disproportionate influence on citizens who do not have strong pro-environment or pro-development values, such as people who are more concerned about high gasoline prices or war in the Middle East. The media in all probability had disproportionate influence on those undecided about ANWR drilling.

Furthermore, scholars have found that new information from the media may alter collective public opinion, which normally is stable. This may occur if several conditions are met for many individuals. These include receiving and understanding credible and relevant information that is inconsistent with a person's past beliefs, views and opinions.[8]

It is unlikely these conditions were met in the ANWR case. The public acquiesced to ANWR's expansion in 1980 and generally continued its opposition to drilling. The tone of print media coverage also continued to oppose drilling. Thus, the findings are consistent with the political science literature on media and public opinion.

7) The unusual case of the Cape Wind project in Nantucket Sound, with environmentalists squaring off against each other, seems likely to pass since this issue is primarily an administrative decision made by the Executive Branch's regulatory apparatus, and it has the support of key elites in the Senate (but not

Senator Kennedy) and pro-environment interest groups. The project has the added advantage of consistent public and media support favoring development. This case was of secondary importance in this book, yet it is worth introducing since it reflects the importance of public and media support to policy outcomes, and similar cases involving environmental trade offs may arise in the future as world leaders strive to reduce global warming through wind power and other alternatives.

Shaping the Future

My purpose in writing this book was to help build a better understanding of the policy-making landscape in environmental-energy policy for students and activists alike. Hopefully, and with the assistance of others, I have achieved this goal.

Looking ahead, scholars may build on this work as a plethora of new or related policies are debated in the public sphere. Party control of Congress may change again as it did in 1994 and 2006; a new President facing new or growing challenges could be elected, events may shift environmental and energy policy agendas; and some of the cases studied here may be debated again. But perhaps, political observers and entrepreneurs will consider some of the patterns of decisions found in this book and advance the common good.

Maybe this sounds naïve. But, academicians in the discipline of political science have a choice; either weigh in on the important issues of our generation or risk perceived irrelevance as we did during the 1960s and 1970s. Why should scholars talk to one another exclusively through scholarly books and journal articles and discount the impact of ideas on real people? Our failures during that earlier period led to the ascension of public policy studies as political science faltered. Let history *not* repeat itself.

Our task is to use empirical, analytical approaches and apply them to real-world policy issues and talk with actors who have normative goals and the capacity to solve problems. For instance, my finding that public forces influence environmental-energy *legislation* perhaps more than elites do might spur political entrepreneurs in and out of government to better educate the public and media on critical issues facing America in the 21st Century. Good deliberation can only be achieved through a competitive media, though, rather than through concentrated corporate control as we have seen increasingly over the past decade. These discussions should include analyses of the *negative externalities*, or unexpected effects of policy proposals.

The American people can make smart decisions, provided they have adequate information, especially on technical issues. They need to be informed and mobilized to act (or not) on important environmental-energy issues including gasoline mileage standards (CAFÉ), global warming, drilling in the waters off northern Alaska, alternative fuels and energy sources, our nation's energy needs, why gas prices sometimes spike (e.g., shareholder pressures), and a host of other topics, not to mention how they can impact decision makers in Washington, DC, and in our neighborhoods. These issues are likely to gain urgency in the next few years.

My grandfather worked all of his adult life repairing pumps at the Atlantic oil refinery in South Philadelphia, beginning just prior to the Great Depression, for a minimal salary. Yet, he and my grandmother managed to raise a family of three children. My family therefore has at least some roots in the oil industry: it has provided for our family's early growth, and today its employees help heat our homes and power our automobiles. The story of oil is inextricably linked with the success and prosperity of twentieth-century America, and with the everyday lives of people.

Yet, environmental protection has become important to millions of people, in the United States and globally. Moreover, it is an issue that has the power to bring together secular and religious forces in American society. In recent years, for instance, some Christian leaders have defined the environment as a spiritual and moral issue, as we are obliged to be "good stewards" of God's gifts.[9]

This position may cause some discomfort to Republican strategists such as Karl Rove, who may prefer "Christian" or "moral" issues to be restricted to abortion and gay rights. But it speaks to the growing reach and complexity of the environmental movement, at a time when demand for traditional and new sources of energy continues to grow worldwide. The need for sound public policy that balances energy needs with environmental protection is likely to become more urgent in the immediate future.

Notes

1. "House Erupts in Chaos," The Crypt's Blog, Politico.com, http://www.politico.com/blogs/thecrypt/0807/House_erupts_in_chaos.html, 3 August 2007.

2. James E. Anderson, *Public Policymaking* (Boston: Houghton Mifflin Company, 1994), 17.

3. (Bond and Fleisher 2000, p. 64). Bond, Jon R., and Richard Fleisher, eds. *Polarized Politics: Congress and the President in a Partisan Era.* Washington, DC: CQ Press, 2000.

4. Walter A. Rosenbaum, *Environmental Politics and Policy*, 5th ed. (Washington, DC: CQ Press, 2002), 57, 58.

5. Charles R. Shipan and William R. Lowry, "Environmental Policy and Party Divergence in Congress," *Political Research Quarterly* 54 (June 2001): 245-47; Rosenbaum, *Environmental Politics*, 59.

6. Doris A. Graber, *Mass Media and American Politics*, 5th ed. (Washington, DC: CQ Press, 1997), 191,201.

7. Graber, *Mass Media*, 194, 201-02.

8. Benjamin I. Page, Robert Y. Shapiro, and Glenn R. Dempsey, "What Moves Public Opinion," in *Media Power in Politics*, 3d ed., ed. Doris A. Graber (Washington, DC: CQ Press, 1994), 123-138.

9.   This position can be summed up in the words of Franciscan scholar Ilia Delio, OSF: Just as Christ became the center of St. Francis's own life, so too Francis realized that Christ is the center of creation. And because all things are united in Christ, one who lives in Christ finds oneself united to all things (Ilea Delio, OSF, *A Franciscan View of Creation: Learning to Live in a Sacramental World*, St. Bonaventure, NY: The Franciscan Institute, 2003, 19).

Methodological Appendix

A. Rice's Index of Cohesion

Rice's Index of Cohesion, which was formulated by sociologist Stuart Rice during the 1920s, is a fundamental means to evaluate partisan voting within a political party and ultimately to compare parties' voting cohesion (see Anderson, Watts, and Wilcox 1966, 32-35). In short, the Rice Index Value measures party cohesion, or unity in voting.

The index ranges from 0 to 100, with the higher number representing greater party unity. A given index value is the absolute value of the difference between the percentage of party members voting "aye" on a motion and the percentage of the same party voting "nay." The following examples illustrate the simple logic of this technique.

Example 1 (Partisanship on a Single Vote)—Large Majorities of Each Party Opposing One Another's Position, and One Party Demonstrating Greater Cohesiveness on a Single Vote:

N=100	Dems 60	(50 aye/60 x 100 = 83.3% in favor)
		(10 nay/60 x 100 = 16.7% opposed)
	Rice Index	
	Value	(83.3 - 16.7 = 66.6)
	Repub. 40	(5 aye/40 x 100 = 12.5% in favor)
		(35 nay/40 x 100 = 87.5% opposed)
	Rice Index	
	Value	(87.5 - 12.5 = 75)

Example 2 (Absence of Partisanship on a Single Vote)—Small Majorities of Each
Party Supporting One Another's Position on a Single Vote:

| | Dems 60 | (32 aye/60 x 100 = 53.3% in favor) |
| | | (28 nay/60 x 100 = 46.7% opposed) |

      N=100   Dems 60   (32 aye/60 x 100 = 53.3% in favor)
                                    (28 nay/60 x 100 = 46.7% opposed)
                     Rice Index
                     Value   (53.3-46.7 = 6.6)
                     Repub. 40   (21 aye/40 x 100 = 52.5% in favor)
                                    (19 nay/40 x 100 = 47.5% opposed)
                     Rice Index
                     Value   (52.5-47.5 = 5)

Example 3 (Absence of Partisanship on a Single Vote)—Large Majorities of Each
Party Supporting One Another's Position on a Single Vote:

      N=100   Dems 60   (57 aye/60 x 100 = 95% in favor)
                                    (3 nay/60 x 100 = 5% opposed)
                     Rice Index
                     Value   (95-5 = 90)
                     Repub. 40   (36 aye/40 x 100 = 90% in favor)
                                    (4 nay/40 x 100 = 10% opposed)
                     Rice Index
                     Value   (90-10 = 80)

Example 4 (Multiple, Related Votes)—Comparing Parties' Cohesiveness across
a Series of Votes (e.g., amendment, procedural vote, final passage) on the Same
Bill:

      N=100   Dems average of Rice Index Values: (66.6 + 6.6 + 90) / 3 = 54.4
              Repub. average of Rice Index Values: (75 + 5 + 80) / 3 = 53.3

B. Roll-Call Voting Data and Rice Index Analyses for ANWR Votes (1978-2006)

This section of the appendix provides detailed information about the roll-call
votes analyzed in chapter 4 using the Rice Index of Cohesion. It provides bill
numbers, chronological voting dates, content, and outcomes, plus calculations for
Rice Index Values.

Importantly, a Rice Index score of 100 means that the party rank-and-file voted
with maximum cohesion. A Rice score of zero means that the party voted with

minimum cohesion, or an evenly divided intra-party vote. I analyzed key votes during the following periods:
Democratic Control during the ANILCA Debate, 1977-1980
Democratic Control during the Post–Gulf War Debate on President Bush's National Energy Policy bill, 1991-1992
Republican Control during the 1995 Budget Reconciliation Debate
Republican Control during Debate on the 2000 Senate Budget Resolution
Republican Control during the 2001 House Debate on the Bush Energy Plan
Democratic Control during the 2002 Senate Debate on Bush Energy Plan
Republican Control during the 2003 Debate on the FY 2004 Budget Resolution
Republican Control during the 2003 Debate on Energy Legislation
Republican Control during the 2005 Debate on the FY 2006 Budget Resolution and Defense Appropriations Bill
Republican Control during the 2005 Debate on Energy Legislation
The Final Year of Republican Majority Control during the 2006 Debates on the Budget and Energy Measures

Democratic Control during the ANILCA Debate, 1977-1980

The Alaska lands bill, or ANILCA, was debated in both chambers from 1978 to 1980. A chronological analysis of votes follows.

1978

House Vote #1 (5/17/78)—The House adopted the rule (H.Res. 1186; 354-42; D250-12; R104-30) for HR 39, the Alaska Lands Bill. This legislation would designate 168 million acres of federal land as national park, national forest, wildlife refuge, wilderness lands, and wild and scenic rivers. The vote was *very bipartisan*, and thus it weakens the PVM. The Rice Index analysis follows.

Democrats 262	(250 aye / 262 x100) = 95.4% in favor)
	(12 nay / 262 x 100) = 4.6% opposed)
Rice Index Value	(95.4 - 4.6 = 90.8)
Republicans 134	(104 aye / 134 x 100 = 77.6% in favor)
	(30 nay / 134 x 100 = 22.4 opposed)
Rice Index Value	(77.6 - 22.4 = 55.2)

House Vote #2 (5/18/78)—Congressman Don Young's (R-AK) amendment to HR 39 was rejected (141-251; D52-208; R89-43). This amendment would remove 5 million acres from the proposed Alaska lands designations in order to permit the State of Alaska to select the land. The vote was *somewhat partisan*. It strengthens the PVM. The Rice Index analysis follows.

Democrats 260   (52 aye / 260 x 100 = 20% in favor)
                             (208 nay / 260 x 100 = 80% opposed)
Rice Index Value   (80 - 20 = 60)
Republicans 132   (89 aye / 132 x 100 = 67.4% in favor)
                             (43 nay / 132 x 100 = 32.6% opposed)
Rice Index Value   (67.4 - 32.6 = 34.8)

House Vote #3 (5/19/78)—The House voted (277-31; D190-16; R87-15) on final passage of the Alaska Lands Bill, HR 39. This version of the bill would protect 102 million acres of federal land in Alaska. This vote was *very bipartisan*. It weakens the PVM. The Rice Index analysis follows.

Democrats 206   (190 aye / 206 x 100 = 92.2% in favor)
                             (16 nay / 206 x 100 = 7.8% opposed)
Rice Index Value   (92.2 - 7.8 = 84.4)
Republicans 102   (87 aye / 102 x 100 = 85.3% in favor)
                             (15 nay / 102 x 100 = 14.7% opposed)
Rice Index Value   (85.3 - 14.7 = 70.6)

1979

House Vote #1 (5/16/79)—The full House adopted the Udall (D-AZ) Amendment (HR 3561) to HR 39, which would designate 125.4 million acres, including the proposed ANWR, for protection in Alaska (268-157; D202-67; R66-90). The vote was *somewhat partisan*. It strengthens the PVM therefore. The Rice Index analysis follows.

Democrats 269   (202 aye / 269 x 100 = 75.1% in favor)
                             (67 nay / 269 x 100 = 24.9% opposed)
Rice Index Value   (75.1 - 24.9 = 50.2)
Republicans 156   (66 aye / 156 x 100 = 42.3% in favor)
                             (90 nay / 156 x 100 = 57.7% opposed)
Rice Index Value   (57.5 - 42.3 = 15.2)

House Vote #2 (5/16/79)—The House voted (360-65; D243-26; R117-39) to pass the Alaska Lands Bill, HR 39. This version of the bill would protect 125.4 million acres of federal land in Alaska and grant ANWR wilderness status, the highest level of environmental protection. The vote was *very bipartisan*. It weakens the PVM. The Rice Index analysis follows.

Democrats 269	(243 aye / 269 x 100 = 90.3% in favor)
	(26 nay / 269 x 100 = 9.7% opposed)
Rice Index Value	(90.3 - 9.7 = 80.6)
Republicans 156	(117 aye / 156 x 100 = 75% in favor)
	(39 nay / 156 x 100 = 25% opposed)
Rice Index Value	(75 - 25 = 50)

1980

Senate Vote #1 (8/18/80)—The Senate agreed to a motion to invoke cloture (i.e., thus limiting debate) on HR 39, the Alaska Lands Bill (63-25; D41-10; R22-15). The vote was *somewhat bipartisan*. It weakens the PVM. The Rice Index analysis follows.

Democrats 51	(41 aye / 51 x 100 = 80.4% in favor)
	(10 nay / 51 x 100 = 19.6% opposed)
Rice Index Value	(80.4 - 19.6 = 60.8)
Republicans 37	(22 aye / 37 x 100 = 59.5% in favor)
	(15 nay / 37 x 100 = 40.5% opposed)
Rice Index Value	(59.5 - 40.5 = 19)

Senate Vote #2 (8/18/80)—The Senate adopted the Tsongas (D-MA) Amendment (72-16; D45-5; R27-11) to HR 39. This amendment would designate 104.3 million acres of Alaska, including the proposed ANWR, into various categories of conservation units. The vote was *very bipartisan*. It weakens the PVM. The Rice Index analysis follows.

Democrats 50	(45 aye / 50 x 100 = 90% in favor)
	(5 nay / 50 x 100 = 10% opposed)
Rice Index Value	(90 - 10 = 80)
Republicans 38	(27 aye / 38 x 100 = 71.1% in favor)
	(11 nay / 38 x 100 = 28.9% opposed)
Rice Index Value	(71.1 - 28.9 = 42.2)

Senate Vote #3 (8/19/80)—The Senate passed its version of HR 39, the Alaska Lands Bill (78-14; D50-3; R28-11), more than a year after the House approved its version. The Senate bill would protect 104.3 million acres of federal land in Alaska and favored development of ANWR more than the House bill since the Senate measure allowed oil exploration on some of the caribou calving grounds. Section 1002 provides for a two-phase program to study the fish and wildlife on the one hand, and the hydrocarbon potential on the other hand, at the coastal plain of ANWR. Section 1003 requires future authorization by Congress for any oil and natural gas development at ANWR. The vote was *very bipartisan*, and the PVM is weak. The Rice Index analysis follows.

Democrats 53	(50 aye / 53 x 100 = 94.3% in favor)
	(3 nay / 53 x 100 = 5.7% opposed)
Rice Index Value	(94.3 - 5.7 = 88.6)
Republicans 39	(28 aye / 39 x 100 = 71.8% in favor)
	(11 nay / 39 x 100 = 28.2% opposed)
Rice Index Value	(71.8 - 28.2 = 43.6)

Democratic Control during the Post–Gulf War Debate on President Bush's National Energy Policy Bill, 1991-1992

Senate Vote #1 (11/1/91)—The Senate rejected a cloture motion on President Bush's entire National Energy Policy, S.1220 (50-44; D18-35; R32-9). The bill included a provision to permit leasing for oil and natural gas exploration at the 1002 Area of ANWR. Senate rules require 60 votes to invoke cloture. This *somewhat partisan* vote strengthens the PVM. The Rice Index analysis follows.

Democrats 53	(18 aye / 53 x 100 = 34% in favor)
	(35 nay / 53 x 100 = 66% opposed)
Rice Index Value	(66 - 34 = 22)
Republicans 41	(32 aye / 41 x 100 = 78% in favor)
	(9 nay / 41 x 100 = 22% opposed)
Rice Index Value	(78 - 22 = 56)

Republican Control during the 1995 Budget Reconciliation Debate

Senate Vote #1 (5/24/95)—The Senate agreed to Senator Domenici's (R-NM) motion to table an amendment by Senator Roth (R-DE) to the budget resolution, S.Con.Res. 13 (56-44; R48-6; D8-38). The amendment would strip ANWR development language from the bill. This *very partisan* vote strengthens the PVM. The Rice Index analysis follows.

Republicans 54	(48 aye / 54 x100) = 88.9% in favor)
	(6 nay / 54 x 100) = 11.1% opposed)

Rice Index Value   (88.9 - 11.1 = 77.8)

Democrats 46   (8 aye / 46 x 100 = 17.4% in favor)

          (38 nay / 46 x 100 = 82.6% opposed)

Rice Index Value   (82.6 - 17.4 = 65.2)

Senate Vote #2 (10/28/95)—The Senate passed HR 2491, the FY 1996 Budget Reconciliation legislation (52-47; R52-1; D0-46). This budget plan was not subject to a filibuster under Senate rules. It aimed to balance the federal budget by 2002 through a combination of spending and tax reductions. Importantly, it included a provision to permit drilling at the ANWR coastal plain. The Rice Index analysis below indicates that this vote was *very partisan*. The PVM is strengthened therefore.

Republicans 53   (52 aye / 53 x100) = 98.11% in favor)

          (1 nay / 53 x 100) = 1.89% opposed)

Rice Index Value   (98.11 - 1.89 = 96.22)

Democrats 46   (0 aye / 46 x 100 = 0% in favor)

          (46 nay / 46 x 100 = 100% opposed)

Rice Index Value   (100 - 0 = 100)

Republican Control during Debate on the 2000 Senate Budget Resolution

Senate Vote #1 (4/6/00)—Senator Frank Murkowski (R-AK), a stalwart supporter of energy development at ANWR, offered a motion to table an amendment offered by a moderate Republican, Senator Bill Roth (DE), to S.Con.Res. 101. The amendment would delete the assumption in the budget resolution that oil exploration at ANWR would generate $1.2 billion in revenue. The motion to table passed (51-49; R47-8; D4-41). The vote was *very partisan* and the PVM is strengthened. Rice Index analysis follows.

Republicans 55   (47 aye / 55 x 100 = 85.5% in favor)

          (8 nay / 55 x 100 = 14.5% opposed)

Rice Index Value   (85.5 - 14.5 = 71)

Democrats 45   (4 aye / 45 x 100 = 8.9% in favor)

          (41 nay / 45 x 100 = 91.1% opposed)

Rice Index Value   (91.1-8.9 = 82.2)

Republican Control during the 2001 House Debate on the Bush Energy Plan

Each of the five votes below strengthens the PVM since each vote was *very partisan* and the majority party won.

House Vote #1 (8/1/01)—The House adopted the rule (H.Res. 216) for its version of President Bush's energy plan (HR 4; 220-206 R218-0; D1-205). This legislation would make numerous changes to current law, including provisions related to supply, conservation, research, and taxation. Importantly, Congress would authorize drilling for oil and natural gas at ANWR. The Rice Index analysis follows.

Republicans 218	(218 aye / 218 x 100 = 100% in favor)
	(0 nay / 218 x 100 = 0% opposed)
Rice Index Value	(100 - 0 = 100)
Democrats 206	(1 aye / 206 x 100 = 0.5% in favor)
	(205 nay / 206 x 100 = 99.5% opposed)
Rice Index Value	(99.5-0.5 = 99)

House Vote #2 (8/1/01)—Congressman John Sununu (R-NH) offered the first of his two key amendments to HR 4. This amendment would require even division of receipts from new oil and gas extracted from ANWR between the State of Alaska and the federal government instead of giving Alaska 90 percent. The federal government would use its portion for research on renewable energy sources and maintenance of federal lands. The aim of this proposal clearly was to provide incentives to moderate members from both parties to support development. The House adopted the amendment (241-186; R200-18; D40-167) and the Rice Index analysis follows.

Republicans 218	(200 aye / 218 x 100 = 91.7% in favor)
	(18 nay / 218 x 100 = 8.3% opposed)
Rice Index Value	(91.7-8.3 = 83.4)
Democrats 207	(40 aye / 207 x 100 = 19.3% in favor)
	(167 nay / 207 x 100 = 80.7% opposed)
Rice Index Value	(80.7-19.3 = 61.4)

House Vote #3 (8/1/01)—Congressman Sununu's (R-NH) second amendment to HR 4 is the one that shocked the environmental community by its unexpected timing and content, according to many environmental insiders in Washington. This amendment would limit to 2,000 acres the amount of surface area for oil and natural gas drilling at ANWR, an idea allegedly conceived by a member of the Bush Administration. The full House adopted this proposal (228-201; R186-34; D41-166). Rice Index analysis follows.

Republicans 220	(186 aye / 220 x 100 = 84.5% in favor)
	(34 nay / 220 x 100 = 15.5% opposed)
Rice Index Value	(84.5-15.5 = 69)
Democrats 207	(41 aye / 207 x 100 = 19.8% in favor)
	(166 nay / 207 x 100 = 80.2% opposed)
Rice Index Value	(80.2-19.8 = 60.2)

House Vote #4 (8/1/01)—The Markey (D-MA) Amendment to HR 4 would strip language from the bill and thus continue the ban on drilling for oil and natural gas at ANWR. The House rejected this proposal (206-223; R34-186; D171-36). Rice Index analysis:

Republicans 220	(34 aye / 220 x 100 = 15.5% in favor)
	(186 nay / 220 x 100 = 84.5% opposed)
Rice Index Value	(84.5-15.5 = 69)
Democrats 207	(171 aye / 207 x 100 = 82.6% in favor)
	(36 nay / 207 x 100 = 17.4% opposed)
Rice Index Value	(82.6-17.4 = 65.2)

House Vote #5 (8/1/01)—A majority of the House voted (240-189; R203-16; D36-172) to support final passage on its version of the President's energy plan (HR 4). This bill would allow oil and natural gas drilling at ANWR, and provide economic incentives for the use of new energy technologies, offshore drilling, production, and conservation. In addition, Corporate Average Fuel Economy (CAFÉ) fuel efficiency standards would increase for sport-utility vehicles and light trucks. The Rice Index analysis follows.

Republicans 219	(203 aye / 219 x 100 = 92.7% in favor)
	(16 nay / 219 x 100 = 7.3% opposed)
Rice Index Value	(92.7-7.3 = 85.4)
Democrats 208	(36 aye / 208 x 100 = 17.3% in favor)
	(172 nay / 208 x 100 = 82.7% opposed)
Rice Index Value	(82.7-17.3 = 65.4)

Democratic Control during the 2002 Senate Debate
on the Bush Energy Plan

Senate Vote #1 (4/18/02)—The Senate rejected a motion to invoke cloture (36-64; D6-44; R30-19) on the Stevens (R-AK) Amendment to the Murkowski (R-AK) Amendment to Senator Daschle's (D-SD) substitute energy bill, S. 517. The Stevens Amendment would permit limited oil and gas development at ANWR and establish a trust fund to assist steel and coal workers. This *somewhat partisan* vote strengthens the PVM. The Rice Index analysis follows.

Democrats 50	(6 aye / 50 x 100 = 12% in favor)
	(44 nay / 50 x 100 = 88% opposed)
Rice Index Value	(88-12 = 76)
Republicans 49	(30 aye / 49 x 100 = 61.2% in favor)
	(19 nay / 49 x 100 = 38.8% opposed)
Rice Index Value	(61.2-38.8 = 22.4)

Senate Vote #2 (4/18/02)—A second cloture motion was rejected (46-54; D5-45; R41-8), aimed at precluding a filibuster on Senator Murkowski's amendment to the Daschle (D-SD) substitute amendment to the Senate energy plan (S. 517). Among other things, Senator Murkowski's amendment would permit oil and natural gas development in a segment of the refuge if the president deems it in the national economic and security interest. It also would limit to 2000 acres the amount of land surface that could be impacted and designate another 1.5 million acres as wilderness in exchange for developing the 1.5-million-acre coastal plain. This *very partisan* vote strengthens the PVM. The Rice Index analysis follows.

Democrats 50	(5 aye / 50 x 100 = 10% in favor)
	(45 nay / 50 x 100 = 90% opposed)
Rice Index Value	(90-10 = 80)
Republicans 49	(41 aye / 49 x 100 = 83.7% in favor)
	(8 nay / 49 x 100 = 16.3% opposed)
Rice Index Value	(83.7-16.3 = 67.4)

Senate Vote #3 (4/23/02)—The Senate voted on a third motion to invoke cloture during this period. It would end debate on the Daschle (D-SD) substitute amendment to overhaul US energy policy by providing $14.1 billion in energy-related tax incentives (i.e., versus $33 billion in the House bill) and provide up to two years to establish new corporate average fuel economy (CAFÉ) standards. The motion passed (86-13; D39-11; R46-2). Unlike the previous two cloture votes, an affirmative vote in this instance would not bring an ANWR drilling provision to a vote because this substitute precluded drilling. This motion has been included in this analysis to help gauge the intensity of preferences for drilling by senators who previously had voted to bring ANWR to the floor. This *very bipartisan* vote weakens the PVM. The Rice Index analysis follows.

Democrats 50	(39 aye / 50 x 100 = 78% in favor)
	(11 nay / 50 x 100 = 22% opposed)
Rice Index Value	(78-22 = 55)
Republicans 48	(46 aye / 48 x 100 = 95.8% in favor)
	(2 nay / 48 x 100 = 4.2% opposed)
Rice Index Value	(95.8-4.2 = 91.6)

Senate Vote #4 (4/25/02)—The Senate version of HR 4, which contained the contents of S. 517 as amended, passed the Senate by a comfortable margin (88-11; D42-8; R45-3). Like the vote on the Daschle substitute amendment, this vote was *very bipartisan*. The PVM is weakened therefore. The Rice Index analysis follows.

Democrats 50	(42 aye / 50 x 100 = 84% in favor)
	(8 nay / 50 x 100 = 16% opposed)
Rice Index Value	(84-16 = 68)
Republicans 48	(45 aye / 48 x 100 = 93.8% in favor)
	(3 nay / 48 x 100 = 6.2% opposed)
Rice Index Value	(93.8-6.2 = 87.6)

Republican Control during the 2003 Debate on the FY 2004 Budget Resolution

Each vote below was *very partisan*. However, the effect on the PVM is indeterminate, at least on the first vote, since the GOP majority failed to win the vote and support for drilling.

Senate Vote #1 (3/19/03)—The Boxer (D-CA) Amendment to the budget resolution (S.Con.Res.23) would strip the ANWR drilling provision from the bill. Environmentalists were pleased when the amendment passed (52-48; R8-43; D43-5). The Rice Index analysis follows.

Republicans 51	(8 aye / 51 x 100 = 15.7% in favor)
	(43 nay / 51 x 100 = 84.3% opposed)

Rice Index Value   (84.3-15.7 = 68.6)
Democrats 48   (43 aye / 48 x 100 = 89.6% in favor)
    (5 nay / 48 x 100 = 10.4% opposed)
Rice Index Value   (89.6-10.4 = 79.2)

Senate Vote #2 (3/26/03)—The Senate subsequently passed the budget resolution, S.Con.Res.23 (56-44; R50-1; D6-42), absent the drilling provision. Rice Index analysis below demonstrates that this vote likewise is *very partisan.*

Republicans 51   (50 aye / 51 x 100 = 98% in favor)
    (1 nay / 51 x 100 = 2% opposed)
Rice Index Value   (98-2 = 96)
Democrats 48   (6 aye / 48 x 100 = 12.5% in favor)
    (42 nay / 48 x 100 = 87.5% opposed)
Rice Index Value   (87.5-12.5 = 75)

House Vote #1 (3/21/03)—Like the aforementioned Senate measure, the FY 2004 House Budget Resolution (H. Con. Res. 95) did not include the drilling provision. This bill likewise passed (215-212; R214-1; D12-199). Rice Index analysis demonstrates a *very partisan* vote.

Republicans 226   (214 aye / 226 x 100 = 94.7% in favor)
    (12 nay / 226 x 100 = 5.3% opposed)
Rice Index Value   (94.7-5.3 = 89.4)
Democrats 200   (1 aye / 200 x 100 = 0.5% in favor)
    (199 nay / 200 x 100 = 99.5% opposed)
Rice Index Value   (99.5-0.5 = 99)

Republican Control during the 2003 Debate on Energy Legislation

Each of the three votes below was *very partisan* and strengthens the PVM.

House Vote #1 (4/10/03)—The House approved the Wilson (R-NM) Amendment (226-202; R196-30; D30-171) aimed at limiting surface area for hydrocarbon production and support facilities at ANWR to 2000 acres. Rice Index analysis follows.

Republicans 226   (196 aye / 226 x 100 = 86.7% in favor)
    (30 nay / 226 x 100 = 13.3% opposed)

Rice Index Value   (86.7-13.3 = 73.4)
Democrats 201   (30 aye / 201 x 100 = 15% in favor)
     (171 nay / 201 x 100 = 85% opposed)
Rice Index Value   (85-15 = 70)

House Vote #2 (4/10/03)—The House rejected the Markey (D-MA) Amendment (197-228; R29-194; D167-34) intended to strike the provision from the energy bill that would authorize the DOI to grant leases for exploration, development, and production of oil and natural gas at ANWR. The Rice Index analysis follows.

Republicans 223   (29 aye / 223 x 100 = 13% in favor)
     (194 nay / 223 x 100 = 87% opposed)
Rice Index Value   (87-13 = 74)
Democrats 201   (167 aye / 201 x 100 = 83% in favor)
     (34 nay / 201 x 100 = 17% opposed)
Rice Index Value   (83-17 = 66)

House Vote #3 (4/11/03)—The House voted to approve the Energy Policy Act of 2003 (HR 6), which included the ANWR drilling provision. Rice Index analysis shed light on the vote on final passage (247-175; R207-17; D40-157).

Republicans 224   (207 aye / 224 x 100 = 92.4% in favor)
     (17 nay / 224 x 100 = 7.6% opposed)
Rice Index Value   (92.4-7.6 = 84.8)
Democrats 197   (40 aye / 197 x 100 = 20.3% in favor)
     (157 nay / 197 x 100 = 79.7% opposed)
Rice Index Value   (79.7-20.3 = 59.4)

Note: This analysis does not detail Senate votes on HR 6 in 2003 because the Senate-passed bill (7/31/03; 84-14) omitted the ANWR-drilling provision. Likewise, the conference report did not include that provision; the bill was filibustered nonetheless and died on 11/21/03 when the Senate failed to invoke cloture on this measure.

Republican Control during the 2005 Debate on the FY 2006 Budget Resolution and Defense Appropriations Bills

Senate Vote #1 (3/16/05)—The Cantwell (D-WA) Amendment to the budget resolution (S.Con.Res.18) would strip the ANWR drilling provision from the bill. Pro-drilling actors were pleased when the amendment failed (49-51; R7-48; D41-3). The Rice Index analysis follows for this *very partisan* vote. The PVM is strengthened since the vote was partisan and the majority party won.

Republicans 55	(7 aye / 55 x 100 = 12.7% in favor)
	(48 nay / 55 x 100 = 87.3% opposed)
Rice Index Value	(87.3-12.7 = 74.6)
Democrats 44	(41 aye / 44 x 100 = 89.6% in favor)
	(3 nay / 44 x 100 = 10.4% opposed)
Rice Index Value	(89.6-10.4 = 79.2)

Senate Vote #2 (3/17/05)—The Senate subsequently passed the budget resolution, S.Con.Res.18 (51-49; R51-4; D0-44), with a provision to drill at ANWR. Rice Index analysis below demonstrates that this vote likewise was *very partisan* and the PVM strong.

Republicans 55	(51 aye / 55 x 100 = 93% in favor)
	(4 nay / 55 x 100 = 7% opposed)
Rice Index Value	(93-7 = 86)
Democrats 44	(0 aye / 44 x 100 = 0% in favor)
	(44 nay / 44 x 100 = 100% opposed)
Rice Index Value	(100-0 = 100)

Senate Vote #3 (4/28/05)—The Senate passed the conference report on the budget resolution, H.Con.Res.95 (52-47; R52-2; D0-44), with a provision to drill at ANWR. Rice Index analysis below demonstrates that this vote likewise was *very partisan* and the PVM strong.

Republicans 54	(52 aye / 54 x 100 = 96% in favor)
	(2 nay / 54 x 100 = 4% opposed)
Rice Index Value	(96-4 = 92)
Democrats 44	(0 aye / 44 x 100 = 0% in favor)
	(44 nay / 44 x 100 = 100% opposed)
Rice Index Value	(100-0 = 100)

Senate Vote #4 (12/21/05)—The Senate defeated a cloture motion to end debate on a defense spending bill (HR 2863) that would have opened ANWR to drilling. The vote was 56 yeas to 44 nays but 60 votes were needed to end debate and take an up-or-down vote on the pro-drilling bill. A yea vote on cloture favors drilling and a nay vote opposes drilling. Rice Index analysis below demonstrates that this vote likewise was *very partisan* and the PVM strong.

Republicans 54	(52 aye / 55 x 100 = 94.5% in favor)
	(3nay / 55 x 100 = 5.5% opposed)
Rice Index Value	(94.5-5.5 = 88)
Democrats 44	(4 aye / 44 x 100 = 9% in favor)
	(40 nay / 44 x 100 = 91% opposed)
Rice Index Value	(91-9 = 82)

House Vote #1 (3/17/05)—Like the aforementioned Senate measure, the FY 2006 House Budget Resolution (H. Con. Res. 95) did not include the drilling provision. This bill likewise passed (218-214; R218-12; D0-201). Rice Index analysis demonstrates a *very partisan* vote, but its impact on the PVM is unclear since the majority party did not include a provision to drill at ANWR.

Republicans 230	(218 aye / 230 x 100 = 95% in favor)
	(12 nay / 230 x 100 = 5% opposed)
Rice Index Value	(95-5 = 90)
Democrats 201	(0 aye / 201 x 100 = 0% in favor)
	(201 nay / 201 x 100 = 100% opposed)
Rice Index Value	(100-0 = 100)

House Vote #2 (4/28/05)—The House passed the conference report for the FY 2006 House Budget Resolution (H. Con. Res. 95; 214-211; R214-15; D0-195), which included the drilling provision. Rice Index analysis demonstrates a *very partisan* vote, and the PVM is strengthened.

Republicans 229	(214 aye / 229 x 100 = 93% in favor)
	(15 nay / 229 x 100 = 7% opposed)
Rice Index Value	(93-7 = 86)
Democrats 201	(0 aye / 195 x 100 = 0% in favor)
	(195 nay / 195 x 100 = 100% opposed)
Rice Index Value	(100-0 = 100)

Republican Control during the 2005 Debate on Energy Legislation

In a repeat of the 2001 and 2003 House debates on an energy plan, the full House rejected an amendment offered by Congressman Edward Markey (D-MA) to strip the energy bill of its provision to drill at ANWR, and then the majority approved an energy plan. These votes strengthen the PVM. Rice Index analyses follow.

House Vote #1 (4/20/05)—The House rejected the Markey (D-MA) Amendment (200-231; R29-201; D170-30) intended to strike the provision from the energy bill (HR 6) that would authorize the drilling at ANWR.

Republicans 230	(29 aye / 230 x 100 = 13% in favor)
	(201 nay / 230 x 100 = 87% opposed)
Rice Index Value	(87-13 = 74)
Democrats 200	(170 aye / 200 x 100 = 85% in favor)
	(30 nay / 200 x 100 = 15% opposed)
Rice Index Value	(85-15 = 70)

House Vote #2 (4/21/05)—The House voted to approve the Energy Policy Act of 2005 (HR 6), which included the ANWR drilling provision. Rice Index analysis follows the vote (249-183; R208-22; D41-160).

Republicans 230	(208 aye / 230 x 100 = 90% in favor)
	(22 nay / 230 x 100 = 10% opposed)
Rice Index Value	(90-10 = 80)
Democrats 201	(41 aye / 201 x 100 = 20% in favor)
	(160 nay / 201 x 100 = 80% opposed)
Rice Index Value	(80-20 = 60)

The Final Year of Republican Majority Control during the 2006 Debate on the Budget and Energy Measures

Senate Vote #1 (3/16/06)—The Senate passed a budget resolution that assumed revenue collection from an ANWR drilling program, S.Con.Res. 83 (51-49; R50-5; D1-43). Rice Index analysis below demonstrates that this vote likewise was *very partisan* and the PVM strong.

Republicans 55   (50 aye / 55 x 100 = 91% in favor)
                          (5 nay / 55 x 100 = 9% opposed)
Rice Index Value   (91-9 = 82)
Democrats 44   (1 aye / 44 x 100 = 2% in favor)
                          (43 nay / 44 x 100 = 98% opposed)
Rice Index Value   (98-2 = 96)

House Vote #1 (5/25/06)—The House approved the American-Made Energy and Good Jobs Act, HR 5429 (R198-30; D27-170), a bill to direct the Secretary of the DOI to establish and execute a drilling plan for ANWR's coastal plain. Rice Index analysis below demonstrates that this vote likewise was *very partisan* and the PVM strong.

Republicans 228   (198 aye / 228 x 100 = 87% in favor)
                          (30 nay / 228 x 100 = 13% opposed)
Rice Index Value   (87-13 = 74)
Democrats 197   (27 aye / 197 x 100 = 14% in favor)
                          (170 nay / 197 x 100 = 86% opposed)
Rice Index Value   (86-14 = 72)

C. Roll-Call Voting Data and Rice Index Analyses for Gulf Drilling and Cape Wind Votes

This section of the appendix provides information about the roll-call votes analyzed in chapter 4 on the Gulf of Mexico and Cape Wind case studies. It also includes Rice Index analyses.

Gulf of Mexico Drilling:

Senate Vote #1 (7/26/06)—The Senate voted to invoke cloture and end debate, thereby proceeding to the bill (S. 3711) that would permit drilling in 8.3 million acres of the Eastern Gulf of Mexico, including 2.5 million acres within "Lease Area 181." It would also use some proceeds for restoring coastal areas. The procedural motion was approved (86-12; R54-1; D31-11), with more than the (60) votes required (*CQ Weekly Report*, 7/31/06, 2136). The PVM is weakened by this *very bipartisan* vote.

Republicans 55   (54 aye / 55 x 100 = 98.2% in favor)
                          (1 nay / 55 x 100 = 1.8% opposed)
Rice Index Value   (98.2-1.8 = 96.4)
Democrats 42   (31 aye / 42 x 100 = 73.8% in favor)

Rice Index Value
(11 nay / 42 x 100 = 26.2% opposed)
(73.8-26.2 = 47.6)

A similar cloture motion passed 72-23 one week later during debate on the bill per se. That procedural vote was *somewhat partisan* and strengthened the PVM (*CQ Weekly Report*, 8/7/06, 2192).

Senate Vote #2 (8/1/06)—The Senate voted to pass S. 3711, its version of the Gulf drilling bill. This measure would limit new drilling to about 8.3 acres in the Gulf of Mexico rather than lift the nationwide ban on drilling off America's shore beyond 100 miles as the House voted to do if each state decided to permit this. In the Senate bill states would receive less in royalty payments than in the House bill. The bill was approved (71-25; R53-1; D18-23). The PVM is strengthened by this *somewhat partisan* vote (*CQ Weekly Report*, 8/7/06; *LA Times*, 8/2/06).

Republicans 54
(53 aye / 54 x 100 = 98.1% in favor)
(1 nay / 54 x 100 = 1.9% opposed)

Rice Index Value
(98.1 - 1.9 = 96.2)

Democrats 41
(18 aye / 41 x 100 = 44% in favor)
(23 nay / 41 x 100 = 56% opposed)

Rice Index Value
(56-44 = 12)

Senate Vote #3 (12/9/06)—This Senate cloture motion would end debate on the ANWR-related bill, HR 6111. The motion passed (78-10; R42-6; D36-4). The vote was *very bipartisan* and the PVM is weak. Rice Index analysis follows.

Republicans 48
(42 aye / 48 x 100 = 87.5% in favor)
(6 nay / 48 x 100 = 12.5% opposed)

Rice Index Value
(87.5 - 12.5 = 75)

Democrats 40
(36 aye / 40 x 100 = 90% in favor)
(4 nay / 40 x 100 = 10% opposed)

Rice Index Value
(90-10 = 80)

Senate Vote #4 (12/9/06)—This Senate motion was the critical vote on Gulf drilling to concur in the House amendment to the Senate Amendment to HR 6111. This bill provides for expanded drilling in the Gulf of Mexico. The motion passed (79-9; R40-8; D39-1). The vote was *very bipartisan* and the PVM is weak. Rice Index analysis follows.

Republicans 48	(40 aye / 48 x 100 = 83.3% in favor)
	(8 nay / 48 x 100 = 16.7% opposed)
Rice Index Value	(83.3 - 16.7 = 66.6)
Democrats 40	(39 aye / 40 x 100 = 97.5% in favor)
	(1 nay / 40 x 100 = 2.5% opposed)
Rice Index Value	(97.5-2.5 = 95)

House Vote #1 (6/29/06)—This was a vote to order the previous question on the rule for HR 4761, thus permitting consideration of a bill to end the federal moratorium on most offshore oil and gas development and affording states more input on these decisions. The motion passed (224-193; R221-0; D3-192). The vote was *very partisan* and the PVM is strengthened. Rice Index analysis follows (<http://library.cqpress.com> accessed 3/8/07).

Republicans 221	(221 aye / 221 x 100 = 100% in favor)
	(0 nay / 221 x 100 = 0% opposed)
Rice Index Value	(100 - 0 = 100)
Democrats 195	(3 aye / 195 x 100 = 1.5% in favor)
	(192 nay / 195 x 100 = 98.5% opposed)
Rice Index Value	(98.5-1.5 = 97)

House Vote #2 (6/29/06)—Congressman Markey's (D-MA) amendment would strike all provisions in HR 4761 ending the federal moratorium on most offshore oil and gas development. The motion was rejected (170-249; R22-201; D147-48). The vote was *very partisan* and strengthens the PVM therefore. Rice Index analysis follows. (<http://library.cqpress.com> accessed 3/8/07).

Republicans 223	(22 aye / 223 x 100 = 9.9% in favor)
	(201 nay / 223 x 100 = 90.1% opposed)
Rice Index Value	(90.1-9.9 = 80.2)
Democrats 195	(147 aye / 195 x 100 = 75.4% in favor)
	(48 nay / 195 x 100 = 24.6% opposed)
Rice Index Value	(75.4-24.6 = 50.8)

House Vote #3 (6/29/06)—Congressman Bilirakis's (R-FL) amendment to HR 4761 would have precluded the DOI from issuing leases for oil and gas development within 125 miles of a state's coast unless requested by the state. The amendment failed (65-353; R32-191; D33-161). The vote was *very bipartisan* and weakens the PVM. Rice Index analysis follows (<http://library.cqpress.com> accessed 3/8/07).

Republicans 223   (32 aye / 223 x 100 = 14.3% in favor)
                           (191 nay / 223 x 100 = 85.7% opposed)
Rice Index Value   (85.7-14.3 = 71.4)
Democrats 194   (33 aye / 194 x 100 = 17% in favor)
                           (161 nay / 194 x 100 = 83% opposed)
Rice Index Value   (83-17 = 66)

House Vote #4 (6/29/06)—This was the critical House vote on final passage of the Deep Ocean Energy Resources Act (HR 4761), a bill to end a federal ban on most offshore oil and natural gas development but give states more control. It would have required the DOI to offer leases for development on 75 percent of the Outer Continental Shelf, although it would have banned drilling out to 50 miles offshore. States could have repealed the ban or extended protection to 100 miles. States likewise would receive royalties increasing from 4.6 percent to 42.5 percent in 2022 for offshore production, lease bids, and royalties. The bill passed (232-187; R192-31; D40-155). The vote was *very partisan* and strengthens the PVM. A much more limited drilling bill ultimately would become law. Rice Index analysis follows. (<http://library.cqpress.com> accessed 3/8/07)

Republicans 223   (192 aye / 223 x 100 = 86% in favor)
                           (31 nay / 223 x 100 = 14% opposed)
Rice Index Value   (86-14 = 72)
Democrats 195   (40 aye / 195 x 100 = 20.5% in favor)
                           (155 nay / 195 x 100 = 79.5% opposed)
Rice Index Value   (79.5-20.5 = 59)

Cape Wind:

The key congressional vote on Cape Wind took place in June 2006 in the House. It was a unanimous and therefore *very bipartisan vote* in which language similar to the Senate's was approved. The upper chamber struck a deal to give the Coast Guard Commandant and other federal agencies a voice in this decision rather than giving the Masschusetts governor veto power.

D. Rice Index Analyses across Multiple ANWR Votes (1978-2005)

This portion of the appendix analyzes average party voting cohesion across similar types of votes. It provides data on the parties' voting cohesion on procedural votes, amendments, and votes on final passage in a given chamber, and average party voting cohesion across all types of votes in the same chamber during voting periods when at least two votes on ANWR were cast.

Interestingly, I found high voting cohesion by the majority party on ANWR votes over time, which seems to support an argument made by Barbara Sinclair (2001, 12) and other scholars on the cohesive nature of congressional majorities. Yet, some of that cohesion had diminished by 2005 on budget votes as the Republican majority had grown in each chamber.

1977-1980 ANILCA Votes

Average Party Voting Cohesion across Similar Types of Votes

Since the Senate cast only one vote of each type, all of them in 1980, we need only summarize those findings. In short, during the ANILCA debate in that body, votes on amendments, procedural votes, and final passage were either *somewhat* or *very bipartisan*. Furthermore, Rice Index analyses above indicate that the Senate Democratic majority tended to vote with greater cohesion than their Republican colleagues on all three types of votes.

Next, consider House votes during the ANILCA period. Combining the Young Amendment in 1978 and the Udall Amendment in 1979, both *somewhat partisan* votes, Democrats' average Rice Index Values are $(60 + 50.2) / 2 = 55.1$. Republicans' average Rice Index Values are $(34.8 + 15.2) / 2 = 25$. Thus, House Democrats voted with twice the cohesion of their Republican colleagues on floor amendments per se.

Since the House cast only one procedural vote during this period, we need only consider the rule on the 1978 House bill, which was *very bipartisan*. As was the case with House floor amendments during the ANILCA debate, Democrats voted with significantly more cohesion than did Republicans on procedural votes.

House votes on final passage analyzed from the ANILCA period were *very bipartisan* and included votes in 1978 and 1979 respectively, but not the voice vote on final passage in 1980. Democrats' average Rice Index Values are $(84.4 + 80.6) / 2 = 82.5$. Republicans' average Rice Index Values are $(70.6 + 50) / 2 = 60.3$.

In all, in each chamber, both parties voted in a cohesive manner on procedural votes, amendments, and final passage. However, Democrats voted with greater cohesion than the GOP minority.

Average Party Voting Cohesion across All Types of Votes

In the Senate, Democratic and Republican voting cohesion averages respectively for key votes on ANILCA are $(60.8 + 80 + 88.6) / 3 = 76.5$ and $(19 +$

42.2 + 43.6) / 3 = 34.9. Thus, Senate Democrats voted twice as cohesively as Republicans did on ANILCA-ANWR votes. House voting cohesion averages for key votes during the ANILCA debate are (90.8 + 60 + 84.4 + 50.2 + 80.6) / 5 = 73.2 for the Democrats, and (55.2 + 34.8 + 70.6 + 15.2 + 50) / 5 = 45.6 for the Republicans. Again, this analysis suggests that House Democratic voting cohesion was higher than that of the GOP.

1991-1992 Energy Votes

There was no analysis conducted since only one key Senate vote occurred.

1995 Budget Votes

Average Party Voting Cohesion across Similar Types of Votes

The lone procedural vote and single vote on final passage were each strongly partisan in the Senate in 1995, and Rice voting cohesion was high for both Democrats and Republicans.

Average Party Voting Cohesion across All Types of Votes

Republican and Democratic voting cohesion averages respectively for key votes on the FY 1996 budget legislation are (77.8 + 96.22) / 2 = 87 and (65.2 + 100) / 2 = 82.6. Thus, Senate Republicans and Democrats voted with high cohesion on ANWR-related votes in 1995, with the Republican majority edging out Democrats.

2000 Budget Votes

There was no analysis conducted since only one key Senate vote occurred.

2001 Energy Votes

Average Party Voting Cohesion across Similar Types of Votes

This section evaluates the lone procedural and final passage votes respectively. These votes were *very partisan* with high voting cohesion for both parties, but slightly higher cohesion for the GOP in both cases. Next, let us examine the three votes on ANWR-related amendments. Republicans' average Rice Index Values are (83.4 + 69 + 69) / 3 = 73.8. Democrats' average Rice Index Values are (61.4 + 60.2

+ 65.2) / 3 = 62.3. Thus, House Republicans voted with slightly greater party cohesion on ANWR-related amendments in 2001 than Democrats did. In all, voting cohesion for both parties in the House in 2001 on procedural, final passage, and amendment roll calls was strong, with the GOP voting together more frequently on each type of vote.

Average Party Voting Cohesion across All Types of Votes

House Republican and Democratic voting cohesion averages respectively for all key votes on the energy bill in 2001 are (100 + 83.4 + 69 + 69 + 85.4) / 5 = 81.4 and (99 + 61.4 + 60.2 + 65.2 + 65.4) / 5 = 70.2. Thus, Republicans and Democrats voted with high cohesion on ANWR-related votes in 2001, but the Republican majority unsurprisingly voted with much more cohesion than Democrats did.

2002 Energy Votes

Average Party Voting Cohesion across Similar Types of Votes

Votes on procedure ranged from *very partisan* to *very bipartisan*. Democrats' average Rice Index Values are (76 + 80 + 55) / 3 = 70.3. Republicans' average Rice Index Values are (22.4 + 67.4 + 91.6) / 3 = 60.5. Thus, Senate Democrats voted with slightly greater party cohesion on key procedural votes in 2002 than Republicans did. Also, Senate Republicans' cohesion surpassed that of the Democrats on the *very bipartisan* final passage vote. In all, voting cohesion for both parties in the Senate in 2002 on both procedural votes and final passage roll calls was moderately strong, with Democratic majorities voting together more frequently on procedural votes and Republicans voting with greater cohesion on final passage.

Average Party Voting Cohesion across All Types of Votes

Democratic and Republican voting cohesion averages respectively for key votes on ANWR in 2002 are (76 + 80 + 55 + 68) / 4 = 69.8 and (22.4 + 67.4 + 91.6 + 87.6) / 4 = 67.3. On average, members tended to show strong support for their respective party positions on ANWR. Democratic voting cohesion was marginally greater than Republican cohesion in the US Senate in 2002. This is not surprising since the Democrats had regained control of the Senate in 2001. We expect the majority party to retain voting unity when its majority is small (see Sinclair 2001).

2003 Budget Votes

Average Party Voting Cohesion across Similar Types of Votes

Votes on ANWR-related amendments in the Senate, and votes on final passage in both chambers were *very partisan* during debate on the FY 2004 budget resolution. Both parties in each body voted in a cohesive manner, regardless of the type of vote cast. Democrats voted with a greater degree of cohesion than Republicans did when the future of the 1002 Area was directly at stake, and they voted with somewhat less cohesion on final passage in the Senate.

Average Party Voting Cohesion across All Types of Votes

We will noow consider party voting cohesion regardless of the type of vote cast. Since only the Senate cast multiple votes, let us combine those two votes here. Republican and Democratic voting cohesion averages respectively for key Senate votes on the FY 2004 budget legislation are (68.6 + 96) / 2 = 82.3 and (79.2 + 75) / 2 = 77.1. Thus, Senate Republicans and Democrats voted with high cohesion on ANWR-budget votes in 2003, with Republicans edging out Democrats. The lone House vote analyzed for this debate indicates that party voting cohesion averages in that body were high for both parties, with Democrats edging out Republicans.

2003 Energy Votes

Average Party Voting Cohesion across Similar Types of Votes

This research analyzed two votes on amendments and one on final passage. All of these votes were *very partisan* with relatively high voting cohesion for both parties, but slightly higher cohesion for the GOP majority. Looking at the aggregate votes on the two amendments, Republicans' average Rice Index Values are (73.4 + 74) / 2 = 73.7. Democrats' average Rice Index Values are (70 + 66) / 2 = 68. Thus, on ANWR amendments on the 2003 energy bill, House Republicans voted with slightly greater party cohesion than Democrats did. In all, voting cohesion for both parties in the House was strong on final passage and amendment roll calls, with the GOP voting together more frequently on each type of vote per se.

Average Party Voting Cohesion across All Types of Votes

House Republican and Democratic voting cohesion averages respectively for key votes on the energy bill in 2001 are (74.3 + 74 + 84.8) / 3 = 77.7 and (70 + 66 + 59.4) / 3 = 65.1. Thus, Republicans and Democrats voted with relatively high cohesion on ANWR-related votes during this debate, but Republicans voted with greater cohesion than Democrats did.

2005 Budget Votes

Average Party Voting Cohesion across Similar Types of Votes

Votes on ANWR-related amendments in the Senate, and votes on the conference report for the FY 2006 budget resolution in both chambers were *very partisan*. Both parties voted cohesively in each body. However, the Democratic minority voted with slightly more cohesion in both chambers of Congress as Republican majorities had grown in recent elections.

Average Party Voting Cohesion across All Types of Votes

Republican and Democratic voting cohesion averages respectively for key Senate votes on the FY 2006 budget resolution are $(74.6 + 86 + 92) / 3 = 84.2$ and $(79.2 + 100 + 100) / 3 = 93.1$. Thus, Senate Republicans and Democrats voted with high cohesion on ANWR-budget votes in 2005, with Democrats edging out Republicans. In the House, the second of two votes (i.e., the conference report that includes a drilling provision) indicates similar levels of voting cohesion for each party.

2005 Energy Votes

This analysis is not detailed here since it repeats the voting patterns found on House energy votes in 2001 and 2003 with high party cohesion for both parties and slightly higher cohesion for the majority Republicans.

E. Interview Questions

The format for general background interview questions below is based on longstanding scholarship (Sudman and Bradbury 1982, 216 and Kingdon 1995, 235). Answers to these questions were used primarily to help identify the ANWR subsystem and its maintenance (see chapters 2 and 3). Many of the questions below following the introductory comments to the interviewee also relate to the Life Cycle Model that was tested in chapter 5.

Hello, I am a researcher here to conduct a survey of key public and private sector officials concerning their feelings about recent efforts to develop energy resources at the Arctic National

Wildlife Refuge (ANWR) in Alaska. You will be asked questions about how this issue was portrayed, the number and types actors involved, the role of the public, and the role of partisanship in both houses of Congress. First, do you have an objection to my using a tape recorder to help me keep better track of our discussion? (Await reply) Now let's get to the substance of the issue.

1)　How does your job relate to decision making about ANWR policy?

2)　In your view, how did the two sides in the ANWR debate leading up to the House (or Senate) votes define this issue?

　　a.　Which definition seemed dominant at the time of the House (or Senate) vote in (specify time period)?

　　b.　In your view, did these portrayals of the ANWR issue change over time? If so, when did these issue definitions begin to shift?

3)　Now I want to ask you some specifics about the congressional committees, executive agencies, White House role, and interest groups involved in making ANWR policy.

　　a.　Did you notice an increase in the number of congressional committees and subcommittees that held hearings on ANWR from the late 1990s until the 2001 (or other) vote?

　　b.　Did you observe a greater role for Executive Branch agencies such as the US Fish and Wildlife Service or the vice president's energy task force in the months or years leading up to the 2001 House vote (or other vote)?

　　c.　In your opinion, did the president play a critical role in the vote, or not?

　　d.　Can you think of any interest groups that were involved with the pro-development vote in the House in 2001 (or pro-environmental vote in the Senate in 2002, for instance) that previously were inactive in the debate?

4)　Did public opinion seem to play a significant role in the outcome of the House or Senate vote in (specify time period)? In your view, did the role of the public change over time?

5)　Some people think that partisan voting led to the protection of the refuge in 1980 and a reversal of that policy by the House when party control of the House and White House changed in 1994 and 2000 respectively. Do you share this view, or not? Why?

F. Methods for Measuring GOP Defections on ANWR

This research used a model for studying ANWR defector voting behavior to help us understand why legislators voted as they did. The three sections below operationalize/measure its three independent variables, and the findings are detailed for each.

The Environmental Constituency Variable

The first independent variable used in this portion of the study, a legislator's concern for pro-environmental constituencies, measures the influence of the environmental community on Republican supporters of ANILCA and the Boxer Amendment by examining interest group ratings published by the League of Conservation Voters (LCV; <www.lcv.org>). It is worth noting that the term "constituency" is a complex one in the literature (see Kingdon 1989, 31-33), but most definitions tend to include the mass public, elites, or both.

The data set lists the LCV scores for defecting and non-defecting Republicans. The spreadsheet lists scores for 1979, 1980, 2001, and 2002; this data includes the most current figures available to analyze the three votes. First identifying whether LCV voting scores are higher for pro-environmental legislators than for pro-development ones operationalizes this independent variable. Descriptive statistics (i.e., LCV scores) are combined for the two years leading up to a given vote on ANWR. Next, the mean score is calculated and then analyzed for its capacity to explain Republican defections and the power of the PVM as an explanation for ANWR policy change.

If we find the mean score to be closer to 100 than to zero, then we infer that this variable is confirmed because a vote to protect ANWR is consistent with the legislator's pro-environmental voting pattern. If we find a mean score closer to zero, then the variable is not confirmed since the pro-environmental ANWR vote is inconsistent with a weak voting record on environmental protection.

The findings for this variable on three key votes are as follows. Combining descriptive statistics for 1978 and 1979 leading up to the House vote in 1979, the mean LCV voting score is relatively low (34.5) for the 117 House defectors and the mean is notably lower (13.2) for the 39 GOP opponents of ANILCA. Thus, although House Republican defectors (i.e., supporters of ANILCA) likely were more favorable to pro-environmental constituencies than opponents of the bill were, defectors' voting scores arguably were not high enough to suggest that GOP defectors voted to satisfy environmental constituencies. An alternative explanation likely exists.

Now we combine descriptive statistics for 1979 and 1980 leading up to the 1980 Senate vote and find the mean LCV voting score is moderate (51) for the 28 Senate defectors but the mean score (16.3) for the 11 GOP opponents of ANILCA is much lower. These scores indicate senators likely cast their vote for ANILCA, in part, due to their concerns about pro-environmental constituencies in their respective states. This variable offers a possible explanation for the votes of these defectors collectively since the gap between the mean LCV voting score for defecting and non-defecting Republicans is relatively high.

Finally, analysis of the Senate vote in 2003 combines descriptive statistics for 2001 and 2002 leading up to the vote. The mean LCV voting score is moderate

(42.5) for the eight GOP Senate defectors but the mean score (6.49) is much lower for the 43 GOP supporters of drilling. Again, the environmental constituency variable is significant since the gap between the mean LCV voting score is high for these two groups of Senate Republicans.

The Good Public Policy Variable

A second possible explanation for GOP defector voting on ANWR concerns a legislator's view of what constitutes good public policy. This study borrows this variable from Kingdon's (1989) model on congressional voting determinants. This study defines a House or Senate member's perception of good public policy just as Kingdon does—namely a "legislator's own policy attitudes" (Kingdon 1989, 8). Kingdon acknowledges that legislators' own policy attitudes can affect their votes, along with external influences, and that the two categories are not mutually exclusive (265, 274).

He utilizes interest group ratings from two groups, the liberal Americans for Democratic Action (ADA) and the conservative Americans for Constitutional Action (ACA), in order to form an index aimed at measuring a legislator's liberal or conservative voting tendencies. That data enables the researcher to compare the legislator's liberal or conservative voting pattern during that session with a given vote from the same session to see whether the two are consistent.

This book assumes Republicans who had a liberal voting pattern before a vote on ANILCA or the Boxer Amendment likely would vote for the motion because it represented "good public policy." A "nay" vote would be inconsistent with their prior voting pattern and thus would weaken this variable as an explanation for ANWR arena change.

Kingdon's (1989) procedure for operationalizing this variable is replicated here and is as follows:

> Operationally, the ADA and ACA scores are used to form an index in which a congressman is considered to be sufficiently extreme if either the ADA or ACA score is 90 to 100 or 0 to 10, and if the opposite score is in the opposite three deciles among [legislators investigated]. If the ADA score is zero, for instance, and the ACA score is in the upper three deciles, the congressman is considered to be conservative; if the ADA score is 100 and the ACA score is in the bottom three deciles, for another example, the congressman is defined as liberal. Congressmen who do not meet these criteria are considered to have a sufficiently moderate record that ADA-ACA position is not a guide to votes, and thus does not evoke the policy goal. [This method is tantamount to] impressionistic scanning... (333).

Table A-1 is largely consistent with Kingdon's methodology for the "good public policy" variable, which he calls a legislator's personal "ideology." This explanation for arena change should not be confused with the party-affiliation rationale.

Table A-1: Measuring the "Good Public Policy" Variable through Interest Group Ratings

If	Member's ADA Score in (Year) is	And	Member's ACA Score in (Same Year) is	Then	Member is Considered to be (Liberal or Conservative)
	0-10		70-100		Conservative
	90-100		0-30		Liberal
	0-30		90-100		Conservative
	70-100		0-10		Liberal

Note: The website <www.adaction.org> lists ADA voting scores, and *The Almanac of American Politics* (1981 and 1982 eds.) lists ACA voting scores. The *Directory of Voting Scores and Interest Group Ratings (2000)* helps to fill in gaps in the data.

The findings for this variable on three key votes are as follows. Combining descriptive statistics for 1978 and 1979 leading up to the House vote in 1979, the mean ADA voting score is relatively low (20.5) for the 117 House Republicans who voted in favor of the pro-environmental ANILCA bill. The mean ADA score for the 39 House Republicans who voted against this measure is (6.37) for the same period.

House Republicans who voted for the ANILCA bill were unlikely to have done so because they believed that their "yes" vote represented good public policy. Although their voting scores are higher than those of non-defecting Republicans, they remained relatively low. An alternative explanation for defectors' votes likely exists.

The mean ACA voting score for the same group of House Republican defectors is relatively high (74) when combining data for 1978 and 1979; the mean for GOP opponents of the ANILCA bill is even higher (93.4). House GOP defectors had a relatively conservative voting pattern leading up to the ANILCA vote. A vote for ANILCA was uncharacteristic of their conservative voting tendencies. Thus, ACA voting data is consistent with ADA data that indicate that defecting Republican legislators probably did not vote for ANILCA because they thought it was good public policy.

Like the House vote in 1979, the "good public policy" explanation for Senate Republican defections in 1980 combines descriptive statistics for the two years preceding the vote, in this case for 1979 and 1980. The mean ADA voting score is relatively low (32.9) for the 28 Senate Republicans who voted in favor of the pro-environmental ANILCA bill. The mean ADA score for the 11 Senate Republicans who voted against this measure is significantly lower (11.95) for the same period.

Based on voting scores from the liberal-leaning ADA, Senate Republicans probably did not vote for the ANILCA bill because they believed that it represented good public policy. Their voting scores, while higher than non-defecting Republicans' scores, remained relatively low. Therefore, an alternative explanation likely exists.

Next, we consider combined ACA scores for 1979 and 1980. Assuming that a high ACA score is granted to Senators who favor conservative issues, and that a low ACA score is granted to those who vote for liberal causes, the mean ACA voting score for the same group of Senate defectors favoring ANILCA is relatively high (60.7); the mean for GOP opponents of ANILCA is even higher (88.9). Although nearly 30 points separate the two groups, both voted conservatively during the two years preceding these votes. Defectors' votes for ANILCA were uncharacteristic of their regular voting pattern. Again, an alternative explanation for GOP defectors' votes likely exists besides voting for good public policy.

Next, we combine descriptive statistics for 2001 and 2002 leading up to the 2003 Senate vote on the Boxer Amendment to the budget bill and find the mean ADA voting score is relatively low (31.8) for the eight Senate Republicans who voted in favor of this pro-environmental amendment. The mean ADA score for the 43 Senate Republicans who voted against this measure is significantly lower (9.36) for the same period.

Based on voting scores from the liberal-leaning ADA, Senate Republicans who voted for the anti-development Boxer Amendment probably did not perceive it to be good public policy. Why? Their voting scores, while higher than non-defecting Republicans' scores, were still relatively low. An alternative explanation for their vote likely exists.

Next, consider conservative ACU scores. Grant a high ACU (i.e., a proxy for ACA) score to senators who favor conservative issues and a low ACU score to senators who vote for liberal causes. The mean ACU voting score for the same group of eight GOP defectors is relatively high (68.9) during the same period; the mean for Republican opponents of the amendment is even higher (92.9).

Republican defectors likely did not cast their vote for the Boxer Amendment because it represented their conception of "good public policy." Why? Their overall voting pattern was conservative rather than liberal during the two years leading up to that vote. A low score would have represented a more liberal voting pattern and thus a vote for ANILCA might have been one of a series of liberal-leaning votes to improve public policies. In sum, this variable does not offer a plausible explanation for defector voting on any of the three key votes examined in this research.

The Regional Variable

A third explanation for Republican defector voting is regional influence. Like Clausen's (1973) study, this study examines regional effects within parties rather than combining Members of Congress from both parties and proceeding to examine the effect of region on voting behavior. Why? Clausen posits that separating the two parties is useful for two reasons.

First, party differences are often strong; thus segmenting Republican from Democratic behavior should reduce distortions of the impact of region on voting behavior. Second, he believes that it is important to give priority to the most critical explanatory variable in voting behavior: namely party (Clausen 1973, 160-161).

This book defines region just as Turner and Schneier (1970, 205), and Clausen (1973, 161) do—that is, by segmenting the region variable into eight elements. I conducted a regional cross tabulation in order to determine whether regional voting patterns are present for GOP defectors and non-defectors on each of the three votes.

Non-defectors are considered in order to increase the integrity of the analysis (i.e., to facilitate comparisons). By calculating the percentage of GOP defectors from each region on each vote, we can draw inferences about whether legislators from certain parts of the country tended to vote for ANWR protection and thus either weaken the PVM or make it indeterminate as an explanation for ANWR voting.

This study found that 63 percent of all House GOP defectors in 1979 (i.e., supporters of ANILCA) came from the Middle Atlantic (19.7 percent), East North Central (27.4 percent), and Southern (16.2 percent) regions. The remaining five regions account for only 36.7 percent of defector votes. At the same time, nearly 3/5 of Republican opponents of ANILCA represent the Pacific (23.1 percent), Southern (20.5 percent), and East North Central (15.4 percent) regions. The remaining five regions account for only about 2/5 of Republican supporters of ANILCA. Taking this data as a whole, it seems that Republican House members from four of eight regions (i.e., Middle Atlantic, East North Central, Pacific, and South) were critical in shaping the Alaska lands debate in 1979 because they comprised a significant portion of one or both of the Republican Party's voting blocs—that is, for or against ANILCA.

Importantly, 76 of the 117 GOP defectors to the winning side came from Mid-Atlantic, East North Central (i.e., Midwestern), or Southern states. Evidently House Republicans from the West, New England, and states separating the old North and South were not overly concerned about protecting Alaska lands.

On the 1980 ANILCA vote, three regions account for 53.6 percent of the 28 Senate GOP defector votes for ANILCA in 1980. Those regions include the West North Central (21.4 percent), Middle Atlantic (17.9 percent), and Border states (14.3 percent). The remaining five regions account for only 46.4 percent of defector votes. As for the 11 Republican senators who took a pro-development position by voting "nay" on the Alaska lands bill, importantly, 81.9 percent of these votes came from only three regions, the Mountain (45.5 percent), Pacific (18.2 percent), and Southern regions (18.2 percent).

The most important inference is that the regional explanation for Senate Republican voting likely mattered much more for opponents of ANILCA in 1980 rather than for those who defected to the pro-environmental position. GOP senators from the Mountain and Pacific states, and from the South voted overwhelmingly against the bill and thus seemed to have intense preferences against protecting Alaska lands.

As for the 2003 Senate vote, a cross tabulation for region finds that 62.5 percent of the eight Senate GOP supporters of the Boxer Amendment came from two regions, the Northeast (i.e., New England) and East North Central (i.e., Midwest) regions. The remaining six regions account for only 37.5 percent of defector votes. Of the 43 Republican senators who voted against the amendment, 72.1 percent of them came from three regions, namely, the Mountain (27.9), Border (18.6 percent), and Southern states (25.6 percent). The most important conclusion is that Republican Senators from New England and Midwestern states were most likely to defect from their party's expected pro-development position on ANWR.

An interesting finding is that moderate Republicans from the Mid-Atlantic and Midwestern states defected from their party's position and therefore influenced ANWR policy decisions on the three key votes above (i.e., in the House in 1979, and in the Senate in 1980 and 2003). This finding is unsurprising, though because it is consistent with other scholarship. For instance, Robin Kolodny (1999) is among the scholars who have studied party unity by region. She found that Republican Members of Congress from states in the East and Midwest had lower mean party unity scores in 1995 and 1996 compared with lawmakers from the South and West and that Republican moderates in the House from those regions often disagreed with the majority (Kolodny 1999, 170).

G. Methods for Investigating Hypotheses of the Life Cycle Model

Media Sampling Procedures

Choice of Publication

The *New York Times* is available online on Lexis-Nexis Academic from 1983 to present. ProQuest database was used as a supplemental tool for the 1977-1982 timeframe.

Internet Sampling Procedures for the *New York Times* Coverage of ANWR (1983-2003):
1) Type in https://web.lexis-nexis.com/universe
2) Click on "news." The "News" database includes the *New York Times.*
3) Select "US News" under "Select a news category."
4) Select "New York News Sources" under "Select a news source."
5) Type "Arctic National Wildlife Refuge" in "Full Text" under "Enter search terms."
6) Select "All available dates" and type from "1977" to "2003" under "Narrow to a specific date range" even though this database begins in 1983.
7) Type "New York Times" under "Search this publication title(s)."
8) The search yields 716 articles, editorials, op-ed pieces, or letters to the editor.
9) Print out all 716 items.
10) Separate articles from editorials/op-eds/letters to the editor.
11) Discard all other types of documents such as corrections.
12) Include every third article (or opinion piece) in sample for years when more than 20 articles (or opinion pieces) were published. Include all articles (or opinion pieces) in sample for years when 20 or fewer items were published.

Internet Sampling Procedures for the *New York Times* Coverage of ANWR (1977-1983)
1) Access the ProQuest database.
2) Click on *New York Times.*
3) Type search terms "Arctic National Wildlife Range" or "Arctic National Wildlife Refuge" or "ANWR" for years "1977" to "1983."
4) Print out all items.
5) Separate articles from editorials/op-eds/letters to the editor.
6) Discard all other types of documents such as corrections.
7) Include every third article (or opinion piece) in sample for years when more than 20 articles (or opinion pieces) were published. Include all articles (or opinion pieces) in sample for years when 20 or fewer items were published.

The total sample of the sum of all articles identified by the two preceding processes is 229, and 149 opinion pieces. Follow similar procedures for the other case studies in this book.

Sampling Procedures for Coverage of ANWR in the *Readers' Guide to Periodical Literature* (1990-1994)
1) Locate bound copies of the *Readers' Guide* from 1990 to 1994.
2) Find all articles listed under the keyword "ANWR."

3) Locate all 14 articles. Omit the single opinion piece listed for this time
period since the sample for opinion pieces is only one.

Media Coding Procedures

The following coding sheet was used to identify the tone of articles and
opinion pieces in the *Times*, in the *Readers' Guide to Periodical Literature*, and
congressional committee hearings on ANWR from 1977 to 2003.

CONTENT ANALYSIS CODING SHEET

ARTICLE/HEARING IDENTIFYING INFORMATION
1. Medium:
    (1) Newspaper   (2) Periodical   (3) Congressional hearing
                                                      (a) House
                                                      (b) Senate

2. Newspaper title or committee/subcommittee name:
(1) NYT   (2) Periodical   (3) Committee / subcommittee
  (a) article   _____   _____
  (b) opinion   _____   _____
      piece

3. Date: _____
Author (for article or opinion piece):   _____

4. Title of article or hearing:
_____
_____

ARTICLE/HEARING ANALYSIS

5. Pro-environmental Issue Definitions	Pro-development Issue Definitions
(A-0) Pristine wilderness or "crown jewel" of the Arctic must be preserved for future generations; environmentally important/special area; protection consistent with our values	(A-1) Movement toward energy independence/prevent an energy crisis if drilling; replaces oil supply from Prudhoe Bay
(B-0) "Big oil" would benefit most from drilling	(B-1) National security would be enhanced if drilling
(C-0) Caribou and other species or habitats must be protected; ecosystem protection; pollution threat with drilling	(C-1) Drilling leaves a small "footprint" on the environment; environmentally sound drilling is feasible; it's only a small portion of ANWR

(D-0) Drilling would yield little recoverable oil; would add little energy security

(D-1) Drilling would create economic benefits (e.g., thousands of jobs; raises federal revenue; decreases the trade deficit; lowers gas prices); Alaskans support its economic benefits

(E-0) Alaska Natives oppose drilling

(E-1) Alaska Natives support drilling

(F-0) Link drilling with Exxon Valdez

(F-1) The coastal plain has a huge spill oil and gas potential

(G-0) Alternatives to drilling are best

(G-1) Drilling would help maintain the TransAlaska Pipeline (TAPS)

(H-0) Drilling will not help the economy

(H-1) Link drilling with CA energy crisis

(I-0) Drilling will take 5-10 years

(I-1) The coastal plain is a desolate / barren wasteland

(J-0) 9 percent of North Slope is already open to development

(J-1) All other pro-development issue definitions

(K-0) Requires a huge infrastructure; another Prudhoe Bay; would scar the land/leave a large "footprint"

(L-0) Develop only as a last resort

(M-0) Involves questionable political tactics; windfall to politicians

(N-0) All other pro-environmental issue definitions

Witness List (Name and organization of person testifying):

_____

_____

_____

_____

Overall tone of the article/hearing:

Pro-drilling 1 2 3 4 5 6 7 Pro-environment   (8) Uncodeable

Coding Tone of Articles and Opinion Pieces

When coding articles for tone, the entire article is the unit of analysis. First, document the number of pro-environmental and pro-development issue definitions for each article. Some definitions may implicitly refer to ANWR; those definitions should be counted as one-half of a definition. Count each definition only once if it is expressed as part of a contiguous idea or expression. However, the same definition may be counted multiple times in the same article when coding for tone. Count the ratio of pro-environmental to pro-development issue definitions.

Next, rate the overall article for tone based on that ratio. A rating of 4 is neutral (i.e., an equal ratio). Ratings above 4 up to 7 are considered to have a tone that favors environmental protection. Ratings below 4 down to 1 are considered to favor ANWR development/drilling. Half-step ratings are permissible. Uncodeable articles are rated 8 and do not define ANWR either as a pro-development or pro-environmental issue. An example of a tone of 5 might have a 7-to-5 ratio of issue definitions favoring ANWR protection. An example of a 2 rating on the tone scale might have a 4-to-0 ratio of issue definitions favoring drilling.

A slightly different method is used for coding the tone of opinion pieces. The rule of thumb is that when reading an opinion piece, first consider whether the author advocates drilling or protection of the coastal plain, and then consider the ratio of pro-environmental to pro-development issue definitions. In short, advocacy trumps the number of issue definitions in opinion pieces. For instance, a given opinion piece might offer intense support for drilling. Thus, we know that the tone rating will be from 1 to less than 4. Select an initial tone on the rating scale. Next, consider the ratio of issue definitions and adjust the rating accordingly. Follow similar procedures for the other case studies in this book.

Two Measures of Issue Definition Frequency in Media Coverage

The overall frequency of issue definitions was measured for the 1977-1994 and 1995-2003 periods for both articles and opinion pieces. Two measures were taken: the percentage of articles or opinion pieces in which a given issue definition appears at least once, and a given definition's appearance once as a percentage of all definitions in articles or opinion pieces (i.e., a definition dominates a certain "percentage of the issue definition market").

Congressional Hearings Sampling and Coding Procedures

This inquiry utilized four databases to identify relevant congressional hearings since preliminary searches found that no single database provides an exhaustive list of hearings on ANWR. As many librarians are aware, no uniform filing system exists for congressional hearings in databases. Instead, each committee decides how to publish its hearings; thus, discretion for committee chairs presents a challenge for researchers.

The Congressional Information Service's (CIS) series was the primary data source used when identifying hearings and is available on CD-Rom at the Library of Congress in Washington, DC. Three additional sources included an internal document from the Senate Committee on Energy and the Environment, the WorldCat database, and the website of the Library of Congress (http://thomas.loc. gov) where full-text hearings are available after 1996. In the latter case, hearings were coded if the keywords were present at least twice in a given hearing.

Searches used the keywords *Arctic National Wildlife Range* and *Arctic National Wildlife Refuge* to identify prospective hearings that subsequently were retrieved at a congressional depository library, searched, and either discarded or retained for further analysis. Searching committee websites is of little value since this issue overlaps with hearings on various issues including national energy policy, revenue generation, oil supply and prices, and environmental protection, all of which relate to possible issue definitions for ANWR.

Congressional Hearings: Coding Procedures for Tone

Congressional hearings were coded for tone and corresponding issue definitions in the ANWR case, but only for tone in the other three case studies. Like Baumgartner and Jones's (1993) work, when coding hearings this study made "every effort to follow [the same procedures for] coding of media coverage" (260), including use of the same coding sheet. Hearings were coded like media opinion pieces rather than newspaper articles. We can assume that both hearings and opinion pieces intend to convey a certain level of advocacy. The tone of articles is based exclusively on the ratio of (total) pro-environmental to pro-development issue definitions. For opinion pieces (and hearings), advocacy of the writer (or witness) is considered first, then the ratio of the total number of issue definitions is factored into the tone.

A given hearing was coded for tone as pro-environment, pro-development, neutral, or uncodeable based on the number of witnesses on each side, not on the total number of issue definitions. In other words, in most cases it was apparent whether a witness during oral summary advocated drilling or environmental protection because he/she said so.

Next, I counted the total number of witnesses on each side to determine the overall tone for the hearing. So, this study used only oral summaries to determine tone by measuring whether a plurality of witnesses favored environmental protection or development of ANWR. This study coded every witness who testified at every identifiable House and Senate hearing on ANWR since passage of ANILCA in 1980 through 2003, but only non-neutral, codeable hearings were counted rather than neutral or uncodeable hearings. Neutral hearings have the same number of witnesses on each side of the issue. Uncodeable hearings are comprised of witnesses that do not define ANWR in their oral testimonies; these tend to be found in secondary hearings in which ANWR is not part of the title.

This large sample likely increases the accuracy of the findings and it is more important than including written testimony/colloquies since that process would yield little additional data as explained in the next section. Finally, coding the tone of congressional hearings, unlike coding media attention, does not require inter-coder reliability since witnesses leave little or no doubt about their position on ANWR drilling.

Measuring Dominant Issue Definitions in Congressional Hearings

Again, this study used a sample of 100 percent of all 58 hearings identified on ANWR to code the tone of congressional hearings and their corresponding issue definitions, unlike the segment on media attention that used a smaller percentage sample. Dominant issue definitions were found by coding 32 House hearings with oral testimonies of 175 witnesses and 26 Senate hearings with oral testimonies of 144 witnesses who testified between 1981 and 2003.

This content analysis omitted several components of hearings insofar as it excluded colloquies between witnesses and congressmen, studies and letters attached to witnesses' testimonies, and prepared statements of minor witnesses who did not testify orally. Adding colloquies will not elucidate tone unless the witnesses are neutral in their oral summaries, and very few are. Colloquies are unlikely to yield more data on the tone of hearings and only a minimal amount of information about issue definitions. Sorting through thousands of additional pages of colloquies would add little to the findings and would be an inefficient use of a researcher's time.

Similarly, studying witnesses' written testimonies, including attached letters and studies of ANWR, would yield little data regarding issue definitions for several reasons. Written testimony either tends to repeat definitions cited in oral summaries or to include technical documentation that fails to define the issue in an emotive way (i.e., fails to influence the policy image of ANWR). Furthermore, written testimony (and its issue definitions) tends to be overlooked by congressmen and senators who are busy professionals who gain the best sense of hearings through oral, personal testimonies. Also, this study excluded testimonies of witnesses who submitted only prepared written statements since the committee or subcommittee did not consider them important enough to testify in person.

On the other hand, both oral and written testimonies were coded for tone and issue definitions for committee and subcommittee chairpersons and their ranking minority members since these key members of Congress can be more influential than other witnesses. This data was compared with data from others who testified.

Tables A-2 and A-3 below list the House and Senate hearings coded in this inquiry.

Table A-2: House Hearings on ANWR (since passage of the 1980 ANILCA)

Date	Committee; Subcommittee	Title	Coded (D, pro-development; E, pro-environment; N,neutral; U,uncodeable)
10/17/85	Interior and Insular Affairs; Public Lands; National Parks and Recreation	Measures Related to Alaska Lands: ANWR	E
4/30/87	Interior and Insular Affairs; Water and Power Resources	Oversight Hearing: Arctic National Wildlife Refuge (ANWR)	D
5/28/87 & 6/23/87	Interior and Insular Affairs; Water and Power Resources	Oversight Hearing: Arctic National Wildlife Refuge (ANWR)	5/28/87 (D) 6/23/87 (D)
6/24/87	Merchant Marine and Fisheries; Fisheries and Wildlife Conservation and the Environment	Arctic National Wildlife Refuge	D
7/21/87	Interior and Insular Affairs; Water and Power Resources	Oversight Hearing: Arctic National Wildlife Refuge (ANWR)	E
7/30/87	Merchant Marine and Fisheries; Fisheries and Wildlife Conservation and the Environment	Arctic National Wildlife Refuge	E
10/6/87	Merchant Marine and Fisheries; Fisheries and Wildlife Conservation and the Environment	Arctic National Wildlife Refuge (Part 2)	N
10/8 & 10/22/87	Interior and Insular Affairs; Water and Power Resources	Oversight Hearing: Arctic National Wildlife Refuge (ANWR)	10/8/87 (D) 10/22/87 (D)

Date	Committee; Subcommittee	Title	Coded (D, pro-development; E, pro-environment; N,neutral; U,uncodeable)
10/29/87	Merchant Marine and Fisheries; Fisheries and Wildlife Conservation and the Environment	Arctic National Wildlife Refuge (Part 2)	D
11/17/87	Joint Hearing - Merchant Marine and Fisheries; Fisheries and Wildlife Conservation and the Environment & Interior and Insular Affairs; Water and Power Resources	Arctic National Wildlife Refuge Development	D
2/24, 3/3 & 3/31/88	Merchant Marine and Fisheries; Fisheries and Wildlife Conservation and the Environment	Arctic National Wildlife Refuge (Part 3)	2/24/88 (N) 3/3/88 (N) 3/31/88 (N)
6/9& 10/88	Interior and Insular Affairs; Water and Power Resources	Arctic National Wildlife Refuge (ANWR)	6/9/88 (D) 6/10/88 (D)
7/7/88	Interior and Insular Affairs; Water and Power Resources	Oversight Hearing: Arctic National Wildlife Refuge (ANWR)	N
5/9/87&6/7, 6/22, 6/28/89	Banking, Finance and Urban Affairs; Economic Stabilization	Long-term Energy Security	5/9/89 (E) 6/7/89 (U) 6/22/89 (U) 6/28/89 (U)
2/27&2/28/ 91	Energy and Commerce; Energy and Power	National Energy Strategy (Part 1)	2/27/91 (E) 2/28/91 (D)
5/9,5/11/91 6/11/91 & 7/16/91	Merchant Marine and Fisheries; Fisheries and Wildlife Conservation and the Environment	Arctic National Wildlife Refuge (Part 1)	5/1/91 (D) 6/11/91 (D) 7/16/91 (D)

Date	Committee; Subcommittee	Title	Coded (D, pro-development; E, pro-environment; N,neutral; U,uncodeable)
8/7/911	Field Hearing (AK) - Merchant Marine and Fisheries; Fisheries and Wildlife Conservation and the Environment	Arctic National Wildlife Refuge (Part 2)	D
8/3/95	Resources (formerly Interior and Insular Affairs)	Arctic Coastal Plain Leasing	D
4/12/00	Resources	Oversight Hearing on Compromising Our National Security by Restricting Domestic Exploration and Development of our Oil and Gas Reserves	D
5/24/00	Energy and Commerce; Energy and Power	National Energy Policy: Ensuring Adequate Supply of Natural Gas and Crude Oil	D
2/28/01	Energy and Commerce; Energy and Air Quality	National Energy Policy	U
3/7& 6/6/01	Resources	National Energy Policy	3/7/01 (D) 6/6/01 (D)
3/15/01	Resources; Energy and Mineral Resources	Domestic Natural Gas Supply and Demand: The Contribution of Public Lands and the OCS	U
3/20& 3/22/01	Energy and Commerce; Energy and Air Quality	Electricity Markets: California	(E) combined

Date	Committee; Subcommittee	Title	Coded (D, pro-development; E, pro-environment; N,neutral; U,uncodeable)
3/22/01	Resources; Energy and Mineral Resources	Estimated Oil and Gas Resource Base on Federal Land and Submerged Land	D
3/30/01	Energy and Commerce; Energy and Air Quality	National Energy Policy: Crude Oil and Refined Petroleum Products	N
5/14/01	Field Hearing (LA) - Resources; Energy and Mineral Resources	Outer Continental Shelf (OCS) Oil and Gas Issues	U
5/22/01	Resources; Energy and Mineral Resources	Short-term Solutions for Increasing Energy Supply from the Public Lands	U
6/13/01	Energy and Commerce; Energy and Air Quality	National Energy Policy Report of the National Energy Policy Development Group	U
6/22/01	Energy and Commerce; Energy and Air Quality	National Energy Policy: Conservation and Energy Efficiency	U
7/11/01	Resources	HR 2436, The Energy Security Act	D
2/14/02	Resources; Energy and Mineral Resources	FY 2003 BLM and USFS Energy and Mineral Program Budget	D
4/18/02	Resources; Energy and Mineral Resources	Oil and Gas Resource Assessment Methodology	U
3/5, 3/12& 3/13/03	Energy and Commerce; Energy and Air Quality	Comprehensive National Energy Policy	3/5/03 (N) 3/12/03 (U) 3/13/03 (U)
3/12/03	Resources	HR 39, Arctic Coastal Plain Domestic Energy Security Act	D

Date	Committee; Subcommittee	Title	Coded (D, pro-development; E, pro-environment; N,neutral; U,uncodeable)
3/19/03	Resources	Enhancing America's Energy Security	D
4/5/03	Field Hearing (AK)—Resources	HR 39, Arctic Coastal Plain Domestic Energy Security Act of 2003; and HR 770, Morris K. Udall Arctic Wilderness Act	D
10/30/03	Resources; Fisheries, Conservation, Wildlife and Oceans	GAO Report on "Opportunities to Improve Management and Oversight of Oil and Gas Activities on Federal Lands"	U

Table A-3: Senate Hearings on ANWR (since passage of the 1980 ANILCA law)

Date	Committee; Subcommittee	Title	Coded (D, pro-development; E, pro-environment; N, neutral; U,uncodeable)
3/19/87	Energy and Natural Resources; Public Land, National Parks and Forests	Alaska Native Claims Settlement Act Amendments of 1987	U

Date	Committee; Subcommittee	Title	Coded (D, pro-development; E, pro-environment; N, neutral; U,uncodeable)
6/2, 6/4, 6/11, 6/12/87	Energy and Natural Resources	Arctic National Wildlife Refuge, Alaska	6/2/87 (D) 6/4/87 (D) 6/11/87 (E) 6/12/87 (D)
7/14/87	Energy and Natural Resources; Public Lands, National Parks and Forests	Land and Water Conservation Fund Act Amendments	N
7/22/87	Energy and Natural Resources	Arctic National Wildlife Refuge, Alaska	N
10/13, 10/14, 10/15, 10/22/87	Energy and Natural Resources	Arctic Coastal Plain Public Lands Leasing Act of 1987	10/13/87 (D) 10/14/87 (D) 10/15/87 (E) 10/22/87 (E)
10/10/87	Environment and Public Works; Environmental Protection	Future Management of the Arctic National Wildlife Refuge	D
2/17/88	Environment and Public Works; Environmental Protection	Future Management of the Arctic National Wildlife Refuge	E
3/6/89	Energy and Natural Resources	Arctic Coastal Plain Competitive Oil and Gas Leasing Act	D
3/12/91	Energy and Natural Resources	National Energy Security Act of 1991 (Title IX)	D

Date	Committee; Subcommittee	Title	Coded (D, pro-development; E, pro-environment; N, neutral; U,uncodeable)
4/19/91	Environment and Public Works; Environmental Protection	Designating a Portion of the Arctic National Wildlife Refuge as Part of the Wilderness Preservation System	E
5/10/91	Joint Hearing—Environment and Public Works; Environmental Protection; Superfund, Ocean, and Water Protection	Developing the Coastal Plain of the Arctic National Wildlife Refuge	D
7/18/95	Energy and Natural Resources	Alaska Oil Reserves	D
8/2/95	Energy and Natural Resources	Arctic National Wildlife Refuge	D
7/23/98	Energy and Natural Resources	Arctic National Wildlife Refuge Resources	D
3/24/00	Governmental Affairs	Rising Oil Prices, Executive Branch Policy, and US Security Implications	U
5/5/00	Energy and Natural Resources	Energy Potential of the 1002 Area; and the Arctic Coastal Plain Domestic Energy Security Act of 2000	D
6/15/00	Energy and Natural Resources	National Energy Security Act	D
1/18, 1/19/01	Energy and Natural Resources	Gail Norton Nomination	D combined

Date	Committee; Subcommittee	Title	Coded (D, pro-development; E, pro-environment; N, neutral; U,uncodeable)
3/21, 4/3, 4/26/01	Energy and Natural Resources	US Energy Trends	3/21/01 (U) 4/3/01 (D) 4/26/01 (U)
6/26, 7/12, 7/12, 7/17, 7/18, 7/19, 7/24, 7/25, 7/26/01	Energy and Natural Resources	National Energy Issues	6/26/01 (U) 7/12/01 (D) 7/13/01 (U) 7/17/01 (U) 7/18/01 (U) 7/19/01 (U) 7/24/01 (U) 7/25/01 (U) 7/26/01 (U)
10/2/01	Energy and Natural Resources	Alaska Natural Gas Pipeline	D
2/1/02	Energy and Natural Resources	FY 2003 Budget Requests for the DOI, USFS, and the DOE	D
2/1/03	Energy and Natural Resources	Oil Supply and Prices	D
2/27/03	Energy and Natural Resources	Energy Production on Federal Lands	D

The following data represents the Bush Administration's most important definitions of ANWR at congressional hearings from 2001 through 2003. Again, I distinguished between testimonies in the House and Senate in order to identify the dynamics of subsystem activity in the two chambers.

Table A-4: President George W. Bush's Administration Defining ANWR through Congressional Hearings in the House and Senate (2001-2003)

Issue Definition: Pro-Environmental	Number and/or (Percentage) of House Hearings in which the Definition Appears (N=8 Hearings)	Number and/or (Percentage) of Senate Hearings in which the Definition Appears (N=4 Hearings)
(Narrowly Defined) Caribou and other species or habitats must be protected; ecosystem protection; pollution threat with drilling	2	0
Drilling would yield little recoverable oil; would add little energy security	1	0
Alaska Natives oppose drilling	1	1
Drilling will take 5-10 years	1	0
Requires a huge infrastructure; another Prudhoe Bay; would scar the land / leave large "footprint"	1	0
Pro-Development		
Movement toward energy independence /prevent an energy crisis if drilling; replace oil supply from Prudhoe Bay	2	1
National security would be enhanced if drilling	3	1
Drilling leaves a small "footprint" on the environment; environmentally sound drilling is feasible; it's only a small portion of ANWR	7 (88%)	4 (100%)
Drilling would create economic benefits (e.g., thousands of jobs; raises federal revenue; decreases the trade deficit; lowers gas prices); Alaskans support its economic benefits	1	0
Alaska Natives support drilling	0	1
The coastal plain has a huge oil and gas potential	5 (63%)	3 (75%)
Drilling would help maintain the Trans Alaska Pipeline (TAPS)	1	0
The coastal plain is a desolate/barren wasteland	1	0
Use drilling revenue for conservation	2	2 (50%)
Caribou calve in Canada	1	0

[Note: Percentages within the table are calculated based on codeable cases only.]

Bibliography

Adams, Rebecca, and John Godfrey. "Nobody Expects to Get What They Want as Energy Bill Heads to Conference." *CQ Weekly Report*, 27 April 2002, 1090-1092.

"A History of the Arctic Refuge." Alaskawild.org. <www.alaskawild.org/ timeline.html> (29 August 2002).

Aldrich, John H. *Why Parties? The Origin and Transformation of Political Parties in America*. Chicago: The University of Chicago Press, 1995.

Aldrich, John H., and David W. Rohde. "The Consequences of Party Organization in the House: The Role of the Majority and Minority Parties in Conditional Party Government." In *Polarized Politics: Congress and the President in a Partisan Era*, edited by Jon R. Bond and Richard Fleisher, 31-72. Washington, DC: CQ Press, 2000.

The Almanac of American Politics. Washington, DC: Sunrise Book, Barone & Co., 1981 and 1982 eds.

American Geological Institute website (1 Jul. 2003).

"Analysis of the Bush Energy Plan." *FOE.org*. 18 May 2001.

Anderson, James E. *Public Policymaking*. Boston: Houghton Mifflin Company, 1994.

Anderson, Lee F., and Meredith W. Watts, and Allen R. Wilcox. *Legislative Roll-Call Analysis*. Evanston, IL: Northwestern University Press, 1966.

"Another Energy Inquiry on Royalties Collection," the *New York Times*, 16 February 2007.

"ANWR Development Gains Momentum: Poll Shows Americans favor ANWR Development." *ANWR.org*. 6 February 2002. <www.anwr.org/ features/poll-anwr-2-6-02.htm> (3 October 2002).

"ANWR Drilling Kills Energy Bill." *CQ Almanac 1991*, 195-209.

"ANWR Reality Lies Far North of Gwich'in," <www.anwr.org> 3 October 2002.

"Arctic National Wildlife Refuge: TimeLine," DOI, USFWS, 1997.

Arnold, R. Douglas. *The Logic of Congressional Action*. New Haven: Yale University Press, 1990.

ASRC.com. <www.asrc.com/page2.html> (3 October 2002).

Audubon.com, http://www.audubon.org>, 6 November 2002.

"Balancing Conservation, Recreation." *CQ Almanac 1997*, 4-15, 4-16.

Barringer, Felicity. "Bush's Record: New Priorities in Environment," the *New York Times*, 14 September 2004.

Battle, N. M. "Hunters Team with Environmentalists," the *Washington Post*, 25 July 2006.

Baumgartner, Frank R., and Bryan D. Jones. *Agendas and Instability in American Politics*. Chicago: The University of Chicago Press, 1993.

Binder, Sarah A. *Minority Rights, Majority Rule : Partisanship and the Development of Congress*.Cambridge; New York: Cambridge University Press, 1997.

Bond, Jon R., and Richard Fleisher, eds. *Polarized Politics: Congress and the President in a Partisan Era*. Washington, DC: CQ Press, 2000.

Bosso, Christopher J. *Environment, Inc. From Grassroots to Beltway*. Lawrence, KS: University of Kansas Press, 2005.

_____.*Pesticides and Politics: The Life Cycle of a Public Issue*. Pittsburgh: University of Pittsburgh Press, 1987.

Bowman, Ann, and Richard C. Kearney. *State and Local Government: The Essentials*. Boston: Houghton Mifflin Company, 2000.

Brady, David W., John F. Cogin, and Morris P. Fiorino, eds. *Continuity and Change in House Elections*. Stanford, Calif. : Stanford University Press/Hoover Institution Press, 2000.

British Petroleum, http://www.bp.com> 8 October 2002.

Bryner, Gary. *Blue Skies, Green Politics: The Clean Air Act of 1990*. Washington, DC: CQ Press, 1993.

"Bush Close to Winning Arctic Drilling Measure." *FoxNews.com*. 11 March 2003. <http://www.foxnews.com/story/0,2933,80847,00.html>

"Cabinet Officials Join Union Leaders Calling for Responsible Energy Policy." Teamsters Union Press Release. 3 October 2001. <www.teamster.org/01newsb/nr 011002_2htm>

Cahn, Robert. *The Fight to Save Wild Alaska*. Washington, DC: National Audubon Society, 1982.

"Capitol Briefs: Arctic Wildlife." *CQ Weekly Report*, 8 May 1959, 624.

Carson, Donald W., and James W. Johnson. *Mo: The Life and Times of Morris K Udall*. Tucson, AZ: The University of Arizona Press, 2001.

Carter, Jimmy. *Keeping Faith: Memoirs of a President*. New York: Bantam Books, 1982.

Cater, Douglass. *Power in Washington: A Critical Look at Today's Struggle to Govern in the Nation's Capital*. New York: Random House, 1964.

Chase, Alston. *Playing God in Yellowstone: The Destruction of America's First National Park*. Boston: The Atlantic Monthly Press, 1986.

Clausen, Aage R. *How Congressmen Decide: A Policy Focus*. New York: St. Martin's Press, 1973.

Clinton, Bill, and Al Gore. *Putting People First: How We Can All Change America*. New York: Times Books, 1992.

Cochran, John, and Rebecca Adams. "Fresh From a Set of Hill Victories, Can Labor Keep the Momentum?" *CQ Weekly Report*, 1 September 2001.

Collie, Melissa P. "Voting Behavior in Legislatures." *Legislative Studies Quarterly* 9 (February 1984): 3-50.

"Congress Admits Alaska as 49th State." *CQ Almanac 1958*, 281-285.
"Congress Approves Offshore Drilling Bill," Reuters, <http://www.msnbc. msn.com/id/16140704/print/1/displaymode/1098/> (10 December 2006)
"Congress Clears Alaska Lands Legislation." *CQ Almanac 1980*, 575-584.
"Congress Completes Action on Alaskan Pipeline Bill." *CQ Almanac 1973*, 596-614.
"Congress Passes Wilderness Act." *CQ Almanac 1964*, 485-490.
Cooper, Joseph, and David W. Brady, and Patricia A. Hurley. "The Electoral Basis of Party Voting: Patterns and Trends in the US House of Representatives, 1877-1969." In *The Impact of the Electoral Process*, edited by Louis Maisel and Joseph Cooper, 133-166. London: Sage Publications, 1977.
Corn, M. Lynne, and Bernard Gelb. "Arctic National Wildlife Refuge: Legislative Issues." Congressional Research Service, 14 May 2002.
_____. "The Arctic National Wildlife Refuge: The Next Chapter." Congressional Research Service, Updated 2 April 2001.
Cox, Gary W. Efficient Secret: The cabinet and the development of political parties in Victorian England. Cambridge; New York: Cambridge University Press, 1987.
Cox, Gary W., and Mathew D. McCubbins. *Legislative Leviathan: Party Government in the House*. Los Angeles: University of California Press, 1993.
CQ Almanac. Washington, D.C.: Congressional Quarterly News Features, Inc. 1977.
_____. 1978.
_____. 1979.
_____. 1980.
_____. 1991.
_____. 1997.
CQ Researcher Online. http://library.cqpress.com> accessed 3/8/07.
CQ Weekly Report. . Washington, D.C.: Congressional Quarterly News Features, Inc. 20 May 1978.
_____. 27 May 1978.
_____. 19 May 1979.
_____. 23 August 1980.
_____. 27 May 1995.
_____. 7 June 1997.
_____. 8 April 2000.
_____. 21 July 2001.
_____. 4 August 2001.
_____. 22 December 2001.
_____. 31 July 2006.
_____.7 August 2006.
"CQ's Presidential Boxscore Through Sept. 1 Adjournment." *CQ Almanac 1960*, 97.
Davidson, Roger ed. *Postreform Congress*. New York : St. Martin's Press, 1992.
Davidson, Roger H., and Walter J. Oleszek. *Congress and its Members*. 6th ed. Washington, DC: CQ Press, 1998.

Delio, Ilea, OSF. *A Franciscan View of Creation: Learning to Live in a Sacramental World*, St. Bonaventure, NY: The Franciscan Institute, 2003.

Department of the Interior, "ANWR: TimeLine."

Downs, Anthony. "Up and Down with Ecology: The Issue Attention Cycle." *Public Interest* 28 (1972): 38-50.

Eckstein, Harry. "Case Study and Theory in Political Science." In *Handbook of Political Science*, Vol. 7, edited by Fred I. Greenstein and Nelson W. Polsby, 79-137, Reading, MA: Addison-Wesley, 1975.

Edelman, Murray. *The Symbolic Uses of Politics*. Urbana, IL: University of Illinois Press, 1995.

Egan, Timothy. "Bush Administration Allows Oil Drilling Near Utah Parks," Common Dreams News Center, 8 February 2002. <http://www. commondreams.org/cgi-bin/print.cgi?file=headlines02/0208-03.htm>.

Eilperin, Juliet. "Growing Coalition Opposes Drilling," In NM Battle, "Hunters Team with Environmentalists," *Washington Post*, 25 July 2006, 01(A).

"Energy." *CQ Weekly Report*, 11 December 2006, 3289.

The Energy Information Administration at the US Department of Energy <www.eia.gov (27 April 2005).

Evans, C. Lawrence, and Walter J. Oleszek. *Congress Under Fire: Reform Politics and the Republican Majority*. New York: Houghton Mifflin Company, 1997.

"Features: The Unions," Arctic Power website, <www.anwr.org> (3 October 2002).

Freeman, J. Leiper. *The Political Process: Executive Bureau-Legislative Committee Relations*. 2d ed. New York: Random House, Inc., 1965.

Fritschler, A. Lee and Bernard H. Ross, *Urban affairs bibliography: an annotated guide to the literature in the field*. Washington: School of Government and Public Administration, College of Public Affairs, American University, 1974.

Fritschler, A. Lee, and James M. Hoefler. *Smoking & Politics: Policy Making and the Federal Bureaucracy*. 5th ed. Upper Saddle River, NJ: Prentice Hall, 1996.

"GAO Report Sparks New Arguments over ANWR drilling." Associated Press State and Local Wire. 15 November.2001.

Graber, Doris A. *Mass Media and American Politics*. 5th ed. Washington, DC: CQ Press, 1997.

Griffith, Ernest S. *The Impasse of Democracy*. New York: Harrison-Hilton Books, Inc., 1939.

"Growing Coalition Opposes Drilling;" In NM Battle, "Hunters Team with Environmentalists," the *Washington Post*, 25 July 2006.

Haycox, Stephen. *Frigid Embrace: Politics, Economics and Environment in Alaska*. Corvallis, OR: Oregon State University Press, 2002.

Hebert, H. Josef. "Senate GOP Renews Arctic Drilling Push." Associated Press. 1 January 2003.

Heclo, Hugh. "Issue Networks and the Executive Establishment." In *The New American Political System*, edited by Anthony King, 87-124. Washington, DC: American Enterprise Institute, 1978.

"Hood Presses Senate Leaders for Energy Plan." Teamsters Union Press Release. 2 November 2001. <www.teamster.org/01newsb/hn_011102_1.htm>.

"House Erupts in Chaos," The Crypt's Blog, Politico.com, http://www.politico. com/blogs/thecrypt/0807/House_erupts_in_chaos.html, 3 August 2007.

"House Passes New Standards for Use of Wildlife Refuges." *CQ Weekly Report*, 7 June 1997, 1313, 1334-1335.

"Hunting and Fishing on Refuges." *CQ Almanac 1996*, 4-22.

Hurley, Patricia A., and Rick K. Wilson. "Partisan Voting Patterns in the US Senate." *Legislative Studies Quarterly* 14 (May 1989): 225-250.

"Inupiat Eskimos First, Best Environmentalists." *ANWR.org*. <www.anwr. org/people/nageak.html> (3 October 2002).

Jenkins-Smith, Hank C., and Gilbert K. St. Clair. "The Politics of Offshore Energy: Empirically Testing the Advocacy Coalition Framework." In *Policy Change and Learning: An Advocacy Coalition Approach*, edited by Paul A. Sabatier and Hank C. Jenkins-Smith, 149-175. San Francisco: Westview Press, 1993.

Judicial Watch v. National Energy Policy Development Group and *Sierra Club v. Vice President Richard B. Cheney*. United States District Court for the District of Columbia. Declaration by Karen Y. Knutson, Deputy Assistant to the Vice President for Domestic Policy, 3 September 2002.

Kiewiet, D. Roderick and Matthew D. McCubbins, eds. *Logic of delegation: Congressional parties and the appropriations process*. Chicago : University of Chicago Press, 1991.

Kingdon, John W. *Agendas, Alternatives, and Public Policies*. 2d ed. New York: Harper Collins College Publishers, 1995.

_____. *Agendas, alternatives and public policies*. New York: Harper Collins, 1984.

_____. *Congressmen's Voting Decisions*. 3d ed. Ann Arbor, MI: The University of Michigan Press, 1989.

"Knowles Slams Senate Democrats' Energy Bill." *ANWR.org*. <www.anwr.org/ features/politics/alaska.htm> (3 October 2002).

Knudson, Tom.. "Fat of the Land: Movement's Prosperity Comes at a High Price." *Sacramento Bee*. 11 April 2001.

Kolodny, Robin. "Moderate Success: Majority Status and the Changing Nature of Factionalism in the House Republican Party." In *New Majority or Old Minority? The Impact of Republicans on Congress*, edited by Nicol C. Rae and Colton C. Campbell, 153-172. New York: Rowman & Littlefield Publishers, Inc., 1999.

Krehbiel, Keith. *Pivotal Politics: A Theory of US Lawmaking*. Chicago: The University of Chicago Press, 1998.

Kurtz, Howard. "Republican Right Rips Jeffords." *Washington Post Online*. 24 May 2001.

LA Times, 8/2/06.

League of Conservation Voters (LCV; <www.lcv.org>)

Lentfer, Hank, and Carolyn Servid, eds. *Arctic Refuge: A Circle of Testimony*. Minneapolis: Milkweed Editions, 2001.

Library of Congress website (www.thomas.loc.gov/).

Linden, Seth "Hood Takes New Role in Nation's Capital" NBC News. 2 February 2005. http://www.ktuu.com/CMS/templates/master.asp?articleid=11441&zoneid=4

Lindblom, Charles E. *Politics and Markets: The World's Political-Economic Systems.* Basic Books, 1977.

Lowell, A. Lawrence. "The Influence of Party Upon Legislation in England and America" (paper presented as part of the *Annual Report of the American Historical Association for 1901*) I: 336-37.

_____. "The Influence of Party Upon Legislation in England and America." *Annual Report of the American Historical Association for 1901* 1: 321-344.

Lowi, Theodore. *The End of Liberalism: The Second Republic of the United States.* 2d ed. New York: WW Norton & Company, 1979.

_____. ed. Private life and public order, the context of modern public policy. New York, Norton, 1968.

_____. "American Business, Public Policy, Case-Studies, and Political Theory." *World Politics* 16 (1964): 677-715.

Maass, Arthur. *Muddy Waters: The Army Engineers and the Nation's Rivers.* Cambridge, MA: Harvard University Press, 1951.

Matlack, Carol. "Taking on the Teamsters." *National Journal*, 7 November 1987, 2782-2788.

McCombs, Maxwell E., and Donald L. Shaw. "The Agenda-Setting Function of Mass Media."

McConnell, Grant. *Private Power & American Democracy.* New York: Alfred A. Knopf, 1966.

McGrath, Susan. "The Last Great Wilderness." *Audubon.org.* <http://magazine. audubon.org/features0109/arctic.html> (2001).

_____. "Problem Definition and Special Interest Politics in Tax Policy and Agriculture." In *The Politics of Problem Definition*, edited by David A. Rochefort and Roger W. Cobb, 117-137. Lawrence, KS: University of Kansas Press, 1994.

Mufson, Steven. "The New Drilling Battle; High Energy Prices Spur Fresh Debate on Offshore Moratorium," *Washington Post*, 15 June 2006, 01(D).

"Oil Company Revives Suit on Avoidance of Royalties," the *New York Times*, 3 March 2007.

Page, Benjamin I. *Who Deliberates? Mass Media in Modern Democracy.* Chicago: The University of Chicago Press, 1996.

Page, Benjamin I., and Shapiro, Robert Y., and Dempsey, Glenn R. "What Moves Public Opinion." In *Media Power in Politics.* 3d ed., edited by Doris A. Graber, 123-138. Washington, DC: CQ Press, 1994.

Paletz, David L. "The Media and Public Policy." In *The Politics of News: The News of Politics.* edited by Doris Graber, Denis McQuail, and Pippa Norris, 218-237. Washington, DC: CQ Press, 1998.

Perloff, Richard M. *Political Communication: Politics, Press, and Public in America.* Mahway, NJ: Lawrence Erlbaum Associates, 1998.

"The Players: Arctic Power, ANWR.org <www.anwr.org/features/players/ apower.htm> (3 Dec. 2002); Telephone interview with Roger Herrera, 3 December 2002.

The Political Arena," Arctic Power website, <www.anwr.org> (3 October 2002).

Poole, Keith T., and Howard Rosenthal. *Congress: A Political-Economic Theory of Roll Call Voting.* Oxford University Press, 1997.

Public Law 105-57, http://www.fws.gov/refuges/policymakers/mandates/hr/420.

Public Opinion Quarterly 36 (Summer 1972): 176-187.

"Recreation in Wildlife Reserves." *CQ Almanac 1962,* 465.

Redford, Emmette S. *Democracy in the Administrative State.* New York: Oxford University Press, 1969.

"Remarks by the President on National Energy Policy in Photo Opportunity with Cabinet Members." *Whitehouse.gov.* 16 May 2001. <http://www.whitehouse.gov/news/releases/2001/05/20010516-7.html>

Rice, Stuart A. *Quantitative Methods in Politics.* New York: Russell & Russell, 1928.

Rohde, David W. *Parties and Leaders in the Postreform House.* Chicago: The University of Chicago Press, 1991.

Rosen, Yereth. "Alaska to Lobby for Oil Drilling." Reuters News Service. 18 March 2001.

Rosenbaum, Walter A. *Environmental Politics and Policy* (5th ed.). Washington, DC: CQ Press, 2002.

Sabatier, Paul A. "Policy Change Over a Decade or More." In *Policy Change and Learning: An Advocacy Coalition Approach,* edited by Paul A. Sabatier and Hank C. Jenkins-Smith, 13-39. Boulder, CO: Westview Press, 1993.

"Saving the Cape Wind Project." *Washington Times* editorial, 5 July 2006, 16(A).

Schattschneider, E.E. *The Semisovereign People: A Realist's View of Democracy in America.* New York: Harcourt Brace Jovanovich College Publishers, 1975.

_____. *Semi-sovereign people: a realist's view of democracy in America.* New York: Holt, Rinehart and Winston, 1960.

Shipan, Charles R., and William R. Lowry. "Environmental Policy and Party Divergence in Congress." *Political Research Quarterly* 54 (June 2001): 245-263.

Siler, Sonja Moore. "Who Deliberates Better? A Comparative Analysis of Media Content During the 2000 US Presidential Election." Dissertation submitted to Temple University, January 2004.

Simon, Richard, and Maura Reynolds, "The Nation; Senate OKs Bill to Expand Oil, Gas Drilling; Measure Opens a Section in the Gulf of Mexico but Must Be Reconciled with a House Version that Allows Production along the Pacific Coast." *LA Times,* 2 August 2006, 17(A).

Sinclair, Barbara. "The New World of US Senators." In *Congress Reconsidered* (7th ed.), edited by Lawrence E. Dodd and Bruce I. Oppenheimer, 1-19. Washington, DC: CQ Press, 2001.

_____. *Legislators, Leaders, and Lawmaking: The US House of Representatives in the Postreform Era.* Baltimore: The Johns Hopkins University Press, 1995.

Smith, Steven S., and Gerald Gamm. "The Dynamics of Party Government in Congress." In *Congress Reconsidered* (7th ed.), edited by Lawrence E. Dodd and Bruce I. Oppenheimer, 245-268. Washington, DC: CQ Press, 2001.

Spiess, Ben. "Arctic Oil Drilling Debate Escalates." *Anchorage Daily News.* 7 May 2001.

"State of Alaska: ANWR Resolution Passes Legislature." *ANWR.org.* <www.anwr.org/features/politics/alaska.htm> (3 October 2002).

Steinberg, Paul F. *Environmental Relations and Biodiversity Policy in Costa Rica and Bolivia.* Cambridge, MA: The MIT Press, 2001.

Suarez, Sandra. *Does Business Learn? Tax Breaks, Uncertainty, and Political Strategies.* Ann Arbor, MI: The University of Michigan Press, 2000.

Sudman, Seymour, and Norman M. Bradburn. *Asking Questions: A Practical Guide to Questionnaire Design.* San Francisco: Jossey-Bass Publishers, 1982.

"2001 Legislative Summary." *CQ Weekly Report,* 22 December 2001, 3037.

Turner, Julius, and Edward V. Schneier, Jr. *Party and Constituency: Pressures on Congress* (revised ed.). Baltimore: The Johns Hopkins Press, 1970.

United States Code: Congressional and Administrative News (92nd Congress-1st Session, 1971, Vol. 2; 96th Congress-2nd Session, 1980, Vol. 5). St. Paul, MN: West Publishing Co.

United States Department of the Interior. *Arctic National Wildlife Refuge, Alaska, Coastal Plain Resource Assessment: Report and Recommendation to the Congress of the United States and Final Legislative Environmental Impact Statement.* 21 April 1987.

United States Department of the Interior. US Fish and Wildlife Service. *Arctic National Wildlife Refuge: Time Line.* 1997.

US Code, 1980, 5057-5059.

USGS website, 1 Jul. 2003, *The National Petroleum Reserve Alaska—Legacy Data Archive.*

Vogel, David. "Representing Diffuse Interests in Environmental Policymaking." In *Do Institutions Matter? Government Capabilities in the United States and Abroad,* edited by R. Kent Weaver and Bert A. Rockman, 237-271. Washington, DC: The Brookings Institution, 1993.

Weart, Spencer .Nuclear fear: a history of images. Cambridge, Mass.: Harvard University Press, 1988.

Weeks, Jennifer. "Domestic Energy Development," *CQ Researcher* 15, no. 34 (30 September 2005): 815.

Wilderness Watch, Spring 1993, 4.

Wilson, James Q., ed. *The Politics of Regulation.* New York: Basic Books, Inc., 1980.

Wiltenburg, Mary. "Who's Got the Power," *Christian Science Monitor,* 28 August 2003, 11.

Interviews

Telephone interview with DOI Secretary Cecil Andrus, Ret., 12/16/02 & 7/24/03.

Telephone interview with Don Barry, 1/6/03.

Telephone interview with USFWS Director Jamie Rappaport Clark, Ret., 1/2/03.

Telephone interview with Chuck Clusen, NRDC (former Chairman of the Alaska Coalition), 11/1/02.

Face-to-face interview with Christine Drager and Daniel Kish, Senate Energy and Natural Resources Committee, Republican Staff, 7/23/02.

Face-to-face interview with Christopher Fluhr, House Resources Committee, Republican staff, 7/22/02.

Telephone interview with Becky Gay, 12/20/02.

Telephone interview with Roger Herrera, 12/3/02.

Telephone interview with Jack Hession, Sierra Club, 11/12/02.

Telephone interview with Alaska State Representative & Majority Leader Jeannette James (R), 12/12/02.

Telephone interview with Adam Kolton, National Wildlife Federation (formerly with Alaska Wilderness League), 9/12/02.

Face-to-face interview with Daniel Lavery, Sierra Club, 7/23/02.

Face-to-face interview with Ken Leonard, American Petroleum Institute, 7/24/02.

Telephone interview with Andrew Lundquist, The Lundquist Group (formerly with the George W. Bush Administration), 1/6/03.

E-mail interview with aide to Congressman George Miller (D-CA), 5/11/05.

Telephone interview with Roger Herrera, 12/3/02.

Face-to-face interview with John Rishel, House Resources Committee, Subcommittee on Energy and Mineral Resources, Republican staff, 7/22/02.

Telephone interview with Dan Ritzman, National Outreach Director, Alaska Coalition, 9/16/02.

Telephone interview with OMB Director Alice Rivlin, Ret., 12/20/02.

Telephone interview with The Honorable John Seiberling, Member of Congress (D-OH), Ret., 9/18/02 & 9/24/02.

Telephone interview with Michael Tubman, Washington, DC, Office of Alaska Governor Tony Knowles, 12/16/02.

Index

About the Author

Dr. Robert J. McMonagle is Assistant Professor of Political Science at Neumann College in Pennsylvania. He earned his Ph.D. in Political Science at Temple University and his M.A. at the University of Chicago's Harris School of Public Policy Studies. Dr. McMonagle formerly served as a congressional staff member on Capitol Hill (1988-91) and later was a candidate for US House of Representatives (1996).